2/05

Lost on the Ocean Floor

LOST

on the Ocean Floor

Diving the World's Ghost Ships

John Christopher Fine

Naval Institute Press

Annapolis, Maryland

Naval Institute Press

291 Wood Road

Annapolis, MD 21402

Library of Congress Cataloging-in-Publication Data

Fine, John Christopher.

    Lost on the ocean floor : diving the world's ghost ships / John Christopher Fine.

        p.   cm.

    Includes bibliographical references (p.).

    ISBN 1-59114-275-X (alk. paper)

    1. Shipwrecks. 2. Treasure-trove. 3. Deep diving. 4. Underwater archaeology. I. Title.

G525.F4949 2004

910.4'52—dc22

                                            2004008445

Printed in the United States of America on acid-free paper ∞

12 11 10 09 08 07 06 05   9 8 7 6 5 4 3 2

First printing

Contents

Introduction

This book is not only about treasure hunting, although great tales of finding sunken treasure are told here. Nor is it is simply about history, although history is uncovered here. It is not purely about underwater archaeology, but there is much to learn here about old ships and wreck sites. Treasure hunting, history, underwater archaeology—all are ingredients in the narrative, as we seek to capture the romance and adventure of discovering the past under the sea.

This book seeks to convey the thrill and the fun of exploring sunken ships and scuttled fleets. It goes behind the scenes of diving adventures great and small. Many projects I worked on have become legendary. Ocean explorers involved in finding and investigating some of the shipwrecks described have become famous as a result of their pioneering discoveries.

From Scapa Flow to Truk Lagoon, from the Scilly Isles to the Florida Keys, join us as we explore the sunken fleets of the world. Warships and treasure-laden galleons, long lost on the ocean floor, come to life again as we travel the globe in search of history, treasure, and adventure. Be you sailor, diver, ship historian, armchair adventurer, undersea explorer, or academic, if you count yourself among those who love the sea, then voyage with us near and far to exotic tropical islands and frigid deep oceans.

Learn, as our divers have learned, that human nature, avarice, cunning, cruelty, and sacrifice remain the foibles and strengths of great conquistadors and humble discoverers. Let us share stories that made the legends and experience the lives of legendary figures who made the stories. Join legions of toilers in the sea and discover with us the lore and fascination of tales lost to time, as we descend beneath the waves with those who seek the ghost ships.

This book, then, is an invitation to adventure: to explore sunken ships alongside divers who have often taken great risks to find history hidden under the sea; to be part of the fellowship of those whose exploits have made this history come alive—sometimes with humor, sometimes with tragedy, and always with the spirit expressed by the credo on coinage from the Spanish Main: PLUS ULTRA. There is "more beyond."

Lost on the Ocean Floor

CHAPTER ONE

Spain's Lost Tierra Firme Fleet

He surfaced gasping for breath. Trying to call out, he could not, struggling to keep his head above water long enough to gulp air. Spain had enslaved a whole village from the island of Santa Margarita, a population of pearl divers who amazed the Spanish conquistadors with their prowess for diving deep and remaining underwater for long periods while gathering oysters. They were driven so hard by their Spanish masters, pressed into the frenzied search and salvage of sunken treasure galleons, that the whole tribe from the village eventually died off.

On 3 June 1626, the slave, diver Juan de Casta Bañon, was not only struggling for breath, he was struggling for life itself. His master promised freedom to the first person that found the shipwreck. Casta Bañon had just found it.

What happened next is reconstructed from the log and official report of Cuban treasure salvor Francisco Nuñez Melián to King Philip IV of Spain. Nuñez Melián was an adventurer, who discovered salvaging after a career that included wine smuggling in the Canary Islands. Nuñez Melián knew how to curry favor with important politicians in much the same way that it is done today, by paying them off with a share of the swag. Narrowly escaping prosecution in Spain, Nuñez Melián landed in Cuba, where he became a favorite of the governor.

Nuñez Melián's providential day would come four years after salvor Gaspar de Vargas—sailing under the mandate of the Marquis de Cadereita, commander of the ill-fated Tierra Firme treasure fleet of 1622—returned without the gold and silver from the *Santa Margarita* and the *Nuestra Señora de Atocha*, two of the fleet's ships that had sunk in a hurricane less than two weeks earlier. The Spanish were quite skilled at salvaging ships. Vargas was dispatched at once to recover what he could for the crown.

Although Vargas had located the galleon *Atocha* he only managed to recover two bronze cannons from its deck. Hoping to come back to the *Atocha,* he sailed to find the *Rosario.* A second storm blew away Vargas's markers, and he was unable to find the *Atocha* again, but he did manage to recover the *Rosario*'s treasure and rescue some of that ship's survivors, who were stranded on one of the keys.

Upon his return to Cuba, a horrible sense of dread spread through the merchant community. The Spanish nobility were stunned. The entire year's output of the silver mine at Potosi, a fortune in Inca gold and oriental treasure, was lost. Spain's debts would be unpaid, its wars unfinanced, the king's creditors unsatisfied. Private fortunes would be wiped out, and the Royal Casa de Contratación, Spain's House of Trade, would have sad news to bear to the king. Without the annual bullion shipment from the Indies, Spain faced near bankruptcy.

Juan de Casta Bañon did not know his fate would be decided on 5 September 1622, when the galleons of the treasure fleet were dashed upon the shoals and sunk in the fury of a hurricane. He did not know it on 16 September 1622, when Gaspar de Vargas sailed in the aftermath of the tragedy, hoping to salvage the gold and silver. Casta Bañon could not have known that the famed commander of the fleet, the Marquis de Cadereita, personally undertook a search for the lost ships but failed. All Casta Bañon knew four years later, in the summer of 1626, was that his master, Nuñez Melián, had ordered him to dive. He knew that if he were successful, he would be freed. With his heart still pounding in his chest, Casta Bañon called out to his companions on board the salvage vessel. "Found. La Santa Margarita, found. A line quickly. A line."

Nuñez Melián took a diving bell aboard his salvage vessel. The kettle-like contraption was constructed with a window that would enable his divers to look out as the massive inverted bronze bell was towed behind his salvage ship. It was an ingenious device for the times, but it proved cruel, indeed fatal, to many divers. The slaves were his property, and when Nuñez Melián sent his accounting to the king he claimed dead slaves as part of his tally. This day he would add Casta Bañon's name to the expense account. Casta Bañon had been the first to discover the lost shipwreck and his freedom would eventually have to be paid for by the Crown. The accounts were not yet rendered and for the moment Nuñez Melián only motioned from the deck of his salvage ship to the slave below, who hung from the dive ladder, gasping for breath.

The carbon dioxide buildup in his system had given Casta Bañon a painful headache, but one thought pulsed through his brain: he would be set free with one more dive. Casta Bañon grasped the rope that was handed down to him and curled his arm around stone weights that would drag him rapidly to the bottom again.

Then he was gone. The salvage master watched from the deck as Casta Bañon's rope played out. A minute, perhaps a minute more, and the men on deck began to haul in on the rope. Then Casta Bañon appeared. He broke the surface, struggling for breath, clinging to the rope and a heavy object it secured. Many hands were there now to help him. They dragged the slave up the dive ladder onto the deck. Nuñez Melián watched as his crew struggled to haul the object aboard.

Black from its four-year immersion under the sea, the object only vaguely resembled a silver bar. A member of the crew scraped the discoloration away. Excitement spread through the ship almost simultaneously, and Juan de Casta Bañon, still lying on the deck, was temporarily forgotten. Nuñez Melián and his men gathered around the silver bar. The slave had indeed found the treasure galleon *Margarita*. When he could stand, Casta Bañon pushed his way through the group of men standing over the silver he had just wrested from the deep.

"Señor. Señor Don Francisco, I beg you, señor," the slave gasped, clutching Nuñez Melián by his shirt. "Your promise, señor. I beg you remember your promise," Casta Bañon said excitedly. He risked his life to deliver treasure up from the sea floor, and now the slave claimed his reward. But the Spanish were notoriously cruel, unfaithful to their word, and more than a century of enslavement had taught the Indians that their Spanish masters were not to be trusted.

Casta Bañon must have feared the worst when Nuñez Melián brushed his hand away, loosing his grasp on his shirt. In that instant, the slave must have remembered his station in life. Now the salvor studied his master's face to see if his promise would be kept.

Nuñez Melián shouted for all the crew to hear. "On the honor of a Spanish gentleman I pledged the man who first discovered the lost ships would have his reward. And you shall." Francisco Nuñez Melián grasped the hilt of his sword and pledged in the sight of his men and Almighty God that henceforth Juan de Casta Bañon was a free man. Then with the spirit of discovery still fresh, Nuñez Melián called his steward to bring wine to toast the freedman and commemorate the provenance of his discovery.

Bañon drank, he breathed deeply, drew his first breath as a free man. It was worth the risk, it had been worth everything, even life itself, to be free. For Nuñez Melián, he would make a mental note to debit the accounts for Casta Bañon's freedom, then set about the task of recovering what he could from the sunken galleon.

Casta Bañon couldn't know, nor could Nuñez Melián even foresee, that this very act, the very accounting for his expenses in freeing this slave, would have momentous importance more than three and a half centuries later. The worm-eaten expense account would be unwrapped and studied by a soft-spoken, unassuming American scholar in the Archives of the Indies in Seville. Casta Bañon's discovery and Nuñez Melián's inflated salvage expense accounts would provide the key that would eventually unlock the secret whereabouts of two of the most fabled treasure ships to the modern world. What began on 3 June 1626 with a slave diver's discovery would cost the lives of four persons in the twentieth century and nearly wreck the lives and hopes of countless others before the treasure of Spain's 1622 Tierra Firme Fleet would be found again.

"Another fellow by the name of Mel 350 years ago dug for it and found it. At one time a mast was even sticking out of the water on one of the wrecks. But they left because they couldn't break into the ship's battened-down holds. When they came back, another storm had wiped out their markers and they couldn't find it again," he told me, hardly able to get a minute free from interruption. On a table near his desk was a working model of his team's favorite treasure hunting boat. His salvage captain and crew barged in to see it and work the electric motor that turned the *Virgalona's* scale model propellers. "It's good. It's a good model," one of his divers called out, and Mel was gone. The men demanded his attention as they toyed with the model ship, marveling at the accurate detail that went into its mailboxes.

"It's just in time. We'll ship it up tomorrow," one of the men in the crowd said while the others continued to work the mailboxes that extended off the stern of the model and were fitted over the ship's two propellers. The two mailboxes were the digging end of the salvage ship, an ingenious improvisation by Mel Fisher—the "other Mel," who had discovered Nuñez Melián's provenance after eleven years of searching. Like his predecessors, this "Mel" was basking in the glory of its discovery and salvage.

"They camped on the Marquesas and planted a coconut tree out there. You'll still see it, only now it fell in the water with the last storm," the modern treasure salvor recounted. He was exuberant. The working model of his salvage ship would be displayed in a museum with gold bars, gold chains, plates and chalices, silver coins, and ingots weighing upwards of seventy pounds each. People from around the world would again, after a lapse of many centuries, marvel at the treasure of the Indies, the wealth of New Spain.

The "other Mel" would not be named governor of Caracas by his grateful king, he would in fact be set upon by creditors and creditors' lawsuits, by government agents and state custodians, defamed, called a fake by his contemporaries, and, like his namesake, have to struggle to clear his "accounts."

Like the salvors of old, Mel Fisher of Key West, Florida, had discovered the wrecks of the *Nuestra Señora de Atocha* and the *Santa Margarita*. For the moment at least, he was basking in public attention, awe, and acclaim for the discovery. His crew enjoyed a moment of lighthearted play with the model of his salvage ship before it and the gold they had brought up joined a museum exhibit, and they went back to sea to find more.

They were ungainly ships. With favorable winds a galleon could make only about four knots, but from 1510, for almost two and a half centuries, the galleon was known throughout the New World and with them Spain conquered and held the Americas and the Indies. When the *Santa Margarita* left Spain on

23 April 1622, it took thirty-nine days to reach its first landfall in the New World at the island of Dominica. The ship that would eventually join it for the trip back to Spain had been built by Alonso Ferrera in Havana. The *Nuestra Señora de Atocha,* although made in the New World, was named for the famed shrine to the Virgin in Madrid. When the six-hundred-ton ship was built, it cost twenty-six thousand ducats (a gold coin used in Europe worth about $2.30).

The *Atocha* was planked with cedar over an oak hull from Cuban forests. Its yard and masts were fashioned from pine imported from Germany. Both the *Atocha* and the *Margarita* carried twenty bronze cannons forged in Spain. The *Atocha's* arsenals were crammed with six and a half tons of gunpowder, more than half a ton of match cord, 60 muskets with more than a ton of shot, 60 hand-cut marble cannonballs and 540 iron. For its day, the *Atocha* was a mighty ship: 110.5 feet long and 32.9 feet wide, with two working decks and 70-foot masts. Thus armed and fitted out, eight mighty galleons sailed out of Havana harbor in a convoy of twenty-eight ships.

Perhaps unsurprisingly, each of the ships in the marquis's fleet was overloaded with passengers, goods, arms, provisions, and gold, the entire year's output of the silver mines at Potosi in the former viceroyalty of Peru, copper, indigo, fine jewels, and oriental porcelain. (Chinese porcelain was transferred from Spain's Pacific galleons engaged in the China trade from the Philippines, brought overland on the backs of mules to Caribbean ports for loading aboard the annual plate fleet.) Once a year the ships would sail, bringing trade goods from Spain, taking back with them the wealth of the New World.

On 4 September 1622, the Marquis de Cadereita, commander of the fleet, gave the order to sail. Almost at once, barely a day's sail out of Havana, the fleet was set upon by the fury of hurricane winds, sinking eight of the ships. An account of the tragedy appeared in a London newspaper in 1623, headlined "A True Relation of That Which Lately Happened to the Great Spanish Fleet." The newspaper account was vivid, "But Munday approaching . . . the weather . . . seemed to change and the winds coming to the North-east raised both a care and a feare in the Admirall. . . . But it should seeme that tempests will have their courses, and are not inexorable: for the winde increased . . . the clouds thickened . . . they could not discerne one ship from another . . . and the passengers, when it was apparent they could not escape saw as little mercy in the sea as they had endured in the winds."

In the aftermath of the disaster the marquis returned to Havana with the remnants of his crippled fleet. Three of the eight treasure galleons were lost: the *Margarita,* the *Rosario,* and the *Atocha,* along with several smaller armed escort ships called pataches. In sum, 550 perished, 259 of them, almost half, went down with the *Atocha.* Of the survivors, 5 survived the *Atocha's* wrecking; 66 were rescued from the *Margarita.* Passengers and crew of the *Rosario* were marooned on a deserted island, their ship thrown up and grounded on the reef.

The Spanish rescuers tried to salvage the *Rosario,* but found that the ship's precarious position on the reef required special caution. In the end the salvage crew, under the orders of Gaspar de Vargas, set fire to the *Rosario.* They burned the ship to the waterline, in the custom of salvors of the day, then recovered all of its precious cargo and cannons.

Unsatisfied with the results, the Marquis de Cadereita personally set up a salvors' camp on islands that were named in his honor—the Cayos de Marques. Modern navigational charts call them the Marquesas Keys; it was the early liberty that report writers took naming the islands that confounded treasure hunters searching for wreck sites. Cadereita's official report to the king, found in the archives of Seville in the *legajo* or folio Santo Domingo 132, became the treasure hunter's guide. The marquis reported that "Dragging her cables, the *Margarita* was lost upon a bank of sand which is to the east of the last Key of the Matecumbe."

It was this last word, copied and reported by archivists engaged by treasure hunters that haunted them. The Matecumbe. Fortunes were raised and expended searching and researching miles of ocean off Matecumbe Key, in Florida's middle keys. Many wrecks were found by Mel Fisher and his divers, who began their operations in the Florida Keys in the sixties. But the fabled galleons *Atocha* and *Margarita* eluded discovery.

A scholar researching the old *legajos* for his doctoral thesis in the Seville archive came upon a stack of revealing financial audits and accounts filed away under *contaduría* number 1112. When Dr. Eugene Lyon picked up the archive records, he found them badly eaten away by *Pollila* worms that left many of the pages too badly damaged to read. Patiently straining to read the series of sometimes illegible waves of Spanish legal script, Dr. Lyon came upon the accounts of Francisco Nuñez Melián. Nuñez Melián's contract with the Crown provided that he would share one-third of the recovered treasure and one-third would go to the king. Nuñez Melián could write off his expenses—provided he could justify his accounts—against the remaining third. This he did, accounted for in the worm-eaten financial records of *contaduría* 1112. Nuñez Melián claimed his slave, Casta Bañon, freed by his master's largesse, and noted that his salvage took place variously in the Cayos de Marques or the Cabeza de los Mártires.

Searching for other documents that would enable him to identify the site of Nuñez Melián's salvage of the *Santa Margarita,* Dr. Lyon went to the Biblioteca Nacional de Madrid, where he found an original map prepared by Capt. Nicholas de Cardona who wrote on the map the following notation: "The Cabeza de los Mártires is the southernmost part of Florida which runs east and west, and is located on a north-south line with the port of Havana, in more than twenty-five degrees Latitude; which is a dangerous place, for there have been drowned in it an infinite number of souls, and for this reason they call it Martires, or because of the innumerable keys which are thus joined together . . . there was lost in this place three silver galleons on the command of the Marquis de Cadereita and other ships of the fleet in which perished many souls and fortunes."

For Dr. Lyon, his tedious work was far from over, but he now knew that the *Margarita* wreck lay nowhere near the middle keys: Matecumbe then was just a generic term that the Spanish used to mean island. The treasure galleons were more than 110 miles south of Matecumbe Key, where treasure hunters, including Dr. Lyon's friend, Mel Fisher, were working.

Dr. Lyon discovered that Nuñez Melián was working in sand when he salvaged 64,750 pieces of eight, silver work, arms, 350 ingots of silver, copper, and 11 of the ship's bronze cannons. Dr. Lyon knew from Nuñez Melián's report to the king, written on 22 April 1627, that Nuñez Melián had not completely salvaged the *Margarita.* The letter read, "The opinion of the pilot-major and of the diver Antonio de Sosa is that the galleon *Santa Margarita* broke in half with the chambers where the silver was stored falling off to the right, and that the missing silver was in the quartel. All excess ballast of the ship was removed leaving hardly anything inside, helping us to further confirm that the majority of the silver was contained in the missing quartel, but when we finally discovered its location, it was so very buried in the sand and so difficult to reach that if God does not help us it will not be possible to retrieve anything."

The archive search for the whereabouts of the two shipwrecks was narrowing. Dr. Lyon found survivor reports that indicated that the *Atocha* sank in sight of the *Margarita*. The Cayos de Marques were obviously translated as the Marquesas Keys. All that was left for the archive detective was to try and narrow the search. His impetuous friend, treasure diver Mel Fisher, already had moved his entire operation to the Marquesas, gambling that Dr. Lyon's deduction was right.

In those early months, Mel Fisher's search efforts were not rewarded. The archive's clues sent Fisher first in one direction, then another. Dr. Lyon went back over documents he had studied years before, still searching for a definitive location of the wreck. The Marquis de Cadereita's official report continued to plague the treasure salvors, ". . . lost on a bank of sand which is to the east of the last key of the Matecumbe."

Matecumbe Key was, of course, discredited. It was the last key in the Marquesas that Cadereita was describing, but east? Mel Fisher has expended hundreds of thousands of dollars and hadn't turned up the wreck. Then Dr. Lyon discovered the problem. The old manuscript, written on both sides of the page with ink long since bled through and faint, was misread by an earlier researcher. In the Old Spanish, west was written "veste" or "ueste," and east "leste." What Dr. Lyon saw under his magnifying class was not an *l* at all but something that looked like a *v* or *u*. There it was, west of the last key of the Marquesas. But where exactly?

For this, Dr. Lyon and the archive documents were only able to help a little. A letter in the archives related how Nuñez Melián's salvors had to row from their camp, on the "last key" for three hours to get to the wreck site. It took them seven hours to row back at the end of their day's work on the shipwreck.

Fisher's treasure hunting ships would leave Key West and remain at sea for a week at a time or until provisions or luck ran low. They were adventurers. Divers were paid $120 per week plus a one-tenth of one-percent share of their finds. At night, anchored at sea or in the lee of a low-lying island, when the lights of Key West and Havana were visible only as a glow on the horizon, the divers would relax, play cards, strum guitars, and then sleep on deck to the sounds of the sea with anticipation of the next day's diving in their dreams.

But already Fisher's divers were making note of the fierce currents in the area of their search, dubbed the "quicksands" because of the shifting sand bottom. After more detective work in the archive, Dr. Lyon was able to tell Fisher that the Spanish salvors probably rowed the equivalent of three miles in one hour. Two large treasure galleons, carrying a king's ransom in gold, silver, and precious cargo sank in sight of each other, a three-hour row west of the last island in the Marquesas. Nine miles out, due west, and Fisher should find his treasure.

In June 1971, almost exactly in the area the armchair detective's research indicated, Fisher's magnetometers located a huge galleon anchor and near it gold chains, bars, Spanish muskets, and silver coins. This was it—they were convinced: they had found the wreck of the *Atocha*. Instead of ending the hunt, however, the anchor Fisher found only marked the beginning of years of work, the result of which has been excavation of the most valuable single treasure shipwreck known in the annals of treasure diving.

Of his discovery of the remains of the *Atocha*, Mel Fisher would comment, "It's the biggest puzzle in my life. I've spent eleven years looking for it. So far we've brought in 40 million dollars worth of treasure from the *Atocha,* and there's $360 million still out there." About the site of the *Margarita* wreck that Fisher and his team found in 1980, he said, "We brought up three to twenty-six million in treasure off the *Margarita.* The valuation depends if you sell it for scrap or fair market value. In weight, we've brought in more than 150 pounds of gold from the *Margarita,* more than two tons of silver, about five tons of copper and thousands of beautiful artifacts—old guns, swords, bronze cannons, a beautiful gold plate for serving Holy Communion, mortars and pestles, navigational instruments," Mel Fisher recounted, adding his inevitable optimistic "and maybe I found the big pile yesterday."

The *Atocha,* apart from its two bronze cannons snagged off the stern castle shortly after its sinking, had remained unsalvaged for centuries. Nuñez Melián and his Indian divers had recovered what they could off the *Margarita,* but Spain's increasingly precarious position in the world—spread thin with wars, including open hostilities with Dutch naval forces in the Caribbean and other concerns after Nuñez Melián was appointed governor of Caracas—along with the lack of modern diving technology, left most of the treasure still buried under the sea, deep inside the *Margarita's* rotting skeleton. And there the treasures of the *Atocha* and *Margarita* lay until Mel Fisher and his divers found them in the 1980s.

Mel Fisher's triumph in the Marquesas didn't come easily, however. Almost as soon as his oldest son discovered numbered bronze cannons that provided conclusive proof that the wreck was the *Atocha,* tragedy struck.

Fisher had bought two used Mississippi River tugs and converted them to treasure salvage vessels. He put his two teenage sons in charge of them. Dirk Fisher, his oldest son, captained the *Northwind.* Diving on one of the magnetometer hits, Dirk found five bronze cannons on 13 July 1975. News was radioed back to Key West and in short order the exultant Fishers converged on the site. When the excitement of the find subsided, the *Northwind* went back to the painstaking routine of digging and sending divers down.

On 20 July 1975, one of the divers sleeping on deck was awakened by an eerie cry, remembered later as a screaming warning in the night. The tug was listing at an odd angle. The diver roused the engineer from his bunk and they investigated the problem, going down into the engine spaces.

It was only when the two divers got down into the engine room that they realized how serious the problem was. The toilet flush line had disconnected, flooding the compartment with water. Fuel in the tanks had shifted, interconnected by an automatic transfer system that was supposed to keep the tug in trim. The transfer system malfunctioned and fuel went over to one side, exaggerating the list. In an instant, the divers in the engine room felt the *Northwind* capsize. One of the men made it through a hatchway, the other was trapped inside the engine room when the tug turned over. On one of the upper decks Mel's son Dirk and his wife, Angel Curry Fisher, were sound asleep. Other members of the crew, sleeping on deck, were thrown clear of the capsizing ship. They woke up in the water.

For one diver in the crew, there was no exit. Rick Gage drowned trying to escape from his cabin. Trapped in a precarious maze of stairways and blocked portholes, Dirk and his wife died. Their bodies were later found in the cabin they shared, Angel wedged in the doorway, Dirk on the bunk. They had no chance to escape.

The divers that managed to escape climbed up on the bottom of the capsized *Northwind*'s hull. They heroically dove down trying to find a way to rescue the diver trapped alive in the engine room. The tug started to sink. The men clinging to its upside-down hull heard the painful cries of their trapped friend, calling to his mother for help, slowly starving for breath as the tug went down.

Miraculously, the diver-engineer, Donnie Jonas, trapped in the engine room, found an air space and was able to locate a floating flashlight that worked. In one last effort, using the thin beam of light, Jonas was able to dive down, find the hatchway, and swim clear of the sinking hulk.

For Mel and his wife Deo Fisher, waiting on a Key West dock for the bodies of their son and daughter-in-law and the other diver to be brought in by rescuers, everything seemed lost. The young Fishers were buried together in the same Hawaiian clothes they had worn at their wedding. Almost immediately, Mel Fisher resolved to continue what he had begun. His outward courage in the aftermath of the tragedy belied the deep pain the Fishers felt. Mel came close to letting go, then marked time to recover from the stunning blow. When it passed, Mel's resolve to continue searching where Dirk had found the cannons could not be shaken, and the work went on.

Counting an earlier accident that took the life National Geographic photographer Bates Littlehales's eleven-year-old son Nikko—who went swimming off the side of one of the treasure salvage ships and was sucked into the propeller by the force of the mailboxes and killed—a total of four lives were now added to the *Atocha*'s roster of dead.

In the months that followed the tragic sinking of *Northwind,* Fisher's divers recovered silver bars that bore serial numbers and identification stamps that matched the *Atocha*'s manifest. The silver bars not only corresponded to the manifest by a number stamped on each bar, but when they were weighed they conformed exactly to the weights taken by the clerk of the Casa de Contratación and the ship's silvermaster when the bars were stowed aboard in 1622.

Continuing his dig, Fisher and his divers found gold bars and chains, coins, and thousands of silver pieces of eight.

It was provenance. Fisher had lost his son and daughter-in-law, a diver, and a close friend's little boy, but he could finally say that in some way their work contributed significantly to the knowledge of civilization. The life of adventure they lived could now be shared with millions who would vicariously enjoy their discovery through the films and articles and traveling museum exhibits that Mel Fisher conceived to make the realization of his and his family's dream accessible to all people. In the fulfillment of this dream, Mel's son still lives, as does the sparkle that burns inside all who believe that El Dorado exists, and that one only has to persist to find it.

For Mel Fisher, his problems didn't end when he found treasure. Almost immediately the state and federal governments interposed lawsuits. Fisher was provoked. The site of the treasure wrecks was approximately forty miles west of Key West, well beyond U.S. and Florida territorial waters. "I've spent eleven years looking for it, and the federal government wants it all. We beat them in the District Court and in the U.S. Court of Appeals. Then the State of Florida took it back to the lower court; then when we won, they appealed it. We won the appeal and now it's in the Supreme Court," Fisher said, describing the extensive litigation that tied up the treasure at a time when his operations most needed money to continue the search. Fisher won in the U.S. Supreme Court.

"I couldn't believe it. The State of Florida claimed it even though it was outside the U.S. It tied up the treasure for a year and a half. We couldn't sell it and we couldn't borrow on it," Fisher lamented. Throughout the years of court battles, Fisher was finding treasure but couldn't liquidate it in order to finance his operations. Finally his cause was vindicated in federal court. The judge, writing the opinion giving Fisher all title and right to the treasure, said: "This Court finds that the property of the wreck involved in this case is neither within the jurisdiction of the United States nor owned or controlled by our government . . . the wreck is located on the outer continental shelf of the United States. . . . Under the facts of this case, possession and title are rightfully conferred, upon the finder of the *res derelictae*."

Fisher won. The case apparently provoked the judges on the United States Court of Appeals to a nostalgic appreciation of the great adventure, for in their opinion confirming Fisher's victory in the lower Federal District Court, the judges wrote, "This action evokes all the romance and danger of the buccaneering days in the West Indies. It is rooted in an ancient tragedy of Imperial Spain, and embraces a modern tragedy as well. The case also presents a story of triumph, a story in which the daring and determination of the colonial settlers are mirrored by contemporary treasure seekers."

The easygoing, soft-spoken Mel Fisher tried to settle with the government and with the State of Florida. It was his wish to donate artifacts for a permanent exhibit. There was annoyance in his voice when he described the expensive court battles he felt were unnecessary, but there was no trace of bitterness. Fisher knew he was right, and the fact that the courts confirmed his own opinion only made it legal, so convinced was he in his purpose.

Mel Fisher died of cancer after a long and debilitating illness, but the wreck sites of the *Atocha* and *Margarita* yielded up their fortune of gold and silver before he died in December 1998. Mel had the satisfaction of knowing that his daughter Taffi and his sons Kane, Kim, and Terry, along with their mother Dolores, known affectionately as Deo, continue the tradition.

The fury of the 1622 hurricane and subsequent storms broke up the ships of Spain's lost Tierra Firme fleet over miles of ocean, strewing treasure along the bottom. All of it may never be found. Yet the drama of the fleet's demise and the struggles of salvors in the days of the Spanish Main and their modern-day counterparts is a story of daring.

The *Margarita* and *Atocha*'s gold has freed men and captured others. As divers set out from Key West in search of Spain's lost fleet, they call to mind the cost of another treasure, piled in a cave on Treasure Island:

> I beheld great heaps of coin and quadrilaterals built of bars of gold. That was Flint's treasure that we had come so far to seek, and that had cost already the lives of seventeen men from the Hispaniola. How many it had cost in the amassing, what blood and sorrow, what good ships scuttled on the deep, what brave men walking the plank blindfold, what shot of cannon, what shame and lies and cruelty, perhaps no man alive could tell. (Robert Louis Stevenson)

CHAPTER TWO

The Shipwrecks of Anegada

Rising up just below the surface, Anegada's reef extends approximately thirteen miles south of the island's last spit of land. With fingers of treacherous coral reaching out into the shipping lanes, the reef has drawn mariners into harm's way for centuries as they negotiated the Anegada Passage, a channel connecting the Atlantic Ocean with the Caribbean.

Christopher Columbus named the island Anegada, meaning the sunken land, in 1493, during his second voyage of discovery. Lying about thirty miles from Tortola, the administrative capital of the British Virgin Islands, Anegada at its highest point rises only about twenty-eight feet above sea level. The fifteen-mile-long by two-to-three-mile-wide island is surrounded by reefs and shallow coral shoals, hardly visible even in clear weather, until a ship is virtually on top of them.

For hundreds of years, Anegadians plied their trade as wreckers, salvaging what they could from the ships that struck the reef. A report sent to the Crown in 1824 described the business of wrecking on Anegada and the need to provide a subsidy to the islanders if the populace was to be expected to save life as well as property. The report stated: "Anegada, though perhaps the largest of the Virgin Islands, being computed to contain upwards of 20,000 acres, is chiefly a barren calcareous rock, with very little soil on the surface. About 100 acres are planted in cotton, and 60 acres in vegetables and corn, cultivated by 22 white inhabitants, all very poor, 29 free black and coloured people, who are still poorer, and 209 slaves belonging to the other two classes. The whole derive their chief means of subsistence from the sea, and their dexterity in assisting vessels wrecked on the dangerous shoals that surround the island, from which they derive a salvage, and sometimes gain, in a manner contrary to strict honesty, as appears by the examinations and inquiries which I have made. At any rate, it may easily be imagined, that people in their situation only expose their own lives to save those of the persons wrecked, and their property, from motives of gain. Now to save the lives of 240 Africans, as free men, as the law now stands relative to shipwrecks, would not only yield no gain to the Anegadians, but would entail upon them an expence for the maintenance of the Africans, which their poverty could not afford, even when aided by the resources of all the other islands. Unless some instructions, therefore, are given in case of another shipwreck of Africans, that a fair salvage will be allowed, and means taken to prevent their becoming burdensome to the community, there is too much reason to fear that many of the Africans would be lost."

The Royal Museum of Ontario conducted a magnetometer search in Anegada waters for three seasons from 1968 to 1970. Researchers took core samples on the sites. Analysis of core samples can help to determine whether a wreck is worth excavating. One of the perils underwater treasure hunters face after finding a shipwreck is that the site has already been plundered of valuable cargo. Indeed, on some of the sites, several of the cannons were in pieces. Blown-apart cannons on a wreck site are normally telltale signs that early wreckers were at work with dynamite, blowing the shipwreck apart to extract its cargo.

Anegada's oldest resident remembered the days when wrecking was the principal occupation on the island. "If one struck anywhere, you would see the people running with their bags and their knives for progging. They might say they were going progging potatoes," said ninety-year-old James Wallace Vanterpool. He described the excitement that spread over the populace when a ship struck the reef.

Born on Anegada on 28 November 1891, James Wallace Vanterpool, or "Uncle Wallace" as he was called out of affection and respect, was the grandson of a sailor whose ship wrecked on Anegada. "Our grandfather was Dutch. He strike here on a vessel and stayed here. That's how we get the name

Vanterpool. My father was his son. My father died before Archie—that was my grandfather's name. Archie lived long after my father died. My grandfather was milk white," Uncle Wallace said, sitting in his rocking chair in the kitchen of his small house in Anegada's settlement.

The locations of shipwrecks were passed down from generation to generation on Anegada. "Uncle Charles showed us the places where they strike when we were children. I was a bit of a boy around twelve or fourteen years, when we used to go to a wreck. After we got to be a certain age we could go where the men went. The people in those days were so accustomed to the wrecks. They used to make their money from those wrecks. There was no hard money on the island. It was only after they opened the sugar cane mills in the Dominican Republic and they could go there to work that there were jobs." Uncle Wallace recounted, reminiscing about the early days on Anegada. The island's wrecks once supported a population of about two thousand, but now only about 125 people, mostly fishermen, reside on Anegada.

Ships continue to wreck on Anegada's treacherous reefs. A Japanese freighter that had been sold in Haiti was renamed the *Ada 1*. It struck the reef in September 1980. Lowell Wheatley, owner of Anegada's only hotel and the first man to arrive at the scene, recalls the incident. "She was coming down the channel because the shipping lane is so close. Her rudder went bad on her. They were just fixing the rudder and the current brought it up on the reef. When they realized it, it was too late to do anything about it. When she hit the reef she really got trapped in there pretty good. There was no way of getting back out."

The ship sits up on the reef canting at an odd angle, a huge gash ripped clean through its hull after winter storms had tossed the ship sideways on the coral. "She held pretty good," Lowell Wheatley continued, describing the wrecking. "There was hardly any water in there at first. Not even worth pumping it out. Two days later they decided to evacuate [the] ship because the weather was getting nasty. So that's when we took off the crew of six and two dogs. They were all Haitians, even the captain. She had just sailed from St. Martin empty after offloading her cargo of concrete blocks and was returning to Haiti when she struck," Lowell concluded, showing off the ship's foghorn, binnacle, wheel, and brass telegraph that he had managed to salvage from the wreckage.

Further down the reef lies the wreckage of a Colombian marijuana runner, the *Rio Negro*. The *Rio Negro* stranded on Horseshoe Reef in February 1979, when its engine failed and the currents drove the ship onto the coral. When authorities arrived to render assistance they impounded the ship's cargo of marijuana and arrested eight crew members.

The islands abound with tales of smuggling and piracy, of illicit cargoes and sunken treasure. Uncle Wallace told an amusing anecdote about a whiskey runner that sank during prohibition.

"It was a small vessel. She had 413 bags of liquor aboard. They had prohibition around the country in those days and she was heading for Puerto Rico. When they'd arrive, they'd put the bags containing the liquor bottles down in the water. Well she never made her destination, striking here on the reef. When the commissioner came over from Tortola, they asked if anyone could dive. I said yes, me and my brother-in-law. So we dived for the commissioner. I came up first and told the commissioner the ship apparently had something like liquor aboard." Uncle Wallace's face beamed with a smile as he recounted the story. "I had dived in the night, before the commissioner came over and we kept out some of the liquor for our own use. It was just a small wooden vessel," he added.

Legend has it that the notorious pirate Edward Teach, better known as Blackbeard, used Anegada as a base to pillage Caribbean shipping. It is said that pirates would ride the beaches with lanterns to lure ships onto the jagged reefs. A tale is told that Blackbeard took a young girl off one of the shipwrecks, fell in love with her, sent her off to England to school and later married her. True or not, the tale adds a romantic allure to this notorious pirate who had a total of fourteen wives.

There is a creek on Anegada called Bone Creek, after the famous pirate captain that quartered there. Others, such as Captain Kidd, Kirke, Prince Rupert, and Captain Norman, after whom Norman Island was named, contribute to the legend and folklore of the region. It is said that Norman Island was the inspiration for Robert Louis Stevenson's Treasure Island.

Plying the Caribbean under letters of commission from King Charles I of England, the privateer Prince Rupert lost one of the ships of his fleet on Anegada's reef in 1652. The *Defiance* was an English ship that Admiral Rupert put under the command of his brother, Prince Maurice. Bert Kilbride, a dive charter captain who has been searching for shipwrecks off Anegada's reef for about thirty years, believes he's found the remains of the *Defiance*.

"She had gold and emeralds aboard," Kilbride said. "I think I found it a couple of years ago. The artifacts are about the right date. I know the *Defiance* is right because the date is right. There's another wreck right on top of it, but it hasn't been dug into yet," Kilbride added as he described a project to locate and excavate the shipwrecks of Anegada.

Nearby is the *San Ignacio,* which wrecked on 31 March 1741, a ship owned by the Caracas Company. "It was one of the privately owned concerns authorized to do business within the Indies. She had aboard several hundred tons of Venezuelan products including gold and crude diamonds when she went against Anegada's reef in 1742," Kilbride said.

Kilbride and a private venture under license from the government of the British Virgin Islands excavated a site they believed to be the *San Ignacio.* "There are eighteen cannons showing and the magnetometer shows more under the sand. There were two cannons on top of the reef that they threw off to lighten ship; then they threw off four more as they came over the reef and sank. When we put in the suction lift we found five more cannons and anchors. [The *San Ignacio*] sank on the other side after bouncing over the reef. The cannons are right," explained Kilbride.

"She had a lead bottom. Spanish had lead bottoms," Kilbride paused, scratched his chin, looked off his veranda on Saba Rock toward Anegada, "English and French had copper bottoms," he added reflectively. "It's in a rough area in forty-five feet of water. That vessel was certainly not salvaged. It's eleven miles from here," Kilbride said pointing. "Nine miles from Anegada, so you couldn't see it. Most you can see is six miles. Closer wrecks may have been salvaged because people were living on Anegada," he added.

Bert Kilbride and others formed a company to survey, map, search, and excavate the shipwrecks lost on Anegada's reef. The company obtained an exclusive contract with the government and ran magnetometer surveys of reef areas. Kilbride reported that more than a hundred contacts were made with the magnetometer survey. This information was extrapolated with shipwreck data and fed into a computer.

Using the computer, sophisticated underwater search techniques, satellite photographs, and coring devices, Kilbride hoped to identify the more important shipwrecks. "There's supposed to be from four hundred to six hundred million dollars in treasure out there," Bert Kilbride said. He pointed toward Anegada's reef. "We plan to make an underwater park, expose the cannons, and leave them there. We'll also preserve the ships' wood and have a little museum in Road Town. But we'll take all the loot, because that's what it's about," Kilbride said. The government of the British Virgin Islands will share fifty-fifty in the finds.

Bert lived in a stone and wood house he built with his own hands on Saba Rock and is something of a legendary figure. Pointing to a bronze cannon he recovered from the *Astrea,* Kilbride described how he struggled to bring the heavy bronze cannon up from the wreck of the British frigate lost on Anegada's Horseshoe Reef on 23 May 1808. "The cannon was made before 1740," Kilbride explained. "After 1740, trunion pins were brought up to center." Kilbride pointed out the unusual features of his cannon. "The barrel was plugged. I never thought anything about it until my son pushed the plug in and I put a screw in it to pull it out. When the plug came out, a hemp cord was attached to it and at the end of the cord was this woven ball smelling of oakum. The plug kept the barrel dry and as clean as the day they sealed it up," Kilbride said. He pulled out the barrel plug and oakum ball to expose the barrel.

George and Luana Marler owned a dive charter business on Tortola. They spent many hours researching and chronicling shipwrecks of the islands. Delving through musty accounts of the sinking of the *Astrea,* the Marlers found that the captain, one Edmund Heywood, thought that the land the crew had spotted was Puerto Rico. Heywood set his course, supposing they would make the safety of Mona Passage by morning. The account the Marlers found poignantly described the tragedy:

"A few minutes before eight o'clock, George Lovet, the gunner, came on deck to stand his watch. Leaning over the port rail, his eyes slowly getting accustomed to the dark evening, he suddenly saw a solid line of white breakers appearing dead ahead. He shouted a warning, and an instant later the captain's command came, 'Helm hard a port.' Having fresh way on, the frigate started to respond to the wheel. But it was too late."

The Marlers' chronicle and discovery of the early reports of the sinking become vivid when diving over the site. Following George Marler out through a narrow passage in the reef, carefully timing it so one can make it through the pass between waves to avoid being dashed upon the shallow coral, then coming upon the *Astrea*'s massive anchors and cannons strewn over the reef, one can imagine the shock Captain Heywood and his men experienced when their vessel sailed headlong onto this precarious reef.

Reef sharks and spotted eagle rays patrolled the reef on the Atlantic Ocean side while George Marler dove down to photograph the wreck site. The *Astrea* struck Anegada's Horseshoe Reef about a mile south of the island. The ship carried another bronze cannon that neither Bert Kilbride nor anyone else have been able to locate. The *Astrea*'s captain threw over many of her thirty-two iron cannons to lighten ship, hoping to get her off the reef. In the crashing surge, the 126-foot long, 704-ton frigate's keel was smashed in two and the crew had to abandon ship. Four of the *Astrea*'s 230 crew members perished in the surge. Today the *Astrea*'s remains are submerged among the surrounding reef. Its cannons and cannonballs are fused with the coral; the *Astrea*'s anchors form picturesque silhouettes against the reef.

Diving on the ship's remains, George Marler would swim down and fan accumulations of sand and bits of coral out of potholes in the reef floor to recover bronze ship fittings, musket balls, copper nails, and assorted ships' accouterments. Great caution had to be exercised while diving over the *Astrea* site; it was necessary to gauge the surf before descending. The wreck is accessible to divers only when the ocean is flat calm, and even on calm days waves and surge can easily throw unsuspecting divers over the reef or smash them against sharp coral.

One of the wrecks discovered by Bert Kilbride in the mid-sixties is simply called the Carronade Wreck because of its large mortar-like cannons. Producing an official-looking document, dated 21 June 1967, from the Tortola administrator's office, Kilbride tells how he was appointed "Receiver of Wreck" by the government after his discovery.

While attempting to identify the Carronade Wreck, Kilbride copied numbers off cannons found on the site and sent the numbers off to England. A reply
came from Comdr. W. R. C. Bennet of the Royal Navy. Commander Bennet
reported "The first item is a 12-pounder cannon registered number S 590 cast
by Messrs. Sturges & Co. in 1805 and proved at Woolwich Arsenal on 18th
January 1805. The second item is a 24-pounder cannon, registered number
53,212, cast by the Carron Co. in 1795 and proved at Woolwich on the
19th/20th October 1795."

This information provided details Kilbride sought. Each detail about a shipwreck has to be sorted and studied. Each small bit of wreckage brought up adds
a piece to the puzzle archaeologists can put together with the goal of identifying
the ship, because wrecks are often found scattered or broken up underwater.

Of the many ships that struck on Anegada's reef, James Wallace Vanterpool
remembered one with a strange cargo. "Some ship strike here loaded with
bones," he began. "She was the *Rocus*. She left South America loaded from stem
to stern with bones. She was a Greek ship. I was the first man to get there on a
little boat. We were going to our fish pots and saw a light. We went toward it,
finally were too far out to turn back. When we got there, the captain called
down to me and I came up. He had a little shorthaired dog that tried to bite me,
but they put him in a room. The captain asked me if this was Anegada. I said
yes, it's the place called Horseshoe. They tried to get a little Danish boat to pull
her off, but couldn't."

Uncle Wallace described the sinking of the 380-foot Greek freighter that
struck the reef at the very southern tip while making for the port of Baltimore.
The *Rocus* was sailing from Trinidad loaded with cattle bones for use in fertil-
izer when her captain misjudged their position and ran up on the reef in 1929.

The *Rocus* was not the first steam-powered vessel to sink off Anegada's reef.
In 1899 the steamer *Ida* was lost. Uncle Wallace was only eight years old when
the *Ida* struck the reef, but he remembers the wrecking. "The *Ida* was the first
steamer that strike on this island in my day. There's been a lot since, but she was
the first I remember. She strike a hole at night," Uncle Wallace recalled. He sat
in his rocking chair, remembering the incident. "In the morning one of the men
saw it and told the people. She was bound from Spain to Puerto Rico. The *Ida*

had everything on board. She had bales of cloth with iron bands around it so when they got them to the bay they had to chop the iron away to get the cloth. She had a cargo of perfume. You could smell the sweet perfume for weeks. Although the tide used to go and come you would go and smell the sweet for weeks around the bay," Uncle Wallace recounted. "The *Ida* had good cheese on her. It was fine cheese, not like the kind you get today. She got lost and passed Puerto Rico. When she turned around to come back she hit the reef."

Uncle Wallace remembered a tragic incident that occurred during a futile attempt to get the *Ida* off the reef. "One of the sailors was just coming out on the tow with a line. The boat he was in capsized, it hit him in his head and killed him. They buried him in the sand. Wrapped him in a Spanish flag and was crying in their Spanish language. Her iron is there where she strike," Uncle Wallace said, offering drink from a jug of sea grapes soaked in rum, an old custom on Anegada.

Ships of the Royal Mail Steam Packet Company regularly plied the Caribbean, carrying mail, cargo, and passengers back and forth between the Indies and England. Two of the most famous shipwrecks in the British Virgins were steamships belonging to the Royal Mail Company. The paddle steamer *Paramatta* had just been launched in England. The *Paramatta* was a finely appointed ship, 330 feet in length with a 44-foot beam, displacing 3,500 tons. When the *Paramatta* set sail from Southampton, England, on 17 June 1859, there were 180 passengers and crew aboard. It was the *Paramatta*'s maiden voyage.

One of the passengers, interviewed by a Jamaica newspaper after the new steamer struck on Anegada's reef, gave the following narrative of the voyage and the events that led up to the ship's collision with the reef on the night of 30 June 1859:

We left Southampton with a fair wind, and were soon running down the Channel at the rate of eleven knots an hour. Her great length, sharp bow, and straight cutwater sent her through every opposing wave without a single spray to wash her deck, or a solitary motion to disturb her steadiness. As a ship she is one of the most perfect models I have ever witnessed, having all that could be conceived, not only

for the supply of every luxury and convenience, but likewise for security in danger.
. . . At the early part of the voyage, when laden with 1,500 tons of coal, we were
running 275 miles a day, which speed increased as we grew lighter (we were burning from 100 to 109 tons of coal per day) until we attained a speed of from 294
to 305 miles a day.

The enormous difficulty with which the captain and officers had to contend in
this, their first voyage in the *Paramatta* was the ship's iron, which caused the compasses
continually to change from their proper points, keeping the officers incessantly cal-
culating and observing local deviation, so as to properly navigate the ship. . . . All proceeded most delightfully until Friday the 24th, when our wheel came upon a sunken
vessel, which being below water, was unobserved by the watch. An iron girder was
wrenched like a wire, and the huge boss was rent to the very axle. The *Paramatta* was
instantly brought to a stand for repair, which occupied some seven hours in the lash-
ing of chains to the axle, to preserve her from further accident by strengthening the
shafts to which the floats were secured.

On the evening of Thursday, the 30th, when anxiously looking for land,
and expecting momentarily to sight Sombrero, the captain refused to leave the
deck, even at the repeated solicitations of the passengers, replying at every
request, "I never go down stairs when we're making land." Thus these officers
continued taking sights and watching for land from three o'clock until ten, when
suddenly the ship struck the ground and told us we were on shore, and for the
first time we discovered we were out of our proper track. Great uneasiness prevailed as to our safety, seeing it was a matter of uncertainty whether the ship was
making water or not; but she was afterwards discovered to be alright, and fear
began to subside.

Vessels were dispatched from St. Thomas to the aid of the *Paramatta*. Unable
to pull her off the reef, the passengers and cargo were transferred and the vessel left to the wreckers of Anegada. The wreck of the *Paramatta* remains partially
intact in forty feet of water. "You can see her whole stern and three decks. She
had square portholes which makes her look like a Spanish galleon," Bert
Kilbride said, describing the wreckage underwater. "You can still see her old
caloric four-cylinder engines," he added.

Flying low over Horseshoe Reef, veteran diver George Marler pointed out the wreckage of the *Paramatta* from the air. The clear water shimmered over the reef. Coral heads rose up nearly to the surface. The iron skeleton of the once regal ship now plays host to a forest of elkhorn coral and a myriad of fish and reef life.

One of the most famous shipwrecks of all time, used as the backdrop for underwater sequences shot for the movie version of Peter Benchley's novel, *The Deep*, is another Royal Mail Company steamship, the *Rhone*. The drama of the sinking of the *Rhone* began on the morning of 29 October 1867, off Peter Island. The narrative is derived from contemporary eyewitness accounts. One report stated:

> On the morning of October 29th, 1867, R.M.S. *Rhone,* latest and finest addition to the Royal Mail fleet, was at anchor near Peter Island, one of the chain of islets bounding Sir Francis Drake Channel to the south and east of Tortola. *Rhone,* under the command of Capt. R. F. Woolley, had left Southampton on October 2nd and was now taking in cargo and stores for the return crossing. The *Conway,* Capt. Hammock, lay alongside.

The stillness of the tropic day was undisturbed, save for the rattle of capstans and occasional voices of sweating negroes at work on the two ships. The sun blazed down from a clear sky, the transfer operations were allowed to go on. The captains were on the alert. At about 11 AM the barometer suddenly fell to 27.95", the sky darkened, and with a mighty roar a fearful hurricane blew from the N.N.W. The howling wind whistled through the shrouds and tore at the rigging. A creamy spume smothered the decks as the surface of the sea was whipped into foam by the force of the hurricane. With engines going at full speed the ships rode the storm. On the *Rhone* a heavy spar fell from aloft, killing the Chief Officer Mr. Topper. His body was found next day on Salt Island and was buried there, together with two of the crew.

At noon there came a lull in the storm and Capt. Woolley weighed and stood away to the south-east where he would have more sea room in which to meet the second onslaught. He had negotiated most of the rocky channels in safety and was rounding the last point when the sky darkened, and a fearful blast struck the *Rhone,* forcing her upon the rocks of Salt Island, where she broke her back, parted amidships, and instantly sank, taking most of her company with her.

Captain Woolley was washed onto a skylight and the next sea took him overside, between the ship and the rocks. He was never seen again.

On Saba Rock, Bert Kilbride's island home, he has accumulated hundreds of artifacts recovered from the wreck of the *Rhone*. Pointing to a skull and leg bones sitting atop an old iron treasure box, Kilbride declared, "That's Steve Kenyon, the ship's carpenter on the *Rhone*. I identified him from a little bronze snuffbox in his shirt pocket. I found that he was the ship's carpenter from the crew list." The bones and skeletal remains were in evidence while Kilbride described how he made the discovery.

"I found his skull and rib cage about ten years ago. I was digging down in the mud. I came upon his toolbox and under it I found his skeleton. I reached my hand down under his rib cage and felt something mushy. I didn't know what it was. When I pulled it out I saw it was his shirt. In the pocket of the shirt was a small snuff box with the name Steve Kenyon engraved on it," Bert Kilbride said.

There is a friendly rivalry between divers on the islands that sometimes results in amusing anecdotes. A story is told about Bert Kilbride. He invited the Marlers to a formal dinner party, and when George and Luana Marler sat down at their places, they found the table set with china from the *Rhone*. Not one to be upstaged, George Marler confided plans to reciprocate. The table will of course be set with *Rhone* china, but Marler plans to set Kilbride's place with dishes marked "second class."

As often as they've dived over the wreckage of the *Rhone,* neither Bert Kilbride nor George Marler were the first salvage divers on the shipwreck, nor the first to dine off its salvage. The *Port of Spain Gazette* published a letter written from Salt Island in May 1870. It described a contemporary salvage of the steamer.

We paid a visit to the Murphys about two weeks ago, they are at Salt Island diving various things out of the wreck of the Steamer *Rhone*. I have never seen a diving dress, it was a novelty to all of us; the children were delighted to see Murphy in his dress, he certainly cut an awful figure, but when he went overboard and we saw him sinking, sinking until we lost sight of him, it was something horrible—the water is 17 fathoms and you can't see the bottom—he was gone for hours, he sent up 12 Bales of Cotton and various other things; amongst other matters a large Scull, which must have belonged to a very large man—the cotton is as good as the day it went down; he also saved the anchor and chains and lots of copper. While he was down he sent a message up to invite the ladies down into the saloon of the *Rhone.* I took a slice of lamb over and we had a first-rate dinner. When dinner was nearly ready, Murphy came up, rested for a few minutes and said "Now ladies, as I have nothing good to offer you, I will take a look into the other half of the ship (she is broke in two pieces) and see what can be got." They begged him not to go but off he went and in half an hour we had as much Champagne, Beer, Soda Water, Lemonade, Seltza, Water and Brandy as we knew what to do with; the liquors were as good as they were the first day and it is nearly three years since they have been down; the Champagne was first rate, as cool as possible, we drank it out of tumblers as we did not have Champagne glasses."

The Murphys (three brothers of them) came to St. Thomas soon after the Hurricane of 1867 and have been there ever since. When the *Rhone* was wrecked they saved the specie and bullion out of her, and got a large sum of money from Mr. Cameron, some $20,000 for their part. The steamer had on board some 60,000 Pounds in specie and bullion. A few months ago the second brother was drowned in St. Thomas harbor; he went down into the hold of the Liverpool Packet and by some means something went wrong and the poor fellow was drowned; the two remaining brothers felt his loss very much. Murphy tells me he sees an enormous Jew fish in the saloon of the Rhone, but the fellow won't come near him.

Reporting on the tragedy that befell the *Rhone* and its sister ship, the *Conway,* Captain and Senior Officer L. Vesey aboard the H.M.S. *Darwin* communicated the following news to the Secretary of the Admiralty at Whitehall while at sea. "Sunday, 3rd November 1867, . . . The *Conway* then cast off and whilst steaming across, was struck by the blast, rose suddenly and burst in her ports—the ship being in danger of foundering—and a lull coming—suddenly he thought the wind was going to shift, and put her head to S.W. He hardly had done so, when the blast struck her, blowing away funnel and mainmast, and if they had not providentially drifted into Tortola Roads and ashore—nothing could have saved them . . . I fear that in the *Rhone* great loss of life occurred—23 only were saved as far as I can yet learn, namely 14 men who were found on the fore top sail yard—which is above water—a few got on shore, and ten others and the 4th Officer were found in the Sound, clinging to the lifeboat."

Several hundred people perished in the tragic sinking of the *Rhone,* believed to be the more seaworthy of the two ships. The *Conway,* originally lying at anchor next to the *Rhone* off Peter Island, had transferred its passengers aboard for safety.

In the film version of *The Deep,* divers vie for sunken treasure and ampoules of morphine deep within the sunken wreckage of the *Rhone.* With a handful of glass ampoules, Bert Kilbride demonstrated the difference between the ones made for the film and the original morphine ampoules actually recovered from another shipwreck sunk off Bermuda.

Divers excavating one of the shipwreck sites inside Anegada's Horseshoe Reef have discovered ships' cannon, valuable hand-blown bottles, shot, a flint-lock pistol in a fairly good state of preservation with the flint still in place, and an assortment of interesting artifacts. The ship is unidentified, designated only as the "Crown Wreck" from a crown discovered stamped on one of the cannon tubes on the site. Archaeologists date the ship to about 1830. Excavation of the shipwreck site is proceeding very slowly in order not to damage fragile arti-facts or destroy the reef.

Besides the *San Ignacio,* other treasure-laden Spanish ships are reported to have sunk off Anegada. *La Victoria,* according to Bert Kilbride, was a Spanish warship carrying a consignment of almost two million dollars worth of gold and silver when it hit the reef in 1738. The 212-ton *Nuestra Señora de Lorento y San Francisco Xavier,* heading for Porto Bello, and the *San Antonio* also struck Anegada's perilous reef, reportedly carrying valuable cargo, as did the 1739 wreck of the *Soledad.*

Not surprisingly, some of the treasure wrecks that struck the reef in shal-low water were discovered by Anegada residents. Uncle Wallace Vanterpool vividly remembers how young men from the settlement recovered gold coins from one of the wrecks. "They brought up doubloons. The young men saved the money in a pail and when they went to share the money—let me show you," Uncle Wallace got up spryly from his rocker and crossed the room to pick up half of a gourd he had on a shelf in the kitchen. "They scooped them out like this," he demonstrated, making a scooping motion with the gourd. "We called it a ladle, and they ladled out each share of the gold coins."

Uncle Wallace has lived most of his ninety years on Anegada except for the time during the two world wars. "We called the first one the Kaiser's war. I was working in the Dominican Republic. In the last war I worked for the U.S. Navy on St. Thomas and stayed until the end of the war," Uncle Wallace related. He did some diving for the Navy during the war. Among his stories about treasure and shipwrecks on Anegada, Uncle Wallace remembered a fierce argument that took place between two men. "They were friends. They got a gold table diving a wreck and squabbled over it. One of the fellas picked up the table and threw it into a salt pond to end the argument before it came to blows. We call it Gold Table Pond to this day, and we go there to get salt out of it," Uncle Wallace related.

One thing is certain, for as long as shipping plies the Caribbean the treacherous reefs of Anegada will claim their share. Even with those selected for excavation by Anegada's modern-day treasure salvors, there will be many more left unfound. In the twenty-one year period between 1811 and 1832, studied by Robert H. Schomburgk for the Royal Geographic Society, some sixty-seven ships met their end trying to negotiate the Anegada Passage.

"You know Mr. Kilbride. I used to show him dozens of them," Uncle Wallace said. "We used to go with him to show him where the vessels strike. Once he brought a fellow from Hollywood to show him where one particular vessel strike. Over the years we showed a few people where the vessels went on the reef. They used to give us just ten dollars for the whole day," Uncle Wallace reminisced. "Then they would come back and take up the anchors. Kilbride knows where a pile of those vessels strike, I showed him. But I guess Kilbride is getting to be a pretty good age too," Uncle Wallace smiled. He sat back in his chair and rocked pensively.

Then, as if describing his island's legacy to the inquisitive world, Uncle Wallace paused, motioned out toward Horseshoe Reef and said, "What I named to you only strike in my day. Anegada had from history dozens and dozens of vessels strike her. In total, I think three hundred and odd. Yes that reef got a lot of wrecks," he concluded, describing the sunken land and its flotilla of lost ships.

CHAPTER THREE

The Terrible Republic:
Privateers and Pirate Ships

"In some respects privateering as waged a century and more ago was a sordid, unlovely business, the ruling motive being rather a greed of gain than an ardent love of country. Shares in lucky ships were bought and sold in the gambling spirit of a stock exchange. Fortunes were won and lost regardless of the public service. It became almost impossible to recruit men for the navy because they preferred the chance of booty in a privateer," read a historical account about the state of the American maritime forces during the Revolutionary War.

At the commencement of hostilities in 1776, the Continental forces had thirty-one vessels in commission. By 1782, according to the reckoning of this same maritime historian, only seven vessels flew the American Navy flag. These statistics mean only that the brunt of the responsibility for American naval warfare was entrusted into private hands, whose competition for profit brought many early sea captains great notoriety and great wealth.

By the close of 1777, it was discovered that 174 private armed vessels had been commissioned mounting two thousand guns and carrying nine thousand men. Casualties inflicted upon the British were enormous. "During this brief period of the war [the Americans] took as prizes 733 British merchantmen and inflicted losses of more than two million pounds sterling. Over ten thousand seamen were made prisoners at a time when England sorely needed them for drafting into the navy. To lose them was a far more serious matter than for General

Washington to capture as many Hessian mercenaries who could be replaced by purchase," the early chronicler reported.

He went on to describe how in these same two years of the Revolutionary War some nine hundred American ships were taken or sunk by the British. Privateers never sailed in defense of an American brig or merchantman. The privateers only went after prizes and spoils of war.

It was an age of swashbuckling adventure. Privateers with their letters of marque from the American Continental Congress plied their trade often in sight of the English coast. The privateers succeeded in disrupting trade with the British colonies in the West Indies as well. A letter written by a merchant on the island of Grenada stated: "A fleet of vessels came from Ireland a few days ago. From sixty vessels that departed from Ireland not above twenty-five arrived in this and neighboring islands, and others, it is thought, being all taken by American privateers. God knows, if this American war continues much longer, we shall all die of hunger."

The difference between pirates and privateers was only one of definition. Many a pirate was hanged who started out his career in noble cause. Their deeds of daring, their outrages, the cunning and bravery of brigands who captured the imagination of the world, acts of gallantry and coolness under fire, their brag and bravado were all exemplified in the challenge of Barbarossa the pirate to King Charles V. "Go tell your King," he said, "he is King of the Land; but I am the King of the Sea."

Such pluck and the great aspirations of greedy governors and backers who stood to gain from the lucrative privateering trade made the definition quite flexible indeed. When war broke out between Great Britain and France in 1803, U.S. ships carried on a brisk commerce, flying a neutral flag and trading with both sides.

This state of affairs was not to be for long. Without a navy, Napoleon conquered the German states and declared a blockade of Britain. U.S. ships trading with the enemy thus were fair game to marauding legions of privateers with French letters of marque. Great Britain began seizing and condemning U.S. ships that carried goods from French colonies in the West Indies. Even if a ship sailed from America, it was sufficient cause for seizure if the privateer captain judged its cargo to come from enemy possessions in the New World.

Reacting to popular demand, Pres. Thomas Jefferson imposed the embargo of 1807, suspending trade in the following terms: "The whole world is thus laid under interdict by these two nations, and our own vessels, their cargoes, and crews, are to be taken by the one or the other for whatever place they may be destined out of our limits. If, therefore, on leaving our harbors we are certain to lose them, is it not better as to vessels, cargoes, and seamen, to keep them at home?"

Then Jefferson's edict was reduced to the balance sheets a year later, and the merchants found foreign commerce had dropped from $108 million to $22 million. The clamor resulted in repeal of the 1807 embargo and passage of a law that only prohibited trade with the two warring nations, France and England. The non-intercourse act infuriated Napoleon, who retaliated by passing secret orders to the Prussians—and other nations the French forces dominated—to seize American vessels. This piracy under the color and guise of law and war resulted in the seizure of more than two hundred American ships.

The British used the ploy—permitted by sea law of the day—of searching vessels for British seamen and contraband. The plight of the American seamen kidnapped from their vessels and illegally impressed under color of law in British ships became a national issue and fanned a fire of resentment, leading eventually to the War of 1812. As evidence, records found in 1807 revealed that six thousand American seamen had been kidnapped from their vessels and impressed in British ships. Yet even before the War of 1812 pirates often attacked merchant ships and kidnapped or persuaded seamen to join them. One such incident involved the *Speaker,* which sank in 1702 off the island of Mauritius in the Indian Ocean.

The search for the *Speaker* began when a French diver, Patrick Lize, found in the dust-covered archives in The Hague a letter referring to the sinking of the ship. His colleague, Jacques Dumas, a Paris lawyer and then-president of the World Underwater Federation, was skeptical at first. Finding a shipwreck from scanty information contained in an old report from the governor of Mauritius could be an impossible task. As luck would have it, Lize found a part in the old letter that contained specific information: "On January 7, 1702 at eight o'clock in the evening, in a sudden gale, the pirate ship *Speaker* sank near Swarte Klip at the mouth of the south east Great river." But before agreeing to mount the search for this pirate ship Dumas needed more convincing. While Lize could find no manifest or log book, he had searched out reports in England, written by victims of the infamous pirate ship.

The story of John Bowen, the *Speaker*'s captain, is an interesting tale discovered by Lize in his research. Captain Bowen's long adventure began in 1697, off the coast of the Carolinas not far from Charleston. He was in command of a small merchant ship sporting only six guns for self-defense. Set upon by pirates, Captain Bowen surrendered both his ship and crew. With their pilot killed, the French pirate captain impressed Bowen to navigate his ship to the Indian Ocean. Captain Bowen agreed to the pirate's demand on the condition that they release his ship and cargo. Thus the hapless merchant captain set off on a long and perilous journey that became one of the most exciting adventures of all time.

Navigating the pirate ship around the Cape of Good Hope to the coast of Madagascar, Bowen and two other English prisoners escaped in the ship's longboat and made for St. Augustin on the coast of Madagascar, an island that had become a pirates' refuge. Captain Bowen with the two men were captured by Vezo tribesmen and put to work. Eventually a pirate ship put in, its crew wasted with scurvy and sickness. The pirate captain struck up a deal with the natives and bought Bowen and the two English sailors out of captivity to crew his vessel. The pirate vessel sailed off and chanced upon another stranded captain and crew on the beach trying to refloat their ship. The pirates embarked the sailors and were guided to a bay at Methelage on the north coast of Madagascar, where the ship was repaired and provisioned.

In April 1700 an English slave ship, the *Speaker,* Captain Eastlake commanding, anchored in the bay. Bowen and the pirates pretended to go along with a plan to sell the English captain two hundred slaves from the island. They tricked the slaver captain and took him captive on the island, boarding his ship.

The pirates set off aboard the captured 40-gun *Speaker,* making a landfall at Zanzibar. Here the pirate captain and some of the crew went ashore. In the citadel they were set upon and murdered by Moslems. John Bowen and some of the crew who had remained on the beach pulled off in the longboat, regained the *Speaker,* up-anchored, and beat a hasty retreat northward. Elected captain by the *Speaker's* crew, John Bowen thus embarked on a new career of piracy in the Indian Ocean preying on merchant shipping.

His trail can be traced through old records in the London maritime archives, where Patrick Lize found letters from Captain Conway, commander of an English merchant ship captured by the *Speaker* off the coast of India. One letter that Lize recovered read: "On October 28, 1701 at 8 o'clock in the morning as we were coming up the Indian coast between Callicaton and Pocka we encountered a pirate ship, the *Speaker* commanded by Bowen, a Bermudian. It mounted 40 cannons and 2 swivel guns with a crew of 200 men of diverse nationality. These men and their captain took my ship and later I have learned sold it for 40,000 rupees."

Not knowing whether they would be able to locate the wreckage of the *Speaker* from the scanty report of the governor of Mauritius, or even if they did find the shipwreck whether any treasure would be left, Jacques Dumas and Patrick Lize set off from Paris to Mauritius.

After searching along the coast in the area now called the Ilot des Roches (the Swarte Klip mentioned in the governor's letter) the divers discovered the *Speaker's* three anchors and some thirty-four cannons. The wooden hull of the pirate ship had long since rotted away. The men began the task of digging through almost three hundred years of coral growth. The divers' patience and research paid off. They recovered gold bars and coins; Venetian, Dutch, Mexican, Yemeni, and Indian silver; navigational equipment; pearls and jewelry; and armaments.

Captain Bowen had been ever mindful of his earlier career as an honest sea captain. He called the Act of Grace of 1698 trickery to "entrap honest pirates." Bowen told the captain of a wealthy East Indiaman he had captured that he would destroy commerce and disrupt sea traffic of the East India Company until he and his men were given full pardon. Bowen finally found safe haven on Mauritius, paid for with generous bribes to the governor.

It was at the same time that Bowen was pirating in the waters of the Indian Ocean that another, and probably one of the best-known legendary pirate figures of all time, was hanged in London on Execution Dock in 1701. Like John Bowen, Capt. William Kidd was an unwilling pirate. A well-respected and propertied New York merchant captain, William Kidd fell in with the Earl of

Bellomont in 1695 during a voyage to London. Captain Kidd, then in his fifties, had been a privateer against the French. Bellomont was to replace the British colonial governor of New York, Benjamin Fletcher, whose trafficking in pirate smuggled goods brought him to the attention of the Crown.

Bellomont, in partnership with some of the most influential men in England—one of whom was Sir Edward Russel, First Lord of the Admiralty, another Sir John Somers, who later became lord chancellor of England—gave Captain Kidd a commission to attack pirate vessels on the high seas and bring back the spoils to England, where they would be divided among the investors. A second commission from the king of England granted him letters of marque against French ships.

In March 1692, furnished with a 30-gun frigate, the *Adventure Galley*, Captain Kidd was to sail from London. But before they left Nore about seventy members of his crew were kidnapped by a press gang for service in the Royal Navy. Captain Kidd was thus forced to sail from England with a decimated crew. He had, however, managed to capture a prize crossing from England to New York. The captured French ship was sold by the Admiralty in New York. The stroke of bad luck in crewing his ship forced Captain Kidd to violate his agreement with Bellomont and raise the crew's share of any plunder from 25 to 50 percent. Even so, he was forced to accept brigands and rejects to man the *Adventure Galley*. Quite unsurprising, this led to problems in discipline on board, and there was near mutiny when Captain Kidd was reluctant to attack friendly shipping.

Captain Kidd's letters from the Crown gave the privateer power to attack pirate ships and French ships or those with "French papers." In 1697 the *Adventure Galley* was plying the same seas as Bowen's *Speaker*, lying off India's Malabar coast. However, when Captain Kidd refused to attack an English merchantman, his crew nearly rebelled. It was in this fracas that Captain Kidd took action that would eventually see him hanged. Railing the crew to mutiny, the ship's chief gunner, William Moore, unable to control his anger at the captain's decision not to attack the English ship, confronted his captain. Kidd picked up a wooden bucket bound with iron bands used for carrying cannon balls and crashed it down upon Moore's head. The man died the next day from the injury. This temporarily quieted the crew.

Captain Kidd was determined now to abate the feelings of the hot-tempered crew by turning to flat-out piracy. He attacked two ships, one, the *Maiden,* a trader with French passes which Kidd renamed *November,* and the other an American-owned vessel, the *Quedah Merchant.* Even though the *Quedah* had a British skipper, Captain Kidd discovered the vessel had French passes, which Kidd thought would justify his actions when he returned to England.

Putting in on an island off Madagascar, probably not far from where John Bowen was marauding, Kidd's crew mutinied and joined another pirate ship at anchor there—the *Mocha Frigate* captained by the pirate Culliford. The mutinous crew plundered the spoils and burned both Kidd's ship, the *Adventure Galley,* and the prize ship he had renamed *November.*

Apparently the wrecks of the *Adventure Galley* and *November* escaped Dumas and Lize's exploration. The explorers preferred instead to concentrate on the shipwrecks located off nearby Mauritius. Although apparently plundered for their loot and any valuables on board, Captain Kidd's two ships would have made adventurous exploration.

Thirteen men remained loyal to Captain Kidd. The mutineers left them the 500-ton captured *Quedah Merchant.* Living up to the original agreement Kidd struck with his crew, the mutineers gave Kidd 40 percent of the spoils and embarked the rest as they sailed off again to pillage merchant shipping aboard the pirate vessel *Mocha Frigate.*

In the meantime, Captain Kidd's aristocratic investors were coming under scrutiny in England. The organizer of the affair Richard Coote, the Earl of Bellomont, was hoping to rid himself of blame and protect his highly placed partners from the taint that had become associated with the venture. Tales of Captain Kidd's piracy had already reached London, and the opposition party was attempting to make political gain and embarrass Kidd's secret backers.

Captain Kidd left the Indian Ocean wearing back around the cape for the West Indies. Once he reached Hispaniola he knew that he would have to account for his brief and relatively unsuccessful pirate ventures. Captain Kidd sold the *Quedah* and purchased a small sloop. Loading his new vessel, the *Antonio,* with the goods and treasure, he sailed for New York. The wily captain figured he would be able to bargain for his life with the treasure and buried it on an island belonging to John Gardiner in New York. He also warehoused the bulky cargo of bales of cloth and sugar in Connecticut.

Kidd then proceeded to present himself before the Royal governor, Lord Bellomont, in Boston. The captain entrusted Bellomont with the French papers he had taken from the ships he captured off the coast of India. As events would have it, Bellomont "mislayed" the papers that could have arguably exonerated Kidd, and the captain was promptly clapped in irons.

Kidd's property was searched, and search parties were also sent to the warehouse and Gardiner's Island, where his booty was unearthed. The three-and-a-half-year-long voyage had produced only meager sums in comparison to the norm in freebooters' trade of the period. Besides the bags of sugar and forty-one bales of silk, the searchers recovered about 20 pounds of gold and some 150 pounds of silver. All of which were sold by the Crown for 6,472 pounds sterling.

Captain Kidd was put in jail where he languished for two years. The Tory opposition to Bellomont and his secret partners in England's House of Commons demanded that Captain Kidd be brought before them. To the end, in spite of the fact that he was apparently betrayed by the Earl of Bellomont Captain Kidd would not blame the backers.

The French papers, Kidd's only hope of redemption, had been sent to the House of Commons by Bellomont, but the evidence was suppressed. The Court of Admiralty refused to produce the passes at Captain Kidd's trial even though it had been ordered to do so by the House of Commons. Indeed in the transcript of Captain Kidd's trial records the presiding judge stated: "If there was a French pass on the ship, you ought to have condemned her as a prize." The jury was charged with the determination of the passes existence as the question "on which the indictment turns."

By the time Kidd was brought to trial, Bellomont was dead. The British court of Admiralty tried Captain Kidd four times on six indictments, one for murder and five for piracy. The Crown produced two witnesses, one Robert Bradinham and Joseph Palmer, deserters from the crew of the *Adventure Galley*.

They testified that Kidd murdered Chief Gunner Moore with the shot bucket. These witnesses, men who had originally joined the pirate vessel *Mocha Frigate,* came in for pardon under a proclamation by the Crown granting amnesty to pirates. Kidd was found guilty of piracy. His secret backers—Bellomont, now dead; Lord Chancellor Somers, the British secretary of state; Earl Romney, the British ordnance master; and Sir Edward Russel, Lord of the Admiralty—must have thought it convenient that Captain Kidd hang.

The unlucky merchant captain turned privateer then unwilling pirate was led to Execution Dock on 23 May 1701. Even his hanging, it was reported, was as imprudently handled as his career as a pirate. The rope broke and the hapless Captain Kidd stuck in the deep mud below the gibbet. He was promptly hanged again and his bones tarred in hoops and swung out over the port where the corpse was left as a warning to pirates. Two centuries later, the French passes Captain Kidd took from the two prize ships were discovered in the archives of London's Public Record Office.

As with most pirate legends, it was enough that Captain Kidd's loot had been buried and only a relatively paltry amount recovered to foster rumors of buried treasure. Captain Kidd himself, probably hoping to win a reprieve, wrote a letter to the speaker of the House of Commons and claimed that if he were allowed to go to Hispaniola he could dig up the hundred thousand pounds worth of treasure.

Since his hanging in 1701, dozens of major expeditions and hundreds of amateur treasure hunts have been mounted to find Captain Kidd's legendary treasure. It was presumably buried somewhere along the coast from New Jersey to Nova Scotia. These rumors have been given credence over the years as caches of gold and silver were unearthed in places where it is supposed the pirate captain put in. And, as late as 1951, a fisherman found a small bronze plaque in the mud along the New Jersey shore that read "William Kidd—Master—Quedagh."

Among the sunken navy of pirate ships and their squadrons of victims is the wreck of the *Whidah,* which went down in a fierce storm off Cape Cod, Massachusetts, in 1717. The *Whidah* was captured by the pirate Samuel Bellamy, who was drowned with 148 of his crew when the ship struck a bar. Only two of Bellamy's crew survived the wrecking.

Bellamy's pirate legend is replete with tales of witchcraft and superstition. Local legend has it that Captain Bellamy seduced a young girl of fifteen, then went to sea. The girl, Goody Maria Hallett, bore Bellamy's child, but the infant died. The superstitious believed that Goody Hallett, with corn-silk hair and yellow eyes, became a witch, and she was in fact flogged for witchcraft. Cape Cod folklore recounts tales of Goody Hallett upon the back of a whale accompanied by an one-eyed goat and a black cat, searching the ocean for her lover.

Whether tales of bewitching are true or not, treasure divers on Cape Cod have found the wreckage of the *Whidah*. Mel Fisher, Key West's famous treasure salvor, was called into the project after an old map discovered in Harvard University's library led the divers to an area off Wellfleet, Massachusetts.

"They went out with the magnetometer and couldn't find anything. Went out again the next day and hit it," Fisher said. "When I was fourteen years old," Mel Fisher recalled, "growing up in Indiana, I had two study hall periods in high school. I used to spend an hour studying my schoolwork and one hour reading about pirates such as Bellamy. . . . What I read about Bellamy didn't sound true. It sounded like a seaman's tale exaggerated through the years. I never dreamed that I'd see his ship found, salvaged, and shown it to the world."

Bellamy had a certain flamboyance, a quick wit, and an ability to talk convincingly. To the pirate, hypocrisy was a worse offense than robbery on the high seas. "Damn ye, you are a sneaking puppy, and so are all those who submit to be governed by laws which rich men have made for their own security, for the cowardly whelps have not the courage otherwise to defend what they get by their knavery. Damn them for a pack of crafty rascals, and you who serve them for a parcel of henhearted numbskulls. They vilify us. The scoundrels do, when there is only this difference: They rob the poor under the cover of the law, forsooth, and we plunder the rich under the protection of our own courage. Had you not better make one of us, than sneak after the arses of those villians for employment?" Bellamy is reported to have said to the captain and crew of a captured ship, impugning their resistance to joining his pirate band.

Ill-treatment aboard ship was often an open invitation for pirate recruiting. Merchant seamen and often those impressed in navy service were much abused by ship masters. Owners' greed frequently cheated the ordinary seamen on merchant ships of their due. Of the sailor's life before the mast, Richard Henry Dana characterized it best when he wrote "A sailor's life is at best but a mixture of a little good with much evil, and a little pleasure with much pain. The beautiful is lumped with the revolting. The sublime with the commonplace, and the solemn with the ludicrous." It was cruel, hard usage that turned men to piracy, and they generally had little difficulty recruiting a crew.

Plying their freebooting trade in the waters of the Caribbean, pirates and privateers plucked rich prizes from merchant ships trading in the New World. Hoisting out a macabre flag of the "Terrible Republic," the infamous Edward Teach preyed upon merchant shipping from Central America to Virginia. The mere sight of Blackbeard's pirate flag depicting a skeleton with an hourglass and a spear pointed at a heart was often enough to compel his victim's surrender. Sailing first under letters of marque from the British Crown, Teach preyed upon Spanish shipping in the West Indies in the early 1700s. Capt. Charles Johnson's 1724 book about the "Most Notorious Pyrates" reported that "Captain Teach assumed the cognomen of Blackbeard from that large quantity of hair which like a frightful meteor, covered his whole face, and frightened America more than an comet that has appeared there a long time."

Blackbeard's notorious marauding began in late 1715 in a 40-gun ship, the *Queen Ann's Revenge*. After more than a year of pirating along the coast of Virginia and Carolina, ranging as far north as New England, Blackbeard came back to North Carolina. Blackbeard and his crew were pardoned in January 1718 by Gov. Charles Eden. The Act of Grace absolved the pirate and his crew of all past offenses. Historians indicate that the corrupt North Carolina officials took a share of the ill-gotten booty in return.

Blackbeard set off again in 1718, and preyed upon shipping in the Caribbean. With two captured prizes the pirate fleet anchored off South Carolina, where they captured six more ships and held wealthy passengers for ransom. With the pirate base of operations in New Providence, the Bahamas was disrupted.

Blackbeard and his crew took refuge in North Carolina, where they were protected by Governor Eden. Dismayed that the pirates were raiding South Carolina shipping with impunity and holding the government for ransom, Gov. Robert Johnson of South Carolina, unable to secure help from the Royal Navy, sent two sloops of war to go against the pirates. Col. William Rhett with the two armed sloops *Henry* and *Sea Nymph* came upon a band of pirates in the Cape Fear River.

A former colleague of Blackbeard's, Stede Bonnet and his crew did battle with the ships in Cape Fear River, lost, and were captured and eventually hanged. Meanwhile Blackbeard took several more prizes, including a French ship that he brought to Bath Inlet where the governor of North Carolina condemned it in Vice-Admiralty Court.

Blackbeard and the governor disembarked the cargoes, sold them, and burned the prize ship at Bath Inlet to destroy the evidence. The carousing of the pirates and their indiscriminate plundering caused the merchant community to complain to Virginia governor Alexander Spotswood. Finding that Blackbeard was installing himself at Ocracoke Inlet, Governor Spotswood had the Virginia Assembly pass an antipirateering act which posted a reward for Blackbeard, dead or alive.

Governor Spotswood's decree issued on 24 November 1718 provided "Whereas, by an Act of Assembly, made at a session of Assembly, begun at the Capital in Williamburgh . . . an Act to Encourage the Apprehending and Destroying of Pyrates: it is amongst other things enacted, that all and every person or persons, who, from and after the fourteenth day of November 1718, and before the fourteenth day of November, which shall be in the Y.O.L. 1719, shall take any pyrate or pyrates on the sea or land, or in the case of resistance, shall kill any such pyrate or pyrates between the degrees of thirty-four and thirty-nine of northern latitude, and within one hundred leagues of the continent of Virginia or within the provinces of Virginia or North Carolina . . . shall be entitled to have . . . for Edward Teach, commonly known as Captain Teach or Blackbeard; one hundred pounds, for every other commander of a pyrate ship, sloop or vessel, forty pounds; for every lieutenant, master or quartermaster, boatswain or carpenter, twenty pounds; for every other inferior officer, fifteen pounds; and for every private man taken aboard such ship, sloop or vessel, ten pounds . . . belonging to this Colony or North Carolina."

Lt. Robert Maynard of the Royal Navy was put in command of a small sloop of war commissioned by Governor Spotswood and attacked Blackbeard's nine-gun sloop. The pirates seemed to have the upper hand, but when Blackbeard and his men boarded Maynard's sloop to do battle, the notorious pirate was engaged in hand-to-hand combat by the lieutenant and killed. Maynard's crew suffered heavy casualties with ten dead and twenty-four wounded but managed to sail back to Bath with Blackbeard's severed head stuck on the bowsprit.

Sunken pirate ships, pirate lore, and buried treasure hid in the ground with the corpses of the men who dug the hole have lured many explorers in their lust for gold. A journal entry attributed to Blackbeard alludes to his colorful pirate life. "Such a day took one with a great deal of liquor on board, so left the company hot, dammed hot, then all things went well again," read the entry.

Legends of Blackbeard's hidden treasure abound. On the small British West Indian island of Cayman Brac, where divers search out shipwrecks on the rocky shores and shoals, there is an oft-repeated tale that Blackbeard came ashore there to bury treasure.

The legend on Cayman Brac is a romantic tale that elder residents delight in telling. A wedge of limestone rock runs along the middle of Cayman Brac cutting the island in half. The Bluff, as it is called, drops off sheer at the East End of the island, 141 feet down to the sea. The Bluff is laced with caves, many of them unexplored by the island's residents. It is said that Blackbeard landed on Cayman Brac one morning and all alone carried a chest filled with $5 million in pirate loot up the Bluff. Blackbeard was next seen again on the other side of the island—without the treasure chest.

Divers on Cayman Brac like Winston McDermot tell stories about pirate treasure that have been passed down by elder relatives, early settlers on Cayman Brac. "He was a Spaniard, a shipwrecked sailor and he used to walk around backwards so nobody could follow him to where he hid out," Winston McDermot began the tale of Dick Sessinger, the only man pirates left alive on the island. Sessinger managed to survive on the island and planted food. He was so successful at it that he began to supply provisions to the pirates that made landfall on the rocky island. A cove on the Brac still bears Sessinger's name

Winston McDermot describes how Sessinger had a small Nassau trading sloop. In a blow Sessinger tried to make it through a pass on the reef near Cayman Brac's West End. The small boat capsized, drowning the crew. Although Sessinger escaped, he was unable to save a chest containing gold coins he had aboard the ship. Winston believes that the gold can still be found in the cut, submerged in less than fifteen feet of water. That the Brac, with a myriad of deep and inaccessible caves, was a pirates' refuge is undisputed. Shipwrecks abound on the island's reefs making it a popular spot for diving enthusiasts.

Perhaps the golden age of privateering occurred during the war of 1812. Privateers shipped from most every port on the American coast and as many as five hundred letters of marque were issued during that period. Yankee captains with their swift clippers and corsairs played havoc with British shipping, and British merchants bemoaned the loss of upwards of $40 million in ships sunk, condemned, and captured by privateers with their crews and cargoes. In all, privateers during the war of 1812 claimed more than thirteen hundred enemy ships as prizes.

British trade was stifled and a public cry went up demanding to know why "a horde of American cruisers should he allowed unresisted and unmolested, to take, burn, or sink our own vessels in our own inlets and almost in sight of our own harbor."

One American privateer sailing out of Baltimore aboard the vessel *Chasseur* sent a self-styled proclamation ashore in a boat that he demanded be posted in Lloyd's attesting to his blockade of the United Kingdom. This same Yankee captain, Thomas Boyle, sported sixteen guns aboard his priveteersman and did battle with English frigates, capturing eighteen prizes during his first privateering voyage.

Other feats of daring by American privateers were equally audacious. Fourteen English ships were attacked, set afire, and sunk in the English Channel by the privateering ship *Governor Tompkins*. An American schooner captured a British cutter on the Irish Sea and other privateer ships brought back prize cargoes worth as much as $3 million, captured in one voyage.

Privateers during the French wars with England, brothers Jean and Pierre Lafitte plied the Atlantic Coast. They were active in Louisiana and trafficked in smuggled booty. Jean Lafitte had at one point insulted the American governor by countering a reward for his capture with a $15,000 bounty on the governor's head after an unsuccessful expedition to capture Lafitte and his pirates. A major expedition was ordered by President Madison to bring the rascal to justice. Lafitte's pirate ships were sunk or taken as prizes at Barataria, but the pirate escaped.

Thinking Lafitte a total renegade, the British confided their plan of attack to the pirate hoping to prevail on him to take command of a frigate for their impending attack on Gen. Andrew Jackson and the defenders of New Orleans. Lafitte informed on the British, joining forces with the Americans to defeat the British in the Battle of New Orleans. Lafitte was pardoned by President Madison and established himself on the Texas coast. Treasure hunters probing Galveston Island have claimed to have discovered the remains of one of Lafitte's sunken ships. It was reported that the ship was destroyed by U.S. Navy frigates in 1821, when they attacked Lafitte's pirate enclave on the Texas coast.

One of the ablest chroniclers of the early merchant marine, Ralph B. Paine, aptly described the waning of the grand era of piracy and privateering.

The War of 1812 was the dividing line between two eras of salt water history. On the farther side lay the turbulent centuries of hazard and bloodshed and piracy, of little ships and indomitable seamen who pursued their voyages in the reek of gunpowder and of legalized pillage by the stronger. . . . They belonged to the rude and lusty youth of a world which lived by the sword and which gloried in action . . . on the hither side of 1812 were seas unvexed by the privateer and the freebooter. The lateen-rigged corsairs had been banished from their lairs . . . ships needed to show no broadsides of cannon in the Atlantic trade. For a time they carried the old armament among the lawless islands of the Orient and off Spanish-American coasts where the vocation of piracy made its last stand, but the great trade routes of the glove were peaceful highways for the white-winged fleets of all nations. The American seamen who had fought for the right to use the open sea were now to display their prowess in another way and in a romance of achievement that was no less large and thrilling.

With the advent of strong navies and fast clippers, piracy and privateering all but vanished from the high seas. Well after pirate bones have turned to dust, rumors persist of gold-laden shipwrecks and buried treasure, romantic tales from a grand era when the Terrible Republic ruled the seas. These legacies persist from the days of swashbuckling high adventure to challenge the imaginations of historians and seekers of fortune. And, every so often, the challenge is rewarded with caches of gold and pirate loot.

CHAPTER FOUR

Legendary Liners

THE TITANIC

"You could smell ice, I knew it. There was a keenness in the air. You can smell it. The weather was perfect and we were flat out; we were trying to make a record. I was talking to a pal of mine sitting on my bunk. Then she came to a halt. I went out on deck. I couldn't see anything over the side, but there was ice in the well deck and I knew we'd hit an iceberg." Frank Prentiss was just eighteen years old when he shipped out on the *Titanic*. His recollection of the tragedy was part of a film documentary that probed the facts and circumstances of the sinking, one of the most poignant maritime disasters of all time.

It was the era of grand luxury. Transatlantic steamship companies vied with each other for the burgeoning passenger traffic between Europe and America. Ocean liners were being built bigger and better than ever before, and Britain's White Star Line was determined to capture a lion's share of the transatlantic trade. Two enormous sister ships, the largest ships ever, the *Titanic* and the *Olympic,* were being built in Ireland.

The *Titanic* would make history for size and prowess when launched on 31 May 1911. The Titanic was the fifty-third ship Harland and Wolff built for the White Star Line. Even before the great liner was conceived, an author, Morgan Robertson, published a novel called *Futility.* The book, which appeared in 1898, was an oracle of sorts. It described the fate of a majestic transatlantic passenger liner, an enormous ship that displaced seventy thousand tons, the largest ship ever constructed and peopled with wealthy passengers, which struck a berg and sank on a cold night in April in the North Atlantic.

Robertson's fictitious ship was called the *Titan.* The similarities of the two ships compared by chroniclers after the *Titanic* disaster were ironic. The fictional *Titan* was proclaimed unsinkable, a ship with far fewer lifeboat places than passengers, a triple-screw vessel that turned at about twenty-five knots. Here the fictional *Titan* fell short of the dimensions of *Titanic,* whose overall length was 882.5 feet compared to *Titan*'s 800.

Fitted out with two reciprocating engines and twenty-nine boilers, the *Titanic* had a dry weight of 46,328 tons and a displacement of 66,000 tons. The ship was 92.5 feet wide, the height of an eleven-story building, 175 feet from keel to the top of its stacks. Each link of the ship's massive anchor chain weighed 175 pounds.

The epic maiden voyage of the *Titanic* began on 10 April 1912, when the ship sailed from Southampton, England, en route to Cherbourg, France, to embark additional passengers. Outward bound, the *Titanic* made a final call at Queenstown, Ireland, where more passengers, specie, and other goods were taken aboard. From Queenstown the *Titanic* set a course across the Atlantic, sweeping southerly some three hundred miles to avoid ice breaking up in the northern Atlantic.

As the *Titanic* made its westward passage reports came over the wireless of ice in the shipping lanes. At 9:00 AM a message was received from the *Caronia.* It read, "Captain Titanic—westbound steamers report bergs, growlers and field ice in 42 degrees N. from 49 degrees to 51 degrees W. 12th April. Compliments, Barr."

At 11:05 the radio operator of a ship lying some ten miles away, shut down and closed in by the ice, sent a message to the *Titanic* about the iceberg. The curt reply he received may have sealed the *Titanic*'s fate. The White Star liner's radio operator, George Philipps, signaled the *Californian*'s operator: "Shut up, shut up, I am busy. I am working Cape Race."

Busy sending and receiving passenger messages, Philipps ignored the urgent warning. At 11:30 PM, the *Californian* closed its radio down. These were two of at least five messages about ice that were received by the *Titanic* on 14 April 1912. In spite of the radio warnings Capt. Edward J. Smith, the fifty-nine-year-old master of the *Titanic* and a thirty-eight-year veteran of the White Star Line, kept the ship steaming ahead at twenty-two and a half knots.

It was Sunday, 14 April 1912, the fifth night of the voyage from Europe to New York. In the *Titanic*'s crow's nest two lookouts stood their watch. Frederick Fleet and Reginald Lee had been ordered to stay alert for ice. At 11:40 PM, Fleet spotted ice dead ahead of the ship. He sounded the alert and called the bridge, "Iceberg right ahead."

William M. Murdoch, the first mate in charge of the bridge, ordered the engines reversed, and the helm was put hard over. As the two lookouts in the crow's nest counted off the seconds a collision seemed imminent. Then, just as the massive berg loomed dead ahead, the *Titanic* veered off to port. The man in the crow's nest watched as the iceberg swept past along the starboard side, then was left astern. The two lookouts felt they had escaped a close call. Belowdecks a very slight jarring sensation, hardly noticed by the passengers, was felt through parts of the ship.

The ship had struck the berg below the waterline, and a three-hundred-foot gash had been cut along its flank, flooding five of the ship's sixteen watertight compartments.

The shipbuilder's managing director, Thomas Andrews, was aboard the ship and was summoned by the captain. He explained that while the *Titanic* could remain afloat if four of the ship's forward compartments were flooded, it would be impossible if the first five compartments flooded because the ship would go down at the bow. The bulkheads in the watertight compartments only went as high as B deck. When the water rose to that level it would spill over from the fifth into the sixth compartment.

The *Titanic* was doomed. At 12:05 AM Captain Smith ordered the lifeboats readied. At 12:15 AM a distress call was sent out. The Morse code signal CQD was sent followed by MGY—the international marine distress signal followed by the ship's call letters. The Cunard liner *Carpathia,* steaming fifty-eight miles away, signaled the *Titanic* at 12:25 AM that messages were waiting to be transmitted from Cape Race. The *Titanic* sent the following message to *Carpathia:* "Come at once. We have struck a berg. It's a CQD, old man. Position 41.46 N 50.14 W." The new international distress call SOS had just been inaugurated to replace CQD. It was reported that the captain told the radio operator to send out the new distress call. At 12:45 AM the *Titanic* tapped out the first SOS ever broadcast from a liner at sea.

There were not enough lifeboats for all of the passengers. In spite of advice to the contrary, the *Titanic* carried only sixteen lifeboats and four collapsible dinghies. All of the boats could carry a maximum of 1,178 persons, although the *Titanic* was licensed to carry 3,500. Aboard on the fateful night of 14 April were some 2,224 passengers and crew. As the crew struggled to release the lifeboats a mad scramble ensued.

"Lower the lifeboats and stand by. That was the orders," crewman Frank Prentiss remembered. "No lifeboat drills, and a list of lifeboats I believe was put up in the galley on the day we struck the iceberg—It was pell-mell, women and children first. The drop from the boat deck to the water was seventy to eighty feet, and people didn't want to go. You couldn't see the water."

The young crewman helped passengers into the boats. "It was so sad to take the wives away from their husbands. I knew then she was sinking," Prentiss said. As the ship started down at 2:15 AM, the bandmaster signaled the musicians to strike up *Autumn,* a church hymn. Prentiss struggled along the listing decks. From the stern he fell into the water and remembered the freezing cold.

"The cold freezing. That's what killed them. They didn't last long. I was eventually all by myself. The cries and prayers were all over with," Prentiss said, a lucky survivor of the shipwreck that claimed more than fifteen hundred lives.

By 8:30 in the morning Captain Rostron of the *Carpathia* took the last of the *Titanic's* victims aboard and headed for New York with the 705 survivors. Investigations conducted by the United States Congress and the British Board of Trade laid the blame for the *Titanic's* sinking on careless navigation in ice danger conditions. The ship owners contested claims by A. M. Carlyle, who had first recommended sixty-four (and later forty-eight) lifeboats to be slung on the special davits that had been designed to accommodate four boats each.

In England the director of the White Star Line, Bruce Ismay, who had been a passenger aboard the *Titanic* and who had insisted on boarding a lifeboat to save himself, denied the claims of insufficient lifeboats for every person aboard. Board of Trade rules in England equated lifeboat requirements with tonnage, relying on an old law that had not been revised as ships increased in size and passenger-carrying capacity.

Claims by White Star Line, owners of the *Titanic,* that they were not told by Carlyle or others to increase the number of boats and that the company had never seen plans to that effect have been proven false by contemporary investigations. When the White Star Line merged with Cunard in 1934 a blueprint was discovered that showed a plan for sixteen additional lifeboats aboard the *Titanic.* To complicate things further, in Bruce Ismay's pocket at the time of his rescue was a radio message warning of ice in the ship's path.

"Some didn't leave their cabins. It was a lingering death. It was murder wasn't it? And the Board of Trade was equally to blame. There were not even enough lifeboats for the crew," Frank Prentiss lamented. The *Titanic* went down in the North Atlantic, approximately three hundred miles southeast of Cape Race, Newfoundland. The depth of the ocean in that area is about twelve thousand feet, a depth thought to be well beyond the limits of salvage.

When an oil wildcatter from Texas announced a project to locate and explore the wreck of the *Titanic* in 1980, many dismissed it as hype from a self-promoter looking for publicity and a tax shelter. However, there was something in the adventure that piqued the curiosity of scientists at Columbia University's Lamont-Doherty Geological Laboratories in Palisades, New York. Deep-ocean technology emerged with increasing application for seabed mining, oil and gas exploration, and strategic military use. Deep-ocean probes in bathyspheres and bathyscaphes and the use of manned submersibles to explore the deepest ocean reaches fathered any number of deep-ocean vehicles. These submarine progeny have both manned and unmanned capability with robots capable of working at great depths. And deep-sea probes with sonar and advanced electronics have enabled scientists to obtain credible pictures and mosaics of the ocean floor.

Thus when Jack Grimm of Abilene, Texas, announced his plan to equip a research vessel and plumb the ocean depths for the remains of the *Titanic,* the quest for riches was discounted by the scientists at Lamont-Doherty Laboratories, but the opportunity to develop and test equipment capable of performing the task prompted them to contact the Texas oilman.

The Lamont scientists wrote Grimm suggesting a collaboration with the oceanographic community since what he proposed to undertake was technically difficult. It never occurred to the Lamont scientists that a project of that magnitude would be announced without the team having been formed, but, as Dr. William B. F. Ryan found out, the scientific complement of Grimm's expedition had not yet been selected. The two men met over dinner in Florida and it was there that a joint undertaking was planned. Lamont-Doherty would provide the scientific and oceanographic expertise with cooperation and assistance from the Scripps Institution of Oceanography of the University of California. Jack Grimm and his backers would provide funding for the research equipment and vessels.

"Jack Grimm is an oil finder and producer. In that sense an adventurer. This is another wildcat. He gets a group of investors together and instead of finding oil, he wants to find the *Titanic*," Dr. Ryan said, explaining the motivation behind the *Titanic* project.

In the United States of tax-sheltered investments for oil field development, films, and other commercial ventures, a project of this magnitude could be easily enough written off as venture capital. Sensational books, big money movies, and cash advances paid for major scoops may have attracted Jack Grimm and his investors to the *Titanic* project, assuming that they would eventually "strike oil."

Grimm's was the first of many projects to locate, explore, film, and in some cases exploit the *Titanic*'s remains. To begin with, simply finding the *Titanic* was no small feat. It was really an immense speculation. Only small odds were given for the chance of locating a "tiny" ship in a huge ocean.

Fortunately, the *Titanic*'s logbook had been secured in a lifeboat before the ship went under, and a plot in the log showed its position. That plot, however, was taken earlier on the night of the sinking. The *Titanic* had continued for another five or six hours at twenty-two and a half knots after its navigator entered the last plot in the log. As it turned out, the researchers depended more on the plot given by the rescue ships that located the survivors. Their plots would not be exact, since survivors were adrift in the lifeboats before being picked up. Navigation at the time of the *Titanic*'s sinking was accomplished by taking celestial fixes. At best these celestial plots, unlike radio or satellite navigational systems of today, would give an approximate or imprecise location.

Taking all of the information together and extrapolating it into a search area, the scientists were left with a chunk of ocean the size of Rhode Island to search. In that part of the ocean there are deep-sea canyons and channels that run through a thick apron of sediment along the margin of the ocean basin. The ocean area where they would search for the *Titanic* is called the Continental Rise. Benthic storms sweep the area making visibility at depth nil. The entire submarine plain south of Newfoundland and east of Nova Scotia is subject to southward sweeping currents of cold water from the Labrador Sea as well as northward meanderings of warm Gulf Stream surface water. The deep ocean currents hug the contour of the North American sedimentary apron and create "abyssal storms" through their pulsing behavior.

"The sea state in that area of the ocean is four or more [on the Beaufort scale] ninety percent of the time," Dr. Ryan said, explaining another problem faced by researchers in this first and all subsequent explorations. "When the ocean gets that strong, it's generally enough to make an oceanographer seasick," he added with a grin.

Navy camera probes in the same general area failed when they ran into deep-ocean storms a year or so before the *Titanic* project was anticipated. Pictures taken some years before, however, showed clear water, so the scientists decided they would risk it. They were developing a new system using acoustic waves that would "see" through cloudy water created by benthic storms in the same way radar "sees" through clouds in the atmosphere. A surveillance vehicle would be towed behind the research vessel on twenty thousand feet of steel cable. Special winches and a complete cable handling system had been loaned to the project by the Scripps Institution. Computers and computer programs were developed and installed aboard the research vessel, capable of interpreting signals from the surveillance vehicle. These computers generated two-dimensional acoustic images and magnetic profiles of the deep-ocean floor in the search area. The acoustic sensors used for the project could detect objects underwater to a resolution equivalent to about a lifeboat davit—approximately three meters. The images would reveal the *Titanic*'s hull and superstructure and enable the scientists to confirm the authenticity of the wreck.

Special closed-circuit television cameras, still cameras, and lights were developed which could be lowered over the site. At the ocean depths where the *Titanic* went down, technology was at its limits. Transmission of television pictures from that depth is a difficult oceanographic feat. Scientists developed multiplexers and signal conditioners that would enhance the quality of the acoustic signals transmitted over a single, long cable. The television camera developed for the project had a special detector tube which required only one–ten thousandth of a foot-candle of faceplate illumination. Low-light techniques would reduce the effect of back scattering of light reflected by sediment suspended in the water. Special rolls of Kodak 400 ASA Ektachrome film were prepared for the still cameras.

Jack Grimm had undertaken unusual ventures before. He fielded expeditions to find Noah's Ark, the Loch Ness Monster, even Bigfoot. In the summer of 1980, the crew set off in the research vessel *Fay* chartered from Tracor Marine in Florida. The trip was plagued with bad luck. The magnetometer malfunctioned, and while more than a dozen promising sonar readings were made, nothing definitive had been accomplished. By June of 1981 Grimm had mounted a second expedition. This time they chartered the research vessel *Gyre*, belonging to Texas A & M University. Scientists from Lamont-Doherty and Scripps stowed a sled, with mounted instruments and deep-towing equipment, aboard.

The scientists studied their charts to map a search area. They had the *Californian*'s plot where the rescue of survivors took place at 40 degrees 45 minutes north and 50 degrees 10 minutes west. They used plots given by the *Carpathia* and the *Mount Temple* as well. The magnetometers, sonar equipment, and all sea cameras were prepared.

Had the *Titanic* broken up? Were its remains crushed by the pressure of seawater? Did the ship slip into one of the enormous rifts in the ocean bottom, hidden from detection by canyon walls? These were all conjectures the scientists pondered, preparing for their search. They waited and watched the instruments as the equipment was towed over sites that had registered on sonar from the previous year, each time eliminating sites with magnetometer surveys. None of the sites produced any positive readings. The research vessel *Gyre* was forced to head back to port. As a last effort, the Lamont-Doherty camera sled was pulled beneath the ship above the bottom at a depth of 12,500 feet, taking pictures of the ocean floor. Suddenly an object appeared on the shipboard television screen resembling a ship's propeller.

The resemblance of the object to a propeller blade and the inability of the researchers to confirm or deny its authenticity was enough for the project's entrepreneur, Jack Grimm: Grimm declared that he had in fact found the last resting place of the legendary and unsinkable *Titanic.* From these first attempts oceanographer Robert Ballard and other groups set out to find the ship. Dr. Ballard, a scientist at the Woods Hole Oceanographic Institute, teamed up with Jean-Louis Michel of France's Institut français de recherche pour l'exploitation de la mer (IFREMER) to search for the *Titanic* in June 1985. On this first exploration to locate the shipwreck Ballard used the research vessel *Knorr* from the Woods Hole Institute. The French joined the project with IFREMER's ship *Le Suroit.* The scientists swept an area narrowed down by their research with deep-search sonar equipment.

On 1 September 1985 the underwater search vehicle located the *Titanic's* boilers thirteen thousand feet down. Videotape records of the find were made by the *Knorr's* submersible, *Argo.*

The wreck of the *Titanic* was found. Ballard and his French-American team brought back remarkable video and photographic images of the ship. Detailed photographs showed the wine cellar with bottles scattered among the debris.

Later, using tethered robotic camera vehicles from deep-ocean submersibles, dramatic images of the *Titanic* were eventually broadcast to television screens all over the world. Other groups sought the *Titanic's* wealth and utilized submersibles with claw-like arms to retrieve artifacts from the ocean floor. Many relics from the *Titanic* have been put on display all over the globe.

THE ANDREA DORIA

Named for the famous Genoese admiral who fought with the Holy League during the Battle of Lepanto, the Italian liner *Andrea Doria* was a popular transatlantic passenger ship. On 26 July 1956, the *Andrea Doria,* eight days out from Genoa, was heading south as it passed Nantucket Island. The ship was scheduled to reach New York, two hundred miles away, the following day, but fog blanketed the Atlantic, severely limiting visibility. Bridge watchers scanned the radar, navigating the ship in crowded Atlantic shipping lanes.

Suddenly Capt. Piero Calami was called to the radar screen. A ship was heading toward them in the fog. The *Doria's* captain radioed the approaching vessel and warned of the danger. A reply was received indicating that the message was understood by the Swedish liner *Stockholm,* stating that they would take proper action. The officers on the bridge of the Italian liner watched the radar screen. The *Stockholm* continued on its course, without decreasing speed. Suddenly knifing out of the fog, the icebreaker prow of the Swedish-American liner sliced into the luxurious passenger ship at about 11:20 PM.

Reacting to the emergency immediately after the collision, the captain of the 12,644-ton *Stockholm* reversed the engines. With a grinding of metal, the liners pulled apart, leaving a gaping hole in the side of the 29,100-ton, 600-foot-long *Andrea Doria.* In an ironic twist, a fourteen-year-old American passenger, Linda Morgan, asleep on the bunk in her cabin on the *Andrea Doria,* awoke unharmed on the prow of the *Stockholm* amid the twisted steel, clad only in her nightgown.

Both ships involved in the collision sent out the SOS call of distress. They were in the middle of the crowded North Atlantic shipping lanes, so help was nearby. While the *Andrea Doria* began taking water and listed to starboard, the *Stockholm* remained out of danger after closing emergency hatches in the flooded bow. As the ships broadcast their distress position at 40 degrees 30 minutes north, 60 degrees 53 minutes west, the *Ile de France,* the freighter *Cape Ann,* and the U.S. Navy ships *William H. Thomas* and *Edward Allen* sped to the rescue. The *Ile de France* rescued 753 passengers and crew from the stricken *Andrea Doria.* The immediate list to starboard made it impossible for the *Doria*'s crew to launch the port lifeboats. The starboard flank was low in the water, and the crew was able to launch eight lifeboats full of passengers.

At ten o'clock the next morning, after Captain Calami and his men came away failing in their efforts to pump water into other parts of the ship in an attempt to level it off, the liner went under. Fifty persons of the complement of 1,241 passengers and 575 crew members perished. The world watched as newsreel photographers documented the *Doria* rolling over on its starboard side, sinking, black hull stark in the morning light, broken by white striping.

The *Andrea Doria,* veteran of more than a hundred transatlantic crossings, went down in 230 feet of water. It was a cold, dark, current-riddled grave, beyond the safe limits of normal compressed air diving. At this depth, just twenty minutes on the bottom requires forty-five minutes in decompression stops, where a diver is required to wait at different depths beneath the surface before being able to come up to avoid a decompression accident known as the bends.

Since its sinking, the shipwreck has challenged divers to brave the perils in quest of both adventure and the supposed riches carried aboard the luxury liner. New York department store heir Peter Gimbel, an inveterate diver, dove on the *Andrea Doria* the day after its sinking. On assignment for *Life* magazine the divers were sent to get a scoop, photographing the shipwreck in its watery grave.

Sport and professional divers continue to lark the Italian liner, hoping for a souvenir, something from the wreck attesting to their prowess in dangerous ocean conditions. A statue of Adm. Andrea Doria was blown off and raised by divers from a professional salvage company in Boston. For a while it was rumored in the diving community that the statue adorned a pub, a watering hole of divers somewhere on Boston's waterfront.

Technology already in use for offshore oil exploration and deep-sea development made it possible for divers to saturate at depth. Divers breathed compressed gas at ambient pressure remaining at depth underwater for protracted periods in a dry habitat. Divers could go out of the underwater habitat attached by umbilicals to work. This system was used in 1973 by a group of young divers who planned to cut through the hull of the *Andrea Doria* to salvage the booty from the purser's safes.

The diver's saturation system worked perfectly. A habitat was lowered over the shipwreck and anchored to the hull, and cutting torches were used to make a hole in the ship's side. But the divers were faced with problems they had not anticipated once inside the ship. The ship's walls and appointments had collapsed. Debris with trailing wires and cables was everywhere. Work, once the divers penetrated the *Doria's* hull, was too dangerous to proceed. The saturation divers were forced to call off their salvage attempt without securing anything of value from the liner. Hoping for a place in the annals of diving history, a small group of divers from New Jersey launched a private salvage attempt. The effort ended in tragedy when one of their team suffered a heart attack and died on the bottom, ending their plans.

Peter Gimbel and his wife Elga Anderson decided to put another project together to dive the *Doria*. With a group of investors they planned to engage the services of a professional diving concern (the men who had participated in the first successful saturation dives on the *Doria*), lower a habitat over the shipwreck, enlarge the hole cut in the hull leading to the foyer in the first-class section made by the previous saturation salvors, and contract cinematographers to document the event on film. If they could recover significant treasure from the *Doria,* the publicity would lend fanfare to their exploit and hopefully boost the film's sales potential.

The team maneuvered over the shipwreck in July 1981. The first divers descended over the wreck on scuba to secure lines reaching to the *Doria's* promenade deck at 160 feet. Once the down lines were attached and the work vessel moored over the site, the divers saturated in a large eight-foot diameter decompression chamber, which was twenty-three feet long. The large decompression chamber remained on the deck of the ship, and divers would transfer back and forth, under pressure, to the diving bell that mated with the chamber.

The diving bell would be lowered off the stern of the ship to the shipwreck. At its deepest, the ship lay in 230 feet of water. Working under pressure and returning to the dry environment of the diving bell, where saturation pressure equivalent to 160 feet of seawater was maintained, enabled the divers to work from four to six hours at a time. Outside water temperature at that depth was about forty-six degrees Fahrenheit. The divers wore hot-water suits, warmed by continuous streams of preheated water passing into and out of the diving dress. The hot water was pumped by hose from the salvage ship on the surface. The saturation divers did not use traditional tanks, rather band masks attached to air hoses to supply their breathing mixture.

The divers enlarged the previous hole cut in a set of doors, giving themselves access into the *Doria* through a hole which measured twenty by eight feet. The divers dropped into the gloom and accumulation of twenty-five years of silt. They sought out the purser's office, the Bank of Rome office, and the *Doria's* jewelry shop. Dangerous debris flanked the divers, and outside the shipwreck visibility varied from almost nil to sixty feet or more. Some divers filmed while others used airlifts to move the silt and debris out of the way so they could access the safes. They also gathered ship's china from first-class dining rooms.

Petty problems plagued the divers. After nearly ten days of saturation, minor ear and health problems began to have their effect. The divers continued their daily descents to the *Doria* from their shipboard decompression chamber, transferring into the saturation diving bell. Finally, two weeks into the project, they located a Bank of Rome safe. Heavy seas prevented the lowering of the diving bell. Peter Gimbel had saturated. The divers were anxious to get to work cutting the safe free of bolts that held it to the deck. They finally managed to cut the safe loose, rigged it, and it was hauled up.

The divers cut into a ventilating shaft and explored the *Doria's* engine compartment. They discovered the generator and engine rooms were open to the sea through holes in the ship's hull. Finally, after more than a month over the grave of the famous Italian liner, the Gimbels called off their project. With thousands of feet of film in the can and a Bank of Rome safe stowed safely aboard, the salvage ship made for port, the secrets of a legendary liner given up by the sea.

The safe was kept immersed in water. With a great deal of publicity, it was finally opened before live television cameras, revealing U.S. silver certificate dollar bills, Italian lire, and traveler's checks.

THE LUSITANIA

The Germans did not want war with the United States. Posted with the sailing notices for the Cunard steamships, the Imperial German embassy inserted a notice in New York City newspapers dated 22 April 1915 warning "Travelers intending to embark on the Atlantic Voyage are reminded that a state of war exists between Germany and her allies and Great Britain."

The notice also specified that the war zone included waters adjacent to the British Isles and ships flying the British flag were liable to destruction, cautioning passengers of the risk. The *Lusitania* was to sail from New York for Europe on 1 May 1915. German submarines had been blockading the English coast for two months. Lying off the southern coast of Ireland, Kapitan-Leutnant Walther Schwieger was patrolling in his U-boat.

The submarine had sunk three ships in the last two days' patrol along the coast. It was 7 May 1915, and Schwieger had three torpedoes left on board. The captain's log records the incident at 2:00 PM: "Right front appears a steamboat with 4 chimneys and 2 masts coming vertically on us (coming from South South North to Galley Head) the ship is a big passenger steamboat."

Minutes later the U-boat commander notes in his log: "We change our course to 11 and with high speed and converging course to the other ship hoping that it would change its course to St. B. along the West Coast. The ship turns to St. B., takes course to Queenstown and makes therefore an approach for shooting possible."

The submariner's log then records the incident that would eventually bring the United States into the war with Germany. "Side shot on 700 meter (G-Torpedo put to 3 Meter depth), Angle 90, estimated run 22 sn. The shot hits the ship's side immediately aft of the bridge behind. Then happens an extraordinary big detonation with a very big cloud (much higher than the chimney in front). There must have been a second explosion besides the torpedo (boiler or coal or powder?). The buildings above the hit area and the bridge explode, fire starts, smoke covers the whole bridge, the ship stops immediately and leans rapidly to starboard, at the same time sinking more in front. It seems to sink in a short time. Big confusion on the ship; the boats were readied and partly lowered to the sea. There must have reigned confusion on board; some boats are full, quickly lowered they touch the water with their front or rear and get immediately full of water."

The U-boat commander watched the panic as the crew attempted to lower away the liner's lifeboats. Continuing his account in the submarine's log, Schwieger noted: "On the back board side the boats cannot be lowered because of the ship's oblique position, only a few. The ship sinks; in front you can see the name *Lusitania* in gold letters. The chimneys are black, no flag at the rear. . . . I could not have fired a second torpedo in this crowd of people trying to save themselves."

In the panic that followed 1,198 passengers perished of a complement of 1,257. Of the 179 Americans on board 128 lost their lives, including millionaire Alfred Vanderbilt. Eighteen minutes after the German torpedo struck, the *Lusitania* sank. Its location was only imprecisely fixed at north latitude 51 degrees 25 minutes and west longitude 8 degrees 35 minutes, about twelve miles off Galley Head lighthouse on the Irish coast.

The newspaper accounts of the sinking at the time stated that the *Lusitania* was hit by two torpedoes. This has since been repudiated as were claims of the *Lusitania*'s neutrality. There were 4,200 cases of ammunition in the ship's holds bound for Britain. Capt. William H. Turner disregarded admiralty directions to steer evasively and keep up speed. Having failed to make out landmarks, the captain brought his ship in toward the coast then ran parallel to shore at decreased speed, giving the German U-boat an easy target.

Surviving Third Officer A. A. Bestic of the *Lusitania* later told how German warnings were delivered to passengers before they embarked. "It was as though a cloud had passed over the sun and one felt a momentary chill. I sensed that feeling as a lady with three children stopped to speak to me as she stepped on board," Bestic recounted. The woman asked him whether he thought there was any truth in rumors of the *Lusitania* being torpedoed. "I don't, madam, because there's no submarine built that could possibly catch the *Lusitania*," he answered, later lamenting that he did not see the woman passenger among the survivors.

In the six days that the *Lusitania* had been outward bound for Britain, German U-boats had sunk twenty-three ships in the war zone around the British Isles. The British Admiralty had ordered ships in the war zone to keep up full speed, to zig zag, and to make landfalls at night, avoiding headlands. Captain Turner ignored all of these Admiralty directives. The fog had lifted, and Captain Turner ordered the *Lusitania*'s lifeboats swung out, but by shortly after two o'clock, when one ship's lookout, Leslie Morton, spotted the foaming wake of the U-boat's torpedo, it was too late. There was a second explosion deep within the *Lusitania*. Later testimony by the lighthouse keeper at Galley Head revealed that he heard five separate explosions. This gave credence to German claims that the *Lusitania* was carrying a cargo of munitions and that the neutrals aboard were just shields to mask the war cargo.

The SOS went out: "Come at once. Big list. Ten miles South of Old Head of Kinsale." The explosions damaged the *Lusitania*'s steam line and steering mechanisms, and the mortally wounded 32,000-ton liner had difficulty launching lifeboats. Within eighteen minutes of the torpedo hit, the ship sank. Keeper Murphy of the Kinsale Lighthouse on the coast looked out and said later he "could see no trace of her, only smoke and a few ship's boats."

Blame and countercharges followed the *Lusitania*'s sinking. Captain Turner asserted that the Admiralty should have provided him with an escort. Winston Churchill, then first Lord of the Admiralty, excused the failure, saying, "Resources do not permit us to provide destroyer escorts." (Churchill's excuse was discredited when it was revealed that escorts had been provided twice prior to the *Lusitania*'s sinking to chaperone vessels carrying horses from the United States.)

Whether or not the *Lusitania* sailed from New York armed with guns became an issue at hearings in both Britain and the United States. It was the position of officials from the Cunard line, Captain Turner—who survived the sinking—the collector of the Port of New York, the president of the United States, his secretary of state, and 109 of the survivors that the *Lusitania* had sailed from New York unarmed.

Even so, the *Lusitania* was designed to be a naval auxiliary ship in wartime, and four witnesses spoke out that the *Lusitania* was in fact armed. One of these, a German named Gustav Stahl, testified that he saw four guns hidden aboard the *Lusitania* when he boarded the ship in New York to visit a friend before the vessel sailed. Thought to be a plant by German agents, Stahl was indicted for perjury, convicted, and sentenced to eighteen months in the Atlanta federal penitentiary.

In the meantime American anti-German sentiment hardened and two years later the United States declared war against Germany. Just what the *Lusitania* was carrying and whether in fact the ship had concealed guns remained a mystery, unresolved by a number of salvage attempts, some of them secretive, some grandiose, most ending in failure. No one conclusively settled the *Lusitania* issue nor has anyone recovered great riches from its sunken remains.

Among the early salvage attempts to reach the *Lusitania,* a well-known inventor, Simon Lake, mounted a grandiose expedition. Lake submitted an article for the November 1931 edition of the *New York Times* describing his proposed salvage attempt. Lake wrote, "In the safe of the purser, which in a salvaging expedition we expect to be able to bring to the surface, there will undoubtedly be documents of vast importance, and as our men go into the depths of the ship they will find effects which may give posterity lasting mementos of one of the great disasters of history."

Lake hoped to take pictures of the *Lusitania*'s dining salon, although just how he expected to be able to portray the original majesty of a furnished room in a ship that had already been on the bottom of the sea for sixteen years was not explained. Lake planned on building a tube that would be lowered over the sunken ship, which he reckoned to be in 240 feet of water to the keel and 175 feet to A deck. An observation chamber would be built at the end of Lake's tube. The plan was for divers to be able to leave the compartment at the end of the tube to work. Lake wrote, "We wish to get everything of value, actual or sentimental, and bring it back to the world above from the sunken *Lusitania*."

With these goals in mind Simon Lake built his enormous steel tube. Engineers know today that the contraption would not have worked because of Lake's miscalculations of the pressure at the *Lusitania*'s depth. The invention was never tested, however, since Lake's expedition failed to locate the wreck.

Many years later a young American diver resolved to locate the *Lusitania* and answer the question of whether the luxury liner was in fact armed as had been reported by the jailed German witness. It was July 1960, and by this time fathometers and other more sophisticated inventions could confirm the shipwreck's location. John Light found the *Lusitania* and had accomplished thirty-eight dives on the hulk, spotting what he thought resembled a ship's cannon. The shipwreck was deep at 270 feet. Diving in 1962 with another American, Palmer Williams, Light hoped to film the gun. The divers would only have ten minutes to explore the *Lusitania* before having to spend long minutes underwater waiting at various shallower depths until the nitrogen saturated in their blood and tissues was breathed out.

The American divers found the *Lusitania* lying on its starboard side. Light had obtained plans from the Cunard Line that showed where guns were to be mounted if the ship were ever to be called up in wartime. Ironically, Light noted that the German's testimony at the hearing pinpointed the area described on Cunard's drawings. Light and Williams found the spot indicated on the plans and discovered an enormous eight-foot-diameter hole torn through the deck. Diving into the hole, the divers saw what appeared to be a gun but may have been a pipe or other cylindrical object. They left the site without positively confirming whether in fact the object was a ship's cannon.

The depth of the sunken liner puts it out of reach of normal diving operations. Deep exploration is the province of professionals using mixed gas and saturation systems. The cost of mounting such an undertaking and the lack of great treasure aboard discouraged expeditions until explorer Bob Ballard filmed the *Lusitania* in its watery grave. There have been other contemporary projects to explore the liner. One recent effort has been held up in court when the government of Ireland intervened claiming jurisdiction since the *Lusitania* is in Irish waters.

CHAPTER FIVE

Volcanic Apocalypse

"Returned from Saint-Pierre. City completely destroyed by mass of fire eight o'clock this morning. Suppose entire population annihilated; brought back the few survivors; thirty people. All ships anchorage burned and lost; I leave for Guadeloupe. The Volcano continues to erupt." The cruiser *Le Suchet* was on station in Martinique when its commander, Captain Le Bris, sent the terse cable to the naval ministry in Paris. The report came in the immediate aftermath of the disaster that killed thirty thousand people and destroyed fourteen ships at anchor in Saint Pierre Bay.

Louis Cyparis, whose true name was Louis Sylbaris, was the only survivor in the city. Accused of fighting and disorderly conduct, he had been sentenced to jail. Bored with his imprisonment Cyparis decided to go to a festival in the city of Precheur and escaped. After Cyparis enjoyed the pleasures of the city, having danced the night away in Precheur, he turned himself in to finish his time. As punishment, he was sentenced to eight days' confinement in a tiny *cachot* behind the main street. Cyparis languished in his solitary confinement. The brick-and-cement *cachot* had only small slits above the door to admit air. When the volcano erupted, Cyparis was alone in his unlit cell.

The thundering explosion and searing flame clapped around him. Intense heat scorched the land, and thousands of people were instantly killed, incinerated by the flames, grotesquely scalded to death by air so hot it too seemed on fire. From his prison cell Cyparis screamed out in pain. The heat turned the small *cachot* into an oven. Scalding ash, blown by the fury of the eruption, sought out every crack in the cell's tiny openings. Cyparis was almost burned alive. Scorched over much of his back, legs, and face, the prisoner lay tormented in his cell.

Although badly burned, Cyparis survived the holocaust that took the lives of everyone else in the city of Saint Pierre. Days later, in the aftermath of the tragedy, searchers heard him moaning in pain, crying out from the little *cachot,* the only structure that remained intact in the city. As news of the tragedy spread, the hopeless prisoner received world notoriety. In time, P. T. Barnum recruited him, and to the end of his days Cyparis was part of the famous circus entrepreneur's traveling show.

Two blocks away along Saint Pierre's devastated waterfront, only one ship remained afloat. The hull was still burning, smoke and ash hung over the city. Not since 24 August in the year 79 AD did history record such a devastating volcanic eruption. Historians of the day compared the destruction of Saint Pierre to the eruption above the Bay of Naples of Mount Vesuvius, which buried the cities of Herculaneum and Pompeii. The description of Vesuvius's eruption by Pliny the Younger as "flashes of fire vivid as lightening and darkness more profound than night" had parallel in witness accounts of the destruction of Saint Pierre.

From the one ship that managed to escape, the captain wrote of a flashing flame then black clouds that plunged the city into darkness. The *Roddam* had only just arrived at the anchorage in Saint Pierre Bay at about 6:45 AM on 8 May 1902. The officers and crew were on deck making preparations to drop anchor. When all was in readiness Capt. E. W. Freeman gave the order, and the heavy chain rattled through the hawsehole, breaking the morning stillness. Two cable lengths away was the *Roddam*'s sister ship—still quiet, the crew not yet roused from their sleep for the new day's work.

The year 1902 saw increasing competition from great iron ships with massive boilers. Yet it was still a time of transition, and wooden ships with masts and sail continued to prevail in ocean commerce. So on the morning of 8 May, two iron ships of the Quebec line rode at anchor with smaller wooden merchant sailing ships. Captain Freeman, commander of the *Roddam,* was still on deck an hour after his vessel made port. Without warning, Mont Pelée exploded, and the surviving captain later gave his eyewitness account.

"Suddenly there was a violent detonation that shook the land and sea. A massive explosion of the mountain (Mont Pelée) which opened on one side from summit to base releasing a flashing flame, pushing before it formidable black clouds, descending from the mountain like a cyclone. It destroyed everything in its path. The explosion reached the city, plunging it into darkness. Finally the explosion force of the eruption reached the ships lined up at anchor in the Bay . . . burning cinders were driven by the fury of the explosion. When the explosion reached the sea, the hurtling mass, the fury of the explosive force, lifted up the ships, immediately sinking the smaller vessels, throwing the *Roraima* over its side, half submerging the *Roddam*. One wooden ship was gone in an instant, it sank immediately."

It is difficult to imagine the fury of Mont Pelée's explosion. The "cyclone of fire" scorched the land and sea with temperatures in excess of one thousand degrees Centigrade. In its wake, a zone fifty-eight kilometers square was completely wiped out. Nothing lived; nothing remained standing. Of all the passengers and crew aboard the ships at anchor in Saint Pierre Bay, only thirty lived, later rescued by the French cruiser *Le Suchet*.

The *Roddam*, too, was swept with burning cinders from the volcano. Crewmen who had been on deck were severely or fatally burned. The dead littered the ship's decks, many buried under tons of volcanic ash. Captain Freeman and some of his men sought refuge in the *Roddam*'s chart room. "The ship became a floating furnace, fire aboard was raging uncontrollably. Worse than the heat and burns on the flesh was the suffocation caused by the air filled with burning dust and cinders," Captain Freeman reported. He also described the wounded, who suffered great torture with burns over most of their bodies.

Only with immense effort did Captain Freeman manage to get the *Roddam* under control. Looking toward the other Quebec liner, Captain Freeman saw the *Roraima* was on fire. Its entire aft decks were engulfed in flames; smoke billowed from the interior of the liner. Looking across, Captain Freeman could see the *Roraima*'s foredecks crowded with passengers and sailors.

Still struggling with their own ship, the men of the *Roddam* could do nothing to help the victims aboard their sister ship. "I heard their cries for help. The *Roraima*'s masts and stacks had been torn away. Her forward anchor was holding. We couldn't approach the *Roraima*—it was impossible to help the unfortunates aboard," Captain Freeman said later, describing the tragedy.

The *Roddam*'s rudder and steering mechanism had been damaged in the explosion. While the ship's surviving mechanics struggled to make repairs for an hour and a half, other crew members tried to battle the flames that were spreading over the ship. The fire was gaining, engulfing the woodwork in the cabins. All of the surviving able bodies aboard the *Roddam* were pressed into service to fight the flames. They were forced to ignore the wounded. Captain Freeman described the scene: "Two men were dead on deck. Fifteen were twisting in horrifying convulsions. We lay them out on the deck, where there was some protection."

When he could steer, Freeman ordered his ship to sea, but because all of the instruments were destroyed by the explosion and fires, Freeman had to navigate by taking sightings from land as he left the Bay of Saint Pierre. Looking back at the city as the *Roddam* pulled away from the anchorage, the captain saw the entire land engulfed in flames.

As the burning and crippled *Roddam* struck out to sea, Captain Freeman thought his vessel would be lost as well. "The sea was rough. We navigated blindly for five hours. It seemed we crossed a great obscurity in our escape. At five o'clock in the evening we made the island of Saint Lucia. Our decks were covered with cinders. The wounded were finally taken off to hospitals. Many had died." Only in his description of what occurred next can one visualize the drama and impact of the events Captain Freeman and the few survivors of the crew of the *Roddam* witnessed. "In the days that followed, we were given permission to clear the ship of debris. It required three days for the ash to sufficiently cool before it could be removed. Layers of ash and cinders covered our decks. Workers removed 120 tons of ash; I can give that figure exactly, because we were not authorized to dump the material in the port, rather it had to be discharged into a barge that held 20 tons. The barge hauled away six full loads of cinders from the *Roddam*'s decks. The ship was in a pitiful state. Only her hull and machinery remained."

Captain Freeman remarked later, "It seemed that I had entered into a long agony. The ship was a floating furnace. The fire raged aboard. . . .We maneuvered back and forth . . . hearing the screams of those trapped aboard the *Roraima*. . . . It was impossible to even dream of helping those unfortunates."

The passengers and crew aboard the *Roraima* fared far worse. M. E. S. Scott, the second officer aboard the steamship, told of their ordeal trapped aboard the burning ship. "I covered my head with a tarred canvas from one of the ventilators. While the cover protected me, the heat melted it and my face felt like it was covered with hot mud, which dried like a plaster mold. . . . At 8:30 AM, we perceived the *Roddam* coming toward us . . . . We brought the passengers up so we could transfer them to the *Roddam*. . . . To our stuperfication [*sic*], the ship moved away, we asked ourselves, how much longer could we stay afloat. . . . The survivors we were able to revive were layed [*sic*] out on the bow deck. They asked for water, but it was impossible for them to drink. Their mouths, throats, stomachs were burned. Several even had the orifices on their face completely blocked. . . . We were able to force our way into one of the iceboxes on board in an area not yet consumed by the flames. We used pieces of ice to soothe our wounds. We tried to put small pieces of ice in the mouths of some of the wounded. Many of them had their tongues burned. One man had an arm cruelly burned from the shoulder to the fingers, but he suffered most from internal burns. . . . One woman clenched and contracted her jaws. Using a small spoon we were able to force a piece of ice into her mouth. She murmured something then died."

It wasn't until six hours later that the French cruiser *Suchet* arrived and rescued Commander Scott and the few survivors from the *Roraima*. The huge iron ship was engulfed in flames. It burned for three days before sinking.

Diving on the wreck of the *Roraima,* the sounds of the regulator's piston drawing compressed air out of the scuba tank sounded dull, far away. At 205 feet the divers were actually well beyond the practical limits of compressed air diving. Eight atmospheres of absolute pressure squeezed their bodies. Their regulators delivered air to their lungs at ambient pressure, compensating for the depth. There was an eerie stillness as the modern-day explorers neared a barren sandy bottom.

Some of the divers were reacting to the effect of nitrogen in the compressed air. Their reflexes and attentiveness to danger were altered. Not able to make it out at first, the shipwreck seemed like a huge brown wall to the divers, blocking out the little sunlight that penetrated. It took great effort for the divers to swim up the side of this undersea "wall," taking with them the dive boat's small anchor and rope.

When they reached the *Roraima,* the divers could not see the length of the entire ship. The *Roraima* is the largest shipwreck in the Bay of Saint Pierre. The ship sits upright on the bottom, leaning over slightly on its port side. As divers swam up the flank of the ship its immense size became apparent.

Saint Pierre Bay is quite deep, even a relatively short distance out from shore, which made it a perfect anchorage. The *Roraima,* anchored farther out than the smaller ships, sank in deep water—its superstructure and deck lie in about 160 feet. Swimming forward, the divers passed the remains of the leviathan's masts and superstructure. Long filaments of black wire coral coiled from the side of the ship, strands eerily extending from the bulwarks and hatchways. The long silenced deck machinery was overgrown with yellow sponges and small trees of black coral. Tiny soldier fish, bright red in the beam of the dive light, darted in and out of winches and coils of cable. Forward, the deck ended, and the divers peered over and into openings in one of the *Roraima's* cargo holds.

At this depth, none of the divers seemed willing to penetrate the eerie darkness of the hold too far, clinging instead to the ladder, peering inside and down as far as the beam from their dive lights permitted vision. The huge holds seemed large enough to devour carriages as well as cargo. Iron ladders linked inner hatchways, connecting different levels in the forward hold, leading down into dark chasms below.

Peering into the steerageway, the divers could see vacuum tubes hanging from their brass fittings. The *Roraima* was an iron steamship with electric generators that powered the lights. Evidence of the fire that raged aboard the ship before it sank was everywhere. None of the fine internal appointments divers usually notice on a shipwreck were evident on the gutted hulk. Even so, the *Roraima's* hull was relatively intact, except for the bow section that broke away from the main structure when it sank.

Many of the shipwrecks in Saint Pierre Bay have been discovered by fishermen. They cast their traps close to the wreckage, which attract fish. Often their trap lines snag in the wreckage, and the fishermen prevail on Michel Metery, a well-known diver, to free them. It was in this way that Metery first became interested in diving on the ships in Saint Pierre's underwater graveyard.

Metery developed a passion for these shipwrecks. Early each morning he would load his dive equipment into his car, drive down to the beach, and swim out from shore to the ships. One morning a fisherman from the village hailed Metery and asked him to free the line of one of the fish traps. In return the elderly fisherman rowed Metery out in his narrow pirogue, saving him the long swim. The fisherman balanced his canoe as the diver rolled overside and descended to the wreck of what turned out to be the *Gabrielle.*

Metery's depth gauge measured 115 feet. The *Gabrielle* was a wooden merchant sailing ship. The wreck was fairly intact, settled down in the sand. All of the masts, superstructure, and deckhouses were gone. The wood was in deteriorated condition, but still held the recognizable ship's outline.

Metery signaled from the *Gabrielle's* stern section, an area that had apparently been enclosed by a deckhouse. As he fanned sand away, clouding visibility, Metery held up a succession of hand-blown French wine bottles. While the corks were intact on some of them, he could see from flocculent matter inside the bottles that their contents had long ago been contaminated with seawater. Metery reached down into the silt and removed china plates.

Metery was fanning away debris in an area that had been the ship's pantry and galley when he abruptly stopped and reached down into the silt to retrieve a long cylindrical object. He waited for the site to clear sufficiently in order to clearly see what he was brushing clear of silt. For a moment Metery seemed startled. In the dimly lit shadows underwater, Metery had found human skeletal remains. The bones must have belonged to a sailor, trapped in the galley when the *Gabrielle* went down. Metery examined the area he had exposed once more, then reverently replaced the human remains in their watery grave and covered them back the way they had been.

The *Gabrielle* was a copper and brass fastened vessel, fashioned by hand by a nineteenth-century shipwright. The captain had stocked the ship with fine china dishes and cups, some of which Michel Metery saved in his collection of artifacts recovered from the wreck.

The *Gabrielle* was a goelette, a two-masted sailing vessel, owned by the Knight mercantile establishment. The "Maison Knight" also operated a warehouse in Saint Pierre, and their ship was moored fore and aft in the "rade," or anchorage in front of the warehouse. The ship was perpendicular to shore, bow facing out to sea, lined up with the other ships anchored in similar fashion.

Dispatched from Paris, the famed French vulcanologist Alfred Lacroix arrived in Martinique several weeks after the tragedy. Lacroix obtained an eyewitness account of what happened aboard the *Gabrielle* from Second Officer Georges-Marie Sainte. Lacroix reported the second officer's observations. "At a point 200 meters below the summit, a black cloud with a loud report, comparable to nothing I ever heard before, descended on the city of Saint Pierre. The cloud required about fifty-five seconds to reach the city. Before the first burning cinder touched the *Gabrielle,* the force of the explosion dismasted her, the ship was thrown over on the side and sank. The *Gabrielle* remained partially afloat underwater because of its empty cargo holds. The captain had time from the moment when he saw the eruption until the force of the explosion struck the ship to get some of the crew into the cabin. It was there that the crew was burned. The portholes had remained open. The burning cinders had an odor of sulphur."

The mechanic aboard the *Teresa Lovico,* another wooden sailing ship anchored in line with the others, managed to survive when the bodies of his mates were thrown on top of him in the initial explosion, only suffering burns in places where the bodies of his fellow sailors did not cover his skin. The *Teresa Lovico* was rendered almost at once by the eruption of the volcano.

Jean Louis, the mechanic, reported that the *Teresa Lovico* had been moored at the foot of Rue d'Orange, at the southern end of Saint Pierre, 160 feet from shore. The ship's mechanic described for Lacroix and French authorities a huge movement of the sea at about eleven o'clock the night before the eruption. At seven o'clock the next morning, a "steam jet" of vapor emanated from the volcano. According to Jean Louis, an hour later "an enormous mass of the crater detached and was hurled toward the city." He also reported that the wind, which had been from the east before the eruption, had shifted to the south.

Abandoning the sinking *Teresa Lovico,* the mechanic jumped into the bay. His beard and hair were intact, his shirt was not burned, but the jersey he wore fell off him in pieces. Jean Louis said that the water of the bay was not hot. Finding a small barque adrift, Jean Louis climbed aboard and rescued his wife, a maid, the captain's wife, and eight wounded sailors. The *Lovico*'s captain was dead.

With great difficulty, Jean Louis rowed the wounded toward the village of Carbet, where they were eventually taken aboard the French cruiser *Suchet.* Most of his colleagues aboard the *Teresa Lovico* were killed except for the cabin boy who was in his room and only slightly burned. The cabin boy said that he had hid his head in a washbasin.

The *Lovico* sank where it was anchored and settled into the sandy bottom. Underwater, at a depth of 122 feet, the ship's deckhouses and wooden super-structure are gone, as is much of the decking. Amidships, construction and building materials are still stacked on the deck. Building tiles covered over with bright sponges host colorful red soldier fish. Coils of rope remain as they had been stacked as cargo in what had once been the ship's hold.

On part of the forward deck, cylindrical pillars stand upright. The *Teresa Lovico* had cement in barrels on board that were scattered by the explosion and sinking of the ship. Over the years, the wood rotted away, and the cement hard-ened into the shape of the barrels.

Curiously, it was the cargo that first enabled Michel Metery to identify the *Teresa Lovico*. Searching through the wreckage, he found other artifacts that confirmed his identification. One can get a great deal of insight into the life and commerce of Saint Pierre in 1902 from the ships' cargoes. The bustling port was a metropolis, where society enjoyed imported French wine and a theater and opera house. The town's magnificent cathedral and fine houses, constructed of tile and cement, remain preserved as ruins, giving testimony to France's gem in the Caribbean.

Sunk near the *Teresa Lovico* is the wreck of the *Diamant*. The wooden sail-ing vessel sank immediately with the force of the eruption. Jean Baptiste, the cabin boy, went under with the ship but managed to survive by diving under the surface of the water many times to avoid being burned by the scalding vol-canic cinders. Finally the *Diamant*'s cabin boy managed to seize a plank float-ing in the water and clung to it until he was rescued by the *Suchet*.

HMS DIAMOND ROCK

It looms ominous, a jagged rock rising 575 feet out of the sea in the wind-ward passage between the coast of Martinique and the island of Saint Lucia, twenty-five miles to the south. This stark island played a crucial role in the battle for control of the Caribbean during the war between the French and British in 1803.

The French call it Le Diamant, a name that seems appropriate on evenings when a red sunset makes the horizon glow and the rock seems to bristle with rays of light. Beneath the surface, sheer rock faces, large boulders, and underwater caves attract fish and marine life. It was from this jagged rock that British forces commanded by Commo. Samuel Hood effectively blockaded the island of Martinique during the war with France using a British naval tactic that remains unique in the annals of maritime warfare.

By hoisting ships' cannons up the sheer cliff face and onto the rock after its capture from the French, the British were able to control access to the entire station from Port Royal on the east coast of Martinique to Saint Pierre on the west. There were very few men-of-war in the British service and they were required to patrol the entire Barbados station. Only one ship was spared to blockade Martinique. The seventy-four-gun frigate *Centaur* had to patrol the entire coast of the island from Diamond Rock to the city of Saint Pierre.

On 2 December 1803, after a twenty-four-hour chase, the *Centaur* managed to capture a French sloop, the *Sophie,* off the coast of Martinique. Pressed into service for the British, the *Sophie* was stationed off Diamond Rock. The *Sophie* was a resupply ship for the men stationed on Diamond Rock and, being an armed sloop-of-war, the *Sophie* enabled the *Centaur* to stretch its patrol area.

There is only one place on Diamond Rock for a small boat to safely accost the land. Landings can only be made in calm seas, otherwise the mariners risk being dashed against the rocks. The British forces initially landed seventy-five men with a 24-pounder carronade on the small rocky island. As the British sailors and mariners explored the island, they discovered many caves.

In one of the larger caves, halfway up the rock, about three hundred feet above the water, the men established a 32-pounder cannon and magazine, which they called Hood's Battery. With only hoists and capstan, it required a major feat to get this cannon into place. Blocks and tackles were secured below on the flat ground and the cannon was pulled up into the cave. Subsequent communication with Hood's Battery was by means of a bucket slung on ropes. This bucket was called the "Royal Mail" by the sailors. In their cave, the men manning the battery were virtually impregnable. If attacked, they had only to cut the jackstay to the Royal Mail, isolating themselves but remaining safe as long as their food and ammunition held out. The British problem of evacuating sick and wounded personnel the long distance to Barbados or Antigua was solved when medical orderlies built a hospital in a large cave on the eastern side of Diamond Rock.

Once the cannons were in place and the rock fortress was manned with a crew of 150 sailors and marines the British dubbed their stronghold HMS Diamond Rock. The island fortress was considered an armed sloop-of-war, equipped with long-range cannons, a hospital, a galley, and the tradition that sailors were accustomed to on shipboard. The men stationed on HMS Diamond Rock were provisioned with a six-month supply of food and obtained fresh water by trapping rain in catchments.

One night, the captured French sloop *Sophie* exploded mysteriously. All but one sailor aboard the sloop were killed in the explosion. With the loss of the *Sophie,* the British decided to increase their fortifications on Diamond Rock. By hoisting cannons up onto the peak, the British forces could not only control the passage between the rock and the island of Martinique but also the approach from the open sea.

To accomplish the feat of rigging the cannons and hoisting them to the summit of the rock, the *Centaur* was anchored fore and aft of the west side. Thick cable was fastened to a projection of rock just below the summit and was run through the *Centaur*'s capstan and extra-heavy-duty purchase. The sailors attached a long 24-pounder, slinging the cannon along the taut cable and hoisting it up with a 5-inch hawser.

Accounts of the feat report sailors heaving the capstan round to tunes played by the ship's military band. The gun was slowly hauled up 575 feet sheer and 400 feet horizontal from the *Centaur.* New crews were put to work hoisting on the capstan every hour. Eyewitness accounts report that even with fresh relief hourly, the cannon slung at 10:30 in the morning was not landed on the rock until 5:00 in the evening. A second 24-pounder was hoisted up the next day in the same fashion, requiring nine hours at the capstans.

On the second day, a wind came up. As the sailors toiled, they feared that the swinging gun would break away and fall into the sea or that the *Centaur* would part its anchor cable. Their concern was justified, for after the second cannon was landed upon the rock, they discovered that one of the *Centaur's* cables was nearly cut through. A short time later the cable parted and the frigate was forced to put to sea.

From their elevation atop Diamond Rock, the long guns not only commanded the channel to the mainland but had sufficient range to force French ships to fetch far off the coast, where winds and currents prevented their access to Port Royal Bay. The French made one attempt to bombard the island fortress from the mainland of Martinique, but the attempt was thwarted by a slave who had escaped his master and sought refuge on the island. The slave, called Black Jack, had been sold by a British family to a French planter. The slave disliked his new master and escaped to Diamond Rock, brought out in a pirogue by native fishermen.

Black Jack informed the British that a French lieutenant colonel of engineers with a contingent of soldiers were quartered at a plantation four miles from the beach. The French planned to install a mortar battery on the shore opposite Diamond Rock. To foil the French attempt, the British put off a barge and landed twenty-five marines on Martinique. Guided to the plantation by Black Jack, the marines knocked on the farmhouse door. A British lieutenant, posing as a Frenchman with dispatches from the governor of Martinique, had the French colonel awakened. While the colonel was being roused from his bed, the British marines surrounded the farmhouse. In short order, the entire French contingent was captured without firing a shot. The French stores and arms were destroyed, and the prisoners were brought to Diamond Rock.

In late 1805, after a year and a half of British occupation, a large French force stormed Diamond Rock and recaptured it. The British put up a valiant struggle, and heavy casualties were suffered on both sides before the rock fell to the French. When the French occupied the rock fortress, they toppled the British cannons into the sea. One of these original cannons was discovered by the author while diving off Diamond Rock. This was a rare find since it was thought that all of the cannons had been salvaged and removed by divers years before.

Diamond Rock remains much as it was when British forces occupied it in 1803. The walls of the large cave, on the rock face above the water near the cove where a small boat can land, are darkened from the smoke of wood fires.

Fishermen have built a small shrine in the cave and remnants of old fishing traps stand in one corner, apparently abandoned.

Diamond Rock is uninhabited except for large fiddler crabs and lush tropical plant growth. Access to the upper caves requires an arduous climb, pulling oneself up by vines and roots, but after climbing for almost an hour it is possible to reach one of the large caves midway up the rock. There is some evidence of a mortared wall, probably part of the British battlements. Early documentary accounts indicate that British sailors, killed in the battle when the French retook the rock in 1805, were buried on the island. There is no evidence of these grave sites, although the markers may have vanished over time. Indeed the stark beauty and austerity of the island provide a dimension of mystery to the unique history of HMS Diamond Rock. An armed sloop-of-war, and at one time Britain's Gibraltar of the Caribbean.

CHAPTER SIX

Ancient Shipwrecks

SPANISH WRECKS

When he surfaced the symptoms were unclear. Two hours later the diver was evacuated by helicopter to a hospital in France. His legs were paralyzed and he had no feeling in his body below the waist. The wreck he had been diving was found in 235 feet, an extreme depth. Surely beyond the limits of safe sport diving and very nearly at the absolute limits of compressed air diving.

It was a Roman shipwreck. The vessel apparently struck the rocks at the Maza de Oro, foundered, and sank in the deep blackness, seaward of the jutting fist of stone. As the doctors struggled to decompress the young diver in a caisson, the story of the shipwreck that very nearly claimed the life of another toiler in the sea more than 2,200 years after the ship went down began to unfold.

While seeking *Corallum rubrum*—blood red Mediterranean coral, almost priceless when found in large thick branches—a different diver stumbled upon the shipwreck of a Roman merchant ship. However, what he saw was not the ship but rather the cargo it was carrying when it went down. Ranged in rows, pottery jars called amphorae lay on the bottom. In ancient times amphorae were used to transport wine and oil, meat, olives, fruit, and other foodstuffs. The jars were carried as deck cargo, stacked and layered with straw to prevent them from breaking. While the wooden hull of the early Roman ship rotted away and almost completely deteriorated with time, the pottery vessels remained intact.

Their outside surfaces were grown over by marine life. To the coral diver, happening upon a Roman shipwreck for the first time, the thrill of discovery would be subdued by thoughts of caution and control.

At a depth of 235 feet, every extra minute spent below results in additional minutes of required decompression before a diver is able to surface safely. On his subsequent attempt to exploit the shipwreck, the diver suffered the paralyzing decompression accident. A nitrogen bubble, coming out of solution in the diver's blood and tissues, lodged against his spine. After long periods of physical therapy and hospital care the unfortunate diver finally regained the partial use of his legs. Using fixes to find the shipwreck's location, almost as carefully guarded as state secrets, other divers returned to the site and photographed the wreck.

The shipwreck contained amphorae and olive jars. There were several different types aboard, indicating that the ship had called at several ports along the coast of what is now Spain's Costa Brava, picking up and discharging cargo. Near the wreckage a large lead anchor weight called the jas lies in the silt. The jas was of enormous size, weighing an estimated six hundred pounds. The form and structure of the ancient anchor also confirmed the origin and period of the shipwreck.

Diving in the area of the shipwreck could only be accomplished in a flat, calm sea, without currents or wind. Visibility at that depth is quite limited, and the diver's underwater light, powerful on the surface, only cuts a narrow yellow beam in the blackness below.

Large amphorae lie on their sides, arranged and spaced for the most part as they must have been stacked on the ship's deck. Some amphorae were broken at the neck, some had broken handles where they received damage when the ship went down. Because the cargo is grouped together underwater, it is relatively certain that the ship sank quickly, intact save for hull or storm damage that must have occurred when the ship apparently struck the jutting rock island of Maza de Oro.

Not far away from the site of this shipwreck lie the remains of another early cargo vessel that tried to round the point of land running between the rock island, Maza de Oro, and the rocks of Encalladora further inshore. The wreckage is scattered over the underwater site in 170 feet of depth. Large amphorae in classical rounded shapes led specialists to believe that this ship predated the Roman wrecks found in the area and most probably was a Greek ship dating from the sixth century BC.

The amphorae are deeply embedded in the sand. Evidence appears to indicate that the ship was violently thrown about prior to its sinking and broke up on the way to the bottom. Because of the depth of this shipwreck, to date no organized scientific project has been undertaken to excavate it. There appears to be no hull structure left, although no deep excavation has been conducted on the site to determine whether any wood remnants of the hull are preserved under the sand.

How Roman and Greek ships, thousands of years old, wrecked off the coast of Spain and how they traveled there is a story of conquest and adventure, pieced together from data gleaned from archaeological excavation of both land and marine sites.

The road is worn smooth, clear tracks where daily wagon traffic and sandaled feet trod through the portal into the ancient city some 2,600 years before. It is the ancient city of Ampurias, built on the Mediterranean Sea near what is today the modern fishing port of La Escala on Spain's Costa Brava—the Catalan Coast. Rugged, stern, and boasting a savage beauty that has defied mariners since humans put to sea and found this magnificent stretch of land, the Costa Brava extends roughly south from the French frontier to Tossa, on the Spanish coast north of Barcelona. The people have their own language, their own customs and traditions, and a seafaring heritage that reaches back in time to the Golden Age of Greece, when galleys and merchant traders plied these waters. Settlements grew up along the coast to exploit the rich lands and accessible coastal ports.

By about 600 BC Greek colonization had spread over Asia Minor. Moving across and along the Iberian peninsula, the Greeks established Emporion in the Gulf of Rosas. (The present name taken from "Rhode.") The colonists built on the site of Palaiapolis around 585 BC, later expanding to Emporion. A short distance from Palaiapolis the colony of Neapolis was built, fronting on the bay. Because the Greeks enjoyed a protected port, a large wall was constructed facing on the sea. Their civilization flourished; trade routes were established;

classical culture, art, and architecture were brought to the Iberian settlements in Greek ships.

The ancient ruins at Ampurias are really two cities, the remains of two different civilizations. The Punic wars between Carthage and Rome began in 264 BC, and it was during the Second Punic War that Hannibal, the great Carthaginian general, crossed the Alps to invade Rome. With the eventual defeat of Hannibal, the Romans pressed forward and took over the Iberian Peninsula. Around 218 BC Roman legions arrived at Ampurias at the start of the Second Punic War. By the start of the second century BC, the Romans had taken over Ampurias and had begun to build their city on slightly higher ground a few hundred yards west of the Greek Neapolis.

Standing on high ground overlooking the sea, there is a commanding view of the Bay of Rosas. In the distance the rock pinnacles of Cap Norfeo can be seen looming off Punta de La Creu. Turning north along the coast, only a few hours' sail from Ampurias, lie the treacherous rocks off Cabo Creus. In the region of Cabo Creus the sun can be shining brightly, while winds whipped to storm force churn the sea in what the Catalans call a *tramontana*. In bad weather, fog and driving rain impair visibility, adding to the danger mariners face on this cape of storms.

The ruins of the ancient cities at Ampurias have been excavated by the Spanish government and are maintained as a national monument. A museum on the site preserves amphorae, jas from ancient lead anchors, and magnificent Roman and Greek artifacts recovered from archaeological digs. The sites at Ampurias provide typology basis for the identification of pottery and artifacts recovered from shipwrecks off the coast. Among some of the most interesting finds unearthed at Ampurias are colorful tile mosaics depicting an underwater scene with a grouper, girelle, moray eel, crab, and the antennae of a lobster. A bird in the mosaic is seen holding a shrimp. The mosaic is done realistically, representations of marine life accurately drawn. On a large panel prepared by the museum to illustrate items found in various stratigraphic levels, bits of red Mediterranean coral pierced with holes at one end indicate that the Romans dove for coral and wore it as jewelry.

Within the Greek city of Neapolis a massive wall dominates the seafront of this essentially maritime settlement. Ruins of many of the buildings show floors tiled with inlaid mosaics. Magnificent Greek sculpture like the statue of Asklepios, busts of Aphrodite and Hermes, headless Hellenistic marble, and assorted Greek ceramic wares with ornate art date to the fifth and fourth centuries BC.

Passing through the gate to Ampurias columns dominate the paths and grassy knolls. The site of the ancient city has a commanding view of the sea, and a cool breeze often wafts through the carefully planted pines. The Romans built cisterns as water storage catchments, preserved today along with magnificent mosaics. One of the Roman floors was tiled in a pattern later copied by the Nazis as the dreaded symbol of their party. Other floors were tiled with elaborate patterns. Some murals are still preserved on walls that have been excavated by Spanish archaeologists.

The Roman city of Ampurias was laid out in a rectangular maze, approximately 2,300 feet long by 985 feet wide. Outside one wall, the Roman amphitheater had been designed in an elliptical shape about ninety-three meters in diameter. It was there where Romans enjoyed games and sports. Inside the wall, a Roman forum was graced with columns as were the temple and mercantile building.

Divers and marine archaeologists with a firm knowledge of the history of settlements, commerce, and conquest can better interpret and understand the importance of artifacts recovered from underwater sites, and the sea around the ancient cities of Ampurias abound with shipwrecks. Even in clear weather, the rocky coast with stark islands offers only narrow passage between them, adding to the perils of navigation. Sudden storms in the area and frequent bad weather have claimed hundreds of ships over the millennia since early Greek times.

A narrow channel between the coast and a long rock island called Encalladora is the site of several shipwrecks. In bad weather fog can close in, making navigation between the rocks treacherous. Even today in high seas the sturdiest of motor launches avoid the narrow passage, heading out to sea around the rocks. If a ship managed to make it past the rocky point into the narrow passage, a protected cove would afford shelter for a small ship to weather a storm. The entrance to the bay is protected by a submerged point of rocks that hooks around into the mouth of the cove. It was here that divers discovered a small Roman shipwreck.

Reconstructing events that caused the tragedy led to an interesting set of hypotheses. From pottery artifacts that were recovered from the site, located in only about fifty feet of water, it appeared that the ship was a merchant trader. Amphorae aboard the ship were definitely dated to the second century BC and identified as Dresel or Italic. This confirmed the ship as Roman. There were several different types of amphorae aboard when it sank, apparently picked up as the merchant captain stopped at various ports along its route.

Evidence of Roman pottery and fused masses of metal were also recovered from the site. Inside the fused masses, pieces of lead, ship's tools, and weights were discovered. Ceramic covers with Roman symbols indicated the stamp of the merchant whose wares were being shipped or traded. Bits of wood from the hull showed tool marks and channels attesting to the craftsmanship put into the small vessel. Wood was preserved against deterioration by the sea and boring worms as a result of being buried in the sand and silt under the remaining cargo.

Underwater, the outline of the wreck site lies parallel to the land on the northern side of the entrance to the bay. It appeared that the ship made it past the rocky point of Encalladora, sought shelter, and while making into the mouth of the bay struck the submerged rocks and sank. Since the wreckage underwater was in the shape of the vessel, the ship did not break up when it sank.

To clear away layers of silt covering the wreckage, divers had to use specialized tools that would disengage the silt without destroying the artifacts. The simplest way to uncover artifacts buried in silt or sand is by fanning the site with the side of one's hand, a ping-pong paddle, or swim fin. Where there is a deep cover of silt, sand, or mud, divers use an airlift powered by a compressor or a water jet, which is simply a water hose whose stream can be deflected by use of a special nozzle. In the case of the shipwreck in the cove, water jets were used to dig a small trench over the wreck site. With the trench dug, divers fanned the site with their hands, to remove artifacts from the silt.

Only a short distance away from this wreck site is the Bay of Culip. This large sheltered harbor is encircled by a tall cliff and volcanic rock faces. The natural shelter of the Bay of Culip is used today by fishermen and mariners seeking refuge from the violence of the *tramontana* and Mediterranean storms. In harsh weather, waves and wind can churn the bay into a fury to be reckoned with. Fishing boats seeking refuge in the bay must be secured with stout lines to prevent them from breaking free and being dashed upon the rocks.

It was in the Bay of Culip that early discoveries of ancient shipwrecks were made. The bay is not deep, about eighty-two feet at most in the center, and much shallower near the volcanic cliffs that box it in. Pottery shards and pieces of amphorae are everywhere. The entrance to Culip is guarded by two rocks that jut up from the sea, their stony points disguising the bulk of rock underneath. One Roman ship hit these rocks and sank at the entrance to the bay, with its cargo of amphorae spilling as the ship sank. Near shore in front of one of the rock faces another small Roman ship went down. Its cargo is now broken— the pottery shards picked over by generations of divers seeking souvenirs from ancient times.

In the middle of the bay, skeletons of sunken ships yield up their history, each a tale from the Golden Age of Greece and Rome and a remnant of civilizations that flourished hundreds of years before the birth of Christ. Historians place the Mediterranean Sea as the cradle of civilization. When one studies a map, the historic importance of coastal ports and cities is immediately apparent: Egypt, Phoenicia, Tyre, Turkey, Cyprus, Greece, and Rome are some of the centers whose power depended on the sea and commerce.

ANTIKYTHERA

One of the most important finds of classical sculptures occurred quite by accident. A violent gale from the southwest battered two small ships returning from the coast of North Africa. The men were Greek sponge divers who had just completed their season and were on their way home. They anchored their sponge fishing boats in the lee of a steep and uninhabited rock island in the Aegean Sea off Crete.

This was the summer of 1900, and the men were helmet divers. Scuba would not be invented until about forty-three years later. The pumps that powered the compressor were worked by hand, and while there was an understanding of decompression sickness and its cause, it would not be until 1904 that decompression tables would be published. In 1900, sponge divers stayed down for what the captain thought would be their limits for the working depths.

Here in the shelter of the rocks of the island of Antikythera, Capt. Dimitios Kondos decided to put his men to work while waiting out the storm. When he put his first diver in the water beneath the cliffs of Antikythera, he sank to a depth of 180 feet. The captain gauged the divers' time with a hand-blown sand glass. When the sand ran through the glass, five minutes would have elapsed and they would bring the diver up.

But Elias Stadiatis did not stay down five minutes. The diver vented the valves on his helmet and shot to the surface. According to reports of those on board the ship, Stadiatis was gasping out incomprehensible phrases about women with syphilis and death and nakedness in a city. Captain Kondos donned the helmet and diving suit and went over the side to investigate. When Captain Kondos surfaced a few minutes later, an amazing odyssey began that made the name Antikythera synonymous with classical art treasures. Kondos brought up a bronze arm from one of the statues he saw on the bottom.

That winter the divers met with Greek authorities and convinced them that they should be supported by the Greek navy and permitted to excavate the Antikythera shipwreck. The Greek government agreed. Marble and bronze statues; the head of a Greek philosopher, dated to the second half of the third century BC; a discus thrower; a well-preserved bronze Ephebus statue; a life-size athlete throwing a ball, cast in the fourth century BC; and a marble horse, eroded but with the head and body fairly intact, were all recovered. Fortunately, marble and bronze statues that were buried under sand at the wreck site were not eroded by the action of waves and seawater. Many pieces of statuary were recovered fairly intact, and busts of Hermes, Zeus, Apollo, Achilles, Philocletus, Heracles, Aphrodite, and others were found. Researchers discovered on the bottom of some of the statues' feet marks indicating they had been soldered. This led researchers to believe the statues had been pulled from their bases and carried off.

Examination of the Antikythera shipwreck much later by marine archaeologists dated the ship to about 80 BC. They reckoned the ship was coming from Asia Minor or Paros, where the marble statues were taken on board. A type of astronomical clock found on the shipwreck, twelve amphorae made in Rhodes, ceramic ware made in Delos, and lead, tiles, and glassware all aided in identifying the ship's route and origin.

Tragedy struck the early sponge divers as they braved thirty fathoms to recover the statuary. Three divers from Kondos's first team were stricken with the bends. One man died painfully on the deck. At the turn of the century there was, of course, no treatment for the bends, nor decompression chambers nor doctors skilled in diving medicine. Yet what the Greek sponge divers accomplished between November 1900 and September 1901 brought the discipline of marine archaeology into being.

Researchers studying ancient manuscripts discovered that a ship was recorded lost carrying a cargo of statues and art. Precise dating of the Antikythera wreck was made possible when divers found the clocklike astronomical calculator. First thought to be an astrolabe or clock, the device was finally identified as an instrument used to measure the rise and fall of stars in the heavens and planets. Study of engravings on the device revealed that it was made in Rhodes in 62 BC, set to the astronomer Geminos's calendar. The calculator when found on the wreck site had been last set to the position of the stars in 80 BC, thus pinpointing the date of the ship's sinking.

Taking note that General Sulla, commanding the Roman legions, conquered Athens in that period and that an ancient report described the loss of one of Sulla's ships transporting art he looted from the Agora in Athens caused historians to conclude that the Antikythera wreck was carrying the spoils of war back to Rome from Greece when it wrecked in a storm in the Aegean. Yet because of its great depth and the ardors of working on the site, many things have yet to be discovered. These are secrets that the sea may forever conceal, having yielded classical marvels in what remains one of the most unique shipwreck discoveries of all time.

THE CAPE GELIDONYA WRECK

The late Peter Throckmorton was an American marine archaeologist who worked on the excavation of a wreck off the coast of Turkey near Finike. Throckmorton spent hours in the ports and fisherman's bars talking with sponge divers and trawler captains. He was convinced that one of the most effective ways of obtaining intelligence about wreck sites was through bits and pieces he could glean from the men who daily plied the waters of the Mediterranean.

The mariners were often secretive. Strict government antiquities laws meant that they would forfeit any rights to their finds. Many would sack shipwreck sites, taking what they could bring to the surface easily, and sell the artifacts secretly on the black market. Intermediaries would then resell the art treasures to collectors at handsome profit. No one asked any questions.

There is a certain pride, however, in finding something in the sea, and Peter Throckmorton was a particularly artful confidante. He listened when men wanted to brag. The adventure of the Cape Gelidonya wreck began inauspiciously as Throckmorton plied Bodrum's waterfront on the Turkish coast.

Finally Throckmorton heard a rumor that a Turkish captain was selling bronze for scrap. The captain had complained that the payment was too small and it hardly paid to bring it up, since the metal was decayed. Tracking down the information, Throckmorton heard the divers describe finding bronze cast in the shape of animal hides along with primitive tools and weapons. Throckmorton extracted the bits of information about where the divers had found this scrap metal and was given the location of the wreck off Cape Gelidonya.

Throckmorton mounted an expedition with George Bass and in 1960 searched the area in the vicinity described by the sponge divers. The archaeologists were confident that they were on the track of a 1200 BC Bronze Age shipwreck. Finally, the scientists spotted what the sponge divers had described as ingots of copper in the shape of ox hides with cast feet.

The explanation for the odd shape of the ingots was that each represented the prevailing value of one oxen. They were cast on the island of Cypress around 1300 BC, according to the researchers.

Diving in ninety feet of water Bass, Throckmorton, and their team set about establishing an underwater dig according to archaeological method. The site was photographed, measurements and grids taken, and items removed carefully, examined, and conserved according to the best available scientific protocol.

For the archaeologists, the discovery of baskets, made from weeds grown in Syria, preserved between the large ingots aided in piecing together the ship's origin and ports of call. Wood from the ship's hull was enough for the scientists to construct drawings of how the ship must have looked. However, most of the excitement arose when researchers found that the ship they had excavated resembled the one which Ulysses built and is described in *The Odyssey*.

The hours divers spent excavating the Cape Gelidonya wreck at ninety feet did not reward them with treasure or gold or silver. Tools, the ship's hull, bronze weapons, and other artifacts gave them the thrill of peering into the oldest shipwreck yet excavated. They recovered artifacts more than 3,260 years old, thus adding to the knowledge of life and commerce from the time of early mythology.

AGDE

"They called me the mad blaster of Agde," Denis Fonquerle said with a smile. "I bought the land and built my house after I cleared away the rocks with dynamite," he added. Had this French pioneer of underwater archaeology not settled in a small town near the Spanish border on the Mediterranean Sea then some of the most important and magnificent statuary, pottery, ceramics, and tools ever found under the sea may never have been discovered.

It stands in a formal hall of the Louvre in Paris. From all of the magazine pictures of this "Pièce Maitresse" recovered by Denis Fonquerle and his colleagues from the Agde shipwrecks, one might imagine that the statue would have been larger than life or at least life-size. And while it is not a small bronze, it stands somewhat smaller than life-size, measuring four and a half feet. There is a quality of realism in the sculptor's work. It is the Ephebe d'Agde, a Hellenistic statue discovered by Denis Fonquerle and other divers at Agde in 1964.

Denis Fonquerle is not a scientist or archaeologist by profession. This pioneer of nautical archaeology, with a group of volunteers—mostly amateur researchers and divers like himself—dived in a remote corner of estuarine tidal basins and offshore areas on the Mediterranean, not far from the shipwrecks described at Maza de Oro. These amateur divers and archaeologists turned the area into one of the richest underwater digs ever made.

The Agde of antiquity was located between the settlements of Massalia, the ancient civilization built around the Gulf of Marseille, or Galactica, and Emporion, or Ampurias. Both Massalia and Ampurias were active ports used by the Greeks in the sixth century BC, and both areas were later colonized by the Romans after their victory in the Punic Wars.

Ships were afforded protection in the bays formed by Agde's littoral zones, connected to the interior by rivers such as the Herault. Agde became a transit and redistribution point for Greek traders between the two larger commercial centers of antiquity while developing trade with the interior. The land area around Agde is also a rich site for archaeological work.

Valuable pre-Roman historical artifacts have been uncovered in excavations on land, as have artifacts from the later Roman period. Among the many artifacts recovered underwater at Agde were ancient lead anchors or jas, Greek pottery and amphorae, Bronze Age tools such as hatchets, knives, and blade handles, a beautifully worked bronze bowl, two bronze seals from the later Roman period along with assorted Roman Iberian pottery.

Fonquerle directed underwater expeditions in the Agde region despite official opposition and academic jealousy. His divers explored and excavated shipwreck sites and in the process carefully preserved artifacts. Fonquerle's work certainly proved the important role amateurs can play in archaeological discovery and excavation.

The young athlete or Ephebe d'Agde dated to the fourth century BC. On loan to the Louvre by the Municipality of Agde, it is perhaps the most famous artifact recovered in French waters. The Louvre displays it with the Apollon recovered underwater off Piombino, Italy.

The Piombino Apollon, much smaller than the Ephebe d'Agde, is attributed to a Greek artist who used red copper for the lips, breasts, and eyebrows. The date of the Apollon has been disputed. Some experts believe that it was a replica made around the fifth century BC. A Doric inscription dedicated to Athena on the top of the Apollon's left foot enabled experts to date it to the latter part of the fifth century BC. Both the Ephebe and Apollon remain among the most magnificent art treasures ever recovered under the sea.

A battleship that has just been brought to the surface in Scapa Flow, Orkney. Many had to be refloated keel up since some of the behemoths turned over as they sank. Divers established caissons on the upside-down hulls, went inside the wrecks to seal holes to make them airtight, pumped compressed air inside the ships, and brought them to the surface. The hulks were then towed out of the Flow to Scotland's mainland and into a dockyard where they were salvaged from the keel down for scrap. During the voyage compressed air was continually pumped into the hull. The high caisson tubes, visible in this photo, were sealed and shortened for the voyage to the wrecking yard. *Courtesy of Bryce Wilson, Stromness Museum*

Bert Kilbride with artifacts he salvaged in the British Virgin Islands.

Wreck of the *Rhone* in the
British Virgin Islands.

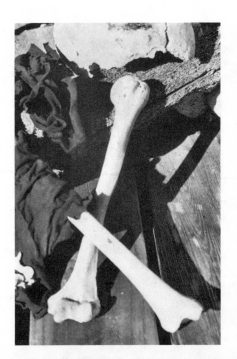

Above left: The bones and remnants of the shirt of the *Rhone*'s carpenter found by Bert Kilbride in the British Virgin Islands.

Above right: Ship's cannon on Anegada's reef, British Virgin Islands.

Bottom: A diver inspects a ship's anchor in the Cayman Islands. Anchors were often tossed over when a ship was caught in a storm, although one can imagine the sailors' difficulty during the fury of a hurricane trying to manipulate a heavy anchor with hand tackle. Researchers follow the anchor's direction because the cable would have paid out in the direction the ship was pushed by wind and waves.

Cannonballs recovered from Napoleon's fleet in Egypt. One (*left*) has been cleaned of encrustations and an electrolytic reduction was used to remove salt crystals that would cause it to break apart if left out of water for any length of time. On the right is a cannonball as it came up.

The hilt of an officer's sword recovered from Aboukir Bay in Egypt. The lion's face hilt symbolized Great Britain, thus it is probably an English officer's sword captured by the French.

Left: Coins recovered from Napoleon's sunken fleet in Egypt. Pay for the troops in Egypt was aboard.

Bottom: The author diving on the shipwrecks in St. Pierre Bay in Martinique. Human remains were found among the wreckage, representative of the holocaust in the immediate aftermath of the eruption of Mt. Pelee's volcano.

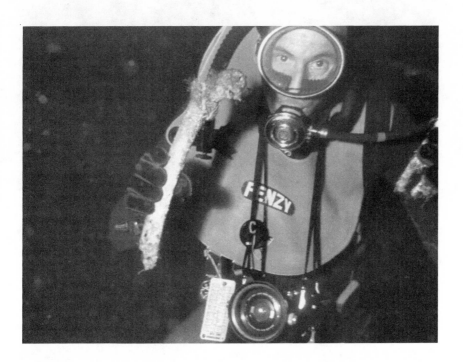

Diver inspecting a cannon that had been hauled up on Diamond Rock. In the battle with the French, the English occupied the rock island and dubbed it HMS Diamond Rock. From the vantage point, cannon could keep French ships at bay.

Matched earrings found by Bob and Margaret Weller and their team of divers on 1 July 1993 on the *Almiranta* of the 1715 fleet sunk south of Sebastian Inlet, Florida. Each earring contained 54 blue-white diamonds. The jewelry consisted of a large gold brooch with 177 diamonds, the top half of a piece of jewelry called a *lazo* with 127 diamonds, a gold dragon toothpick, gold rings, and the bottom section of the *lazo* with 17 diamonds. The treasure came up from a site just in front of Kip Wagner's cabin. Wagner was Florida's legendary beachcomber and diver who found a fortune in gold and silver coins on the beach just in front of his cabin. The site, only 175 feet from shore, was worked in shallow water by generations of divers. This treasure trove, dubbed by the Wellers and their team as "The Queen's Jewels," proves that sunken treasure can be overlooked and there is no such thing as finding everything.

The author snorkeling on the wreckage of a sunken destroyer in Truk Lagoon.

Left: Gold coins recovered from the wreckage of Sir Cloudesley Shovell's HMS *Association* shipwreck off the Isles of Scilly.

Bottom: The author (*center*) flanked by British Royal Navy divers about to explore the wreck of the HMS *Royal Oak* in Scapa Flow. The water is dark and cold and requires dry suit diving. The *Royal Oak* is a war grave, and diving is prohibited on the shipwreck. The author received special permission from the Crown to film the shipwreck when the Royal Navy divers inspected the hull and put a flag on the stern in commemoration of the dead sailors, many of whom remain entombed inside the sunken battleship.

Soldiers pose on shore after the scuttling of the German High Seas Fleet in Scapa Flow, Orkney. *Courtesy of Bryce Wilson, Stromness Museum*

Scapa Flow in the aftermath of the scuttling of the German High Seas Fleet. *Courtesy of Bryce Wilson, Stromness Museum*

Diver snorkeling above an anchor from the *Jupiter* shipwreck. This "Aviso" or courier ship was wrecked in shallow water just off the beach in Jupiter, Florida.

One of Mel Fisher's divers using a metal detector underwater to locate artifacts.

Molly the dolphin with a coin in her mouth. Molly learned how to use her echolocation abilities to find coins under the sand. The dolphin would locate the coin by sending signals into the sandy bottom, snap her jaws to move the sand, snap again when the coin was uncovered, and grab it with her lips and bring it back to the divers.

Coins being removed from a clump or fused mass by archaeologist Jim Sinclair working for Mel Fisher. This is what a clump of coins looks like when it is brought up from the ocean floor. When silver coins are in contact with each other in a clump, the inside coins come out in perfect, mint condition.

Above: Diver Tom Ford, one of Mel Fisher's divers and salvage vessel captains, surfaces with gold found on the legendary wreck of the *Atocha.*

Below: A delicate ivory box recovered by Mel Fisher's divers and conserved by the Fisher team of archaeologists.

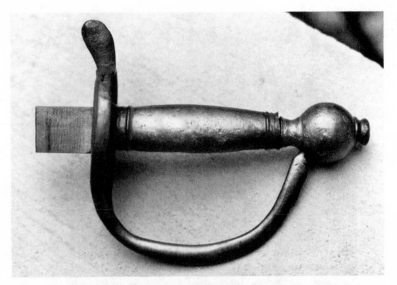

A sword handle found on the wreckage of Napoleon's fleet in Egypt. Often the iron blade has rusted away or is badly corroded. The brass hilt can be beautifully restored.

A triptych, a golden religious artifact, found amid sunken wreckage.

Anchor lost on Anegada's reef in the British Virgin Islands.

Diver exploring a cave where wreckage may have spilled.

A wooden cross found on a shipwreck in Bermuda. The Spanish
arrived with trade goods and priests
to convert the native peoples. The
priests brought wooden crosses to the
New World but returned to Spain
with gold crosses that were often
studded with emeralds.

Mel Fisher's legendary gold chain.
The Spanish taxed bullion and specie,
coins and treasure at 20 percent—the
royal fifth. Jewelry was not taxed. To
avoid paying the tax Spanish merchants carried massive chains of pure
gold like this one. Each link weighs
an ounce and the links could be
removed and used in trade. This is
the chain the author and his team lost
then found again while filming Mel's
exploits in the Keys.

A gold-and-emerald studded cross found on the *Atocha* by
Mel Fisher and his divers.

A minted pillar dollar. Spain established screw presses in the New World mints that prevented the clipping or shaving of cob coins by dishonest merchants. The pillar dollars bore a warning to all other nations who might dare encroach on Spain's colonization of the New World: Utraque Unum, which means "And we are one." Pillar dollars were minted first in Mexico in 1732.

CHAPTER SEVEN

The Holocaust of War

TRUK LAGOON

"The skeletons are piled up in there like a corned beef factory. Bones and heads. Those guys didn't have time to get out. It sank in one minute." Kimiuo Aisek was only seventeen years old when American forces attacked the Japanese fleet at anchor in Truk Lagoon. What he saw and heard, had it been timely communicated to American intelligence, would have surely influenced the historical events that led up to the Japanese attack on Pearl Harbor and America's eventual entry into the war in the Pacific.

Kimiuo, however was just a youth, working for the Japanese, befriended by a Japanese chief petty officer. What he found out and what he observed would only come to light many years later as Kimiuo began diving and discovering the many wrecks of the ships that he saw destroyed in the American bombing raids.

The *Aikoku Maru* was an armed merchant ship. It was built in 1939, by Tama Zosensho shipbuilders in Okijima, Japan. A huge cargo ship—some 492 feet long, displacing 10,437 tons—the *Aikoku Maru* had special meaning for Kimiuo Aisek. He was fourteen when Chief Petty Officer Uchita stopped him on a roadway on Dublon Island. Kimiuo was fluent in Japanese, having studied under Japanese teachers at his Trukese school. Uchita was an officer on the *Aikoku Maru*.

A friendship developed between the Japanese sailor and the Aisek family and the officer would often dine at the Aisek household. It was through Uchita that Kimiuo learned about the destination of the ship and its cargo of munitions.

Softened by effects of drink, good food, and the company of Kimiuo's family, the chief petty officer reminisced about his wife and four children at home in Japan.

As time passed Kimiuo began working for the Japanese navy, loading supplies. One of the ships the Trukese youth loaded with ammunition was the *Aikoku Maru*. Kimiuo ate in the ship's mess while they loaded the dangerous cargo. On one trip the *Aikoku* took on ammunition for Rabaul. Kimiuo and his fellow Trukese worked three days loading the ship. Meanwhile, the war in the Pacific intensified. Having recovered from the devastating blow suffered at Pearl Harbor, the U.S. Navy was taking the offensive and pushing across the Pacific.

On 4 February 1944, Kimiuo was aware that reconnaissance flights were being made over the Japanese anchorage in Truk lagoon by two American PB4Y Liberators. The commander of the Japanese Combined Fleet, Adm. Mineichi Koga, fearing an all-out assault on Truk, ordered his larger military ships out to Palau on 10 February. About sixty merchant ships, armed escorts, and tankers remained, stalled by high seas and delays in transferring cargo. Six days later the Americans launched their attack.

Hiding in a cave, young Kimiuo left his family to go down to the shore. "I was sleeping in the house of my parents. My uncle was with me. The noise of the attack woke me up. I wasn't really expecting that something went wrong. When the Japanese did target practice they shot real ships, so at first I didn't think something went wrong. Then when I saw the ships on fire and the shooting bombs that's when I realized something was wrong. I first ran into a cave. We have built it ourselves. After two hours I went out from the cave and hid in the trees, and I watched the American planes, how they released the bombs," he related.

As the young man watched, wave after wave attacked the Japanese ships riding at anchor in the lagoon. Kimiuo saw his friend's ship, the *Aikoku Maru,* being attacked. "They were diving, three bombers and two torpedo planes. They went for the *Aikoku,* the torpedo planes coming in just above the water. It looked like they all hit at once. There was smoke and a tremendous explosion as the ammunition went off. One American plane went up with the exploding ship—it happened so fast. There was nothing left. By the time the smoke was gone there was just nothing. Nobody had any time to get out. My friend Uchita was trapped in the ship. I went down to the hospital in Dublon later to try and see if there were any survivors. A small boat picked up three survivors and the bodies of seven dead. I asked about Uchita. A survivor from the *Aikoku* told me that she sank immediately. There was no chance," Kimiuo recounted.

Many years later diver Kimiuo Aisek returned to the *Aikoku Maru*. The wreckage sits upright on the bottom at about 170 feet to its deck. The bow section aft for about 200 feet is destroyed. As Kimiuo pushed in at a compartment hatch, bones of dead sailors began to tumble out. The macabre spectacle reminded him of the remnants in a corned beef factory.

The history of Micronesia is replete with adventurous tales and traditions of brave men in sailing canoes traveling vast distances across uncharted open ocean to settle the islands. In the eighteenth century the Spanish ruled the region, exploiting the colonial wealth in their Pacific trade, which encompassed the Philippine Islands.

Germany took advantage of Spain's weakened position after the Spanish-American War and took over Micronesia until 1914, when Japan forced the Germans out.

The seeds of World War II were perhaps planted just after World War I ended. Secret treaties were negotiated with Japan wherein the allies granted the Imperial government all former German colonies north of the equator. The Treaty of Versailles in 1919 awarded Japan a mandate over the Marianas, Caroline, and Marshall Islands. In the fall of 1940, the League of Nations gave Japan a "mandate" to administer the islands. The mandate, in its famous Article IV, strictly prohibited establishment of military or naval bases or the erection of fortifications in the territories. Veiled with secrecy, Japan almost immediately began construction of underground tunnels, bunkers, and gun emplacements.

Had young Kimiuo Aisek been able to timely communicate what he saw happening on his homeland, then the shape of world history may have been far different. Kimiuo was born on Dublon Island inside Truk, a large fringing reef, on 13 September 1927. His father worked for the Japanese as a stevedore. The Japanese were by this time well entrenched in the islands and schools were staffed by Japanese teachers. That is where Kimiuo learned Japanese; he attended the Japanese school for only three years then worked for the Japanese as a house-boy, carrying water from the well to the houses.

Kimiuo's narration of the events he observed in Truk begins in 1936. "The Japanese construction started on Dublon. All kinds of construction came at that time. Building roads, gun emplacements. The Japanese always said they were going to develop the island. Nothing was said about the military. In those years from 1936 to 1939 they also worked on the mountain of Dublon and those small islands on the outer reef. The Japanese navy sent a special intelligence man to choose the place for those guns." At this point in his narrative Kimiuo paused, his voice became softer, more confidential.

"What I am telling now all writers never get this story," his eyes focused on the lagoon and he returned to his tale of intrigue and the secret fortification which was the prelude to war. "The sizes of the guns are six inches," Kimiuo continued. "This guy came to Truk as a civilian but later someone told me he is a commander in the Japanese navy. He's a gunner. That's why they sent him over: To place the guns in a good position. His name, I found out, was Mr. Tsugawa. By 1940, all was near completion—the gun emplacements and air-field. By the middle of 1941, the Japanese started to bring in their military men. Their navy, they moved in their Fourth Fleet, their Pacific fleet from Japan to Truk. At that time I didn't really think something was wrong until December. By December 1941, World War II blew up," Kimiuo related his eyewitness account of the events on Truk's island. "This was very secret. The Japanese never told any people on the island, only discussed it among themselves."

"Up to that time the Japanese were O.K. They were strict because of the military rule, but person-to-person they were fine. In December 1941 I was working for the Japanese military in the shipping yard. We found out about Pearl Harbor that day. They had a big shout. I did not think anything. The Japanese always told the Trukese people that America was no good. It was a no good country that was going to try to take everything away. The Japanese said they were going to win the war in eight months," Kimiuo said.

The events in February 1944, changed everything. The war in the Pacific was being pushed toward the Japanese homeland. A powerful armed merchant and supply fleet of some fifty ships was sunk in two days of fighting. Hundreds of Japanese planes were destroyed on the ground and in the air over Truk Lagoon. The might of Imperial Japan was being challenged and their fortifications on Truk were in flames.

Kimiuo described the change after the American air attacks. "The Japanese attitude changed after we got attacked in 1944. They became strict on almost everything. When they thought they were going to win the war everything belonged to you. The coconut trees, the taro beds, property. After the 17 February 1944 attack they took everything away from us. You didn't own anything anymore," Kimiuo related.

Parallel stories about the war and the sinking of Japan's Imperial Fleet are told by others, older residents of the islands who lived through the holocaust of war and destruction and were eyewitnesses to the battle for Truk Lagoon.

James Sellem and his wife Nikku sat under a makeshift shelter on a point of land in front of their home on Fefen Island as he pounded breadfruit with a stone pestle. Perspiration streamed down his face and forehead, running into his eyes from the exertion in the tropic heat. Sellem could not switch the heavy pounding stone from hand to hand because one arm was gone from just below the elbow. He lost it in 1944, in one of the American air attacks on his island as he was standing just outside a cave.

Sellem worked for the Japanese in 1934, beginning at the airfield with the crews handling gasoline and supplies. The Japanese constructed the sea wall that now runs in front of his house. They completed the airfield in 1939. Continuing his work, Sellem pointed with his chin toward the lagoon. In the distance, iron sticks protruded from the water. The masts marked the final resting place of the *Fujikawa Maru,* a 434-foot long armed cargo ship that sits upright on the bottom off Fefen Island in about seventy feet of water.

"The American ships stayed off well outside the reef," Sellem said, describing what he saw during the attack. "The *Fujikawa Maru* was the last wreck to sink. I saw the planes throw down bombs and torpedoes on the *Fujikawa,*" he remembered, looking at his wife Nikku who also lived through the war. "I saw houses burned. The sea was burning from oil. I could not see the ship because of smoke. In the first air raid, the Trukese people didn't know what was happening; they were excited and came out to watch the planes. Then they saw others being killed and began digging caves. The Japanese hid in caves where the Americans could not throw down bombs. More than a hundred people were hiding in one cave—in another cave more than a thousand were hiding. In the cave behind the church more than 1,500 people were hiding. The Trukese cave was small, only thirty people could go in," Sellem added. He paused in his work, kneading breadfruit with his one hand and the stump of his other arm. Nikku stirred the steaming breadfruit and handed her husband another piece to pound soft.

The ship that Sellem saw go down remains virtually intact on the sandy bottom. The *Fujikawa Maru,* whose name translated means Fuji River, was used as an aircraft ferry. Its six huge cargo holds had been stowed with new cargo, equipment that never saw service nor fueled Japan's mighty war machine.

In the *Fujikawa*'s number two hold Japanese Zero fighter planes lie helter-skelter in the accumulation of silt. The Mitsubishi Zero had been the fastest and most maneuverable fighter plane of World War II. With speeds upwards of 340 miles per hour and a range of 1,500 miles, the Zero ruled the sky for a time.

In the solemn quiet of the massive cargo hold the planes seem like toys. Some damaged, thrown aside, as if a pernicious child had discarded his playthings in a sandbox and had gone on to play somewhere else. Squeezing into the narrow iron pilot's seat, divers often play with the instruments of war—abstract, inert objects silenced by the sea. Gauges and instruments can still be read in some of the cockpits. In others the instrument panel is empty, apparently to have been assembled at their ultimate destination. In the *Fujikawa*'s forward hold, propeller blades are stacked along with machine-gun ammunition.

The *Fujikawa* was struck by a torpedo on its starboard side. The explosion tore through the ship's steel plate, peeling back the metal. Divers can easily swim through the hole in the ship's side, coming out amidships. Colorful soft coral festoon the decks and passageways of the *Fujikawa Maru,* and fish patrol the action stations where sailors stood, readying bow and stern guns to fend off the fateful attack.

From a distance, the *Fujikawa*'s cannons fore and aft are hardly recognizable, so overgrown with coral, rooster comb oysters, sponges, and other attaching marine life. Close inspection of the guns reveals their firing mechanisms and breach plugs. Live ammunition is stocked in nearby holds.

On the bridge level, remnants of a ship's pantry litter the floor. Large tiled tubs further along the ship's superstructure reveal the Japanese fondness for soaking and bathing. Clark Graham, a former Peace Corps volunteer on Truk who became a licensed dive guide on the island described the *Fujikawa Maru* as his favorite shipwreck. "I found a rubber boot with a U.S. trademark on it. I found a book once. I think about the men getting their ship here to Truk Lagoon. I discovered a navigational sextant. There is a great deal of life on the *Fujikawa*. It instills a sense of discovery," Clark said, describing the wreck.

The Japanese are slowly coming back to the islands they once mastered in Micronesia. They have recently built memorials to their war dead and have contributed money in some cases to restore the remnants of their religious shrines. American former combatants, too, have returned to the islands. The islanders greet the influx of visitors with mixed emotions. "We were forced to work for the Japanese and not paid," James Sellem said. "The Japanese army was all over our island. You had to work. If you didn't work one time, the Japanese hit you," he added, remembering part of the ordeal of occupation.

Another visitor, a physician from Kansas who journeyed to Micronesia with his wife, Dr. James Lee served as ship's doctor aboard the USS *Boyd* in the Pacific. While Dr. Lee and his wife did not dive, Dr. Lee swam over the shallow wrecks and looked down through the faceplate of a dive mask, balancing himself on the bow gun of an armed cargo ship sunk off Uman Island. The cannon loomed up to just a few feet under the surface. It was one of the smaller armed cargo ships, and its superstructure and after section were almost completely destroyed in the bombing raid. The *Dai Na Hino Maru*'s bow section and gun emplacement remain intact, and the wreck sits upright on the bottom. Built before the war by the Nakamura Steamship Company, *Dai Na Hino Maru,* or the "Circle of the Sun," seemed to hold a particular fascination for Dr. Lee.

Perhaps as a former destroyer man he identified with the smaller ship. Davits hang empty over the twisted steel of the hull. It appears that the intense heat of the explosion melted one of the ship's masts, which bends in two on one section of the sunken hull. The ship is overgrown with coral and marine life, its chains and machinery forming colorful patterns in the mottled light filtering down from the surface.

Dr. Lee said very little when he finally climbed back aboard the fiberglass runabout. There is a certain awe about the shipwrecks on the bottom of Truk Lagoon. It is a ghost fleet—the largest navy in the world—that never sails.

"I've carried this for thirty-seven years," Paul O'Leary, a lawyer from Brownsville, Texas, said. He reached into his wallet and produced a small yellowed piece of paper protected by plastic. In neat small handwriting, the lawyer had a tabulated running account of his bombing missions as a nineteen-year-old aviator in World War II. On the small piece of paper, in the first column, was the date, 8 February, then under Place on the chart, Truk. It was 8 February 1945, almost a year after the initial air raids destroyed the Japanese fleet.

"I think we only bombed Truk once. It was kind of a warm-up for us," O'Leary remembers. The missions were being regularly flown from Tinian, and by this time it seemed that the Americans were using the Japanese fortification on Truk for target practice. Under "duration" on the small paper, O'Leary had noted 6:38—the elapsed flight time for his bomber from Tinian. The last column was headed by the notation "Exp." Following across the top line for O'Leary's first bombing mission, he wrote "G.P." "That means we used General Purpose bombs," O'Leary said. "By March 8, we were going into the mainland," he looked at his yellowed record. "We hit Osaka. It was 15 hours 20 minutes elapsed flight time, dropping 'I', or incendiaries," he continued.

O'Leary had left his wife in Hawaii and was flying back to meet her after a trip to the islands in Micronesia to reminisce and revisit places where he was stationed during the war. As the commercial passenger jet overflew Truk, O'Leary intently peered out the porthole. "Years passing probably changed me more than it's changed that island. I was only nineteen years old," he said reflectively.

The scars of war have been covered by nature. On land the Japanese fortifications, airfields, and tunnels have been reclaimed by lush tropical foliage. Underwater soft coral, in bright red and yellow, surround ships' guns and catwalks. Pastel sponges crowd out rooster comb oysters and algae, vying for space amid the mass of twisted steel and deck machinery.

One of the wrecks on the bottom of Truk Lagoon was not sunk by American bombs. The I-169 was built in the Mitsubishi submarine yards in Kobe, Japan, in 1935. The Japanese I-class submarines were the biggest submarines of World

War II. While the I-169 had an overall length of 331 feet and displaced 1,400 tons, later-built I-class subs were more than 400 feet long, with a cruising range of 37,500 miles surface running at a speed of fourteen knots.

Some of the huge I-class submarines had hanger space for floatplanes on their forward decks. The larger submarines had 115 feet of hangar space and held three airplanes. One of these submarine-launched planes flew a reconnaissance mission over Pearl Harbor on 4 January 1942 in preparation for a second attack on America's fleet anchorage.

The Japanese decided to fly the second bombing mission against Pearl Harbor using huge "Emily" flying boats—the Kawanishi H8K. The Emilys had a range of 2,900 miles flying at 15,000 feet with an airspeed of 250 knots. They could carry two tons of bombs. The Japanese would fly the mission with refueling stops at French Frigate Shoals. The hangers in the submarines were loaded with aviation fuel, and rendezvous points were arranged. On 3 March 1942, the two Emily bombers were refueled by the I-class submarines inside the reef at French Frigate Shoals. Both planes successfully reached Oahu but because of thick cloud cover over the island missed their targets and the bombs dropped harmlessly into the sea or on a mountain slope. Both Emily bombers made it safely back.

On 9 September 1942, the large submarine I-25 surfaced and launched a floatplane off the coast of Oregon in a forest area east of the Cape Blanco lighthouse. The pilots dropped two 170-pound incendiary bombs to create forest fires in order to destroy valuable timberland. The floatplane returned to the submarine after its mission and was safely stowed in the I-25's hanger before it submerged. The submarine went back on patrol, having inflicted only minimal damage to the woodlands yet having claimed a victory for Japan's first and only air strike on the American mainland.

The I-169 was not so fortunate. At anchor in Truk Lagoon with five other submarines, the I-169 submerged on 2 April 1944 after being warned of a second major air attack on Truk's anchorage. The I-169, like its I-class counterparts in the Japanese fleet, was among the largest submarines ever built, powered by two 4,500 horsepower diesel engines. Able to obtain a surface speed of twenty knots, the submarine had a cruising range of sixteen thousand miles. Once submerged, the I-169 could attain a speed of nine knots.

When the sub crash-dived to avoid the impending air strike a ventilation hatch tube had been left open by human error, flooding the ship. The Japanese sent rescue divers down when the I-169 was noticed missing. The divers swam along the undamaged pressure hull, banging on the outside, hoping to discover the reason for the problem. The sub lies upright on the sand in approximately 140 feet of water. At this extreme depth the rescue divers had to wait long periods at decompression stops before being able to surface to avoid the dreaded bends. The divers' signals were returned by a sailor trapped inside the submarine. It appeared that the conning tower and control room were flooded.

Working as quickly as possible to free their trapped shipmates, the Japanese attached a steel cable to the sub, hoping to be able to bring the boat to the surface using a barge crane. An air hose was eventually taken below and attempts were made to connect it to the sunken ship. Partway up to the surface the cable separated and the I-169 slipped back down to its watery grave. Divers continued to tap out messages to their comrades still trapped inside the sub. Finally the struggling seamen succumbed, and all eighty-seven crewmen were lost with their ship.

When all rescue efforts failed, the Japanese decided to destroy the I-169 to prevent it from falling into enemy hands. They were apparently then unaware of the Allied strategy to neutralize Truk and the islands in Micronesia, then to bypass them in the push toward the Japanese homeland. The Japanese naval command on Truk ordered depth charges dropped on the submarine, destroying the entire forward section of the boat.

Exploring the wreckage of the I-169 remains difficult because of its tremendous depth. The wreckage is upright on the bottom listing slightly on its port side but intact from an area behind where the conning tower would have been, to the propellers and after torpedo tubes.

The submarine is sunk in the channel between Moen and Dublon islands. Finding its location using bearings off the land is not a simple matter. Watching his dive guides attempt to get a fix on the sub's location and then throw in a grappling hook to make the dive boat fast, Kimiuo Aisek's face was immobile, only his eyes smiled. "Bet you two dollars you don't make it," he said quietly. Then after each attempt he would add it up. "You owe me four dollars," he would laugh. Finally

Truk's master diver signaled the pilot, his eyes intent on taking bearings. In an instant he was over the wreckage and the grappling hook snagged into the I-169.

For a time diving on the submarine was restricted after two American sport divers died after losing their way inside the wreckage. The engine room hatch had been welded shut but over time the hatch was pried free by adventuresome sport divers. It was Kimiuo who, with underwater cinematographers, made the first dive of discovery on the I-169.

Penetrating the submarine's hull through the narrow after hatch, the divers found the remains of possibly thirty Japanese seamen who lost their lives when the I-169 sank, trapped inside and suffocated. The divers did not at first disturb the remains but rather contacted the authorities. The Japanese government sent navy divers to work with the Americans and the remains were removed and cremated in a special memorial service. Ceremonial sake brought from Japan was sprinkled on the water and many of the relatives and a surviving shipmate of I-169, a sailor who had been on shore when the submarine sank, blew taps as the flames consumed the mortal remains of his fallen comrades who lost their lives many years before.

Kimiuo glided over the wreckage, familiar landmarks catching his eye. He dropped down to the sand on the lagoon floor to examine the propeller blades and aft torpedo tubes. Long strands of black wire coral spiraled upwards and a school of reef fish parted as the diver swam through then.

The first American air attack on Truk lasted two days, 17–18 February 1944. The raid, dubbed "Operation Hailstone," was launched by carrier-based planes from a U.S. task force sailing ninety miles northeast of Truk. Five aircraft carriers under the command of Vice Adm. R. A. Spruance took part in the attack. In the first wave of the attack, seventy-two Hellcat fighters were launched from the carriers *Yorktown, Enterprise, Bunker Hill, Intrepid,* and *Essex.* In the first hours of fighting, thirty Japanese planes were shot down in the air over the lagoon and approximately 260 Japanese aircraft were destroyed on the ground. The fighter attack was followed by waves of Dauntless dive bombers and torpedo planes.

The intensity of the air attack on Truk prompted historians to assert that the attack was fifteen times more severe than the Japanese assault on Pearl Harbor.

On the first day alone the American planes loosed 369 1,000-pound bombs, 498 500-pound bombs, and 76 torpedoes.

In the darkness of 18 February, the Americans launched a second attack on the Japanese fleet, said to be the first time that aircraft were launched from U.S. carriers at night. When the smoke cleared fifteen Japanese naval ships, seventeen cargo ships, and six tankers lay on the bottom of Truk lagoon amounting to some 200,000 tons.

The Americans crippled the Japanese support fleet but missed Adm. Mineichi Koga's main combat force. Warned of the impending attack by the 4 February 1944 reconnaissance flight over Truk, Admiral Koga left Truk aboard the battleship *Musashi*, the sister ship of the battleship *Yamato*, on 10 February. Sailing with him to Palau were five heavy cruisers, twelve submarines, some twenty destroyers, and two aircraft carriers.

Aircraft wreckage is strewn about on the sandy lagoon bottom. Shot down taking off from the Japanese airfield on Eten Island, a twin engine Mitsubishi bomber crashed and sank in sixty-five feet of water. The G4MI bomber, a "Betty Bomber" as the series was called by the Allies, is fairly intact save for the cockpit which must have received the impact of the crash.

Divers can enter the airplane from hatches in the fuselage and move forward to the cockpit. The plane's shortwave radio set remains intact and there is space in the shattered cockpit for divers to pass out through the twisted aluminum windscreen frame.

During the war, the Japanese relied heavily on their 4,500-mile long-range Kawanishi flying boats. These huge four-engine seaplanes could be used for supply or reconnaissance missions. The wreck of one of these Kawanishi seaplanes lies just off the southern point of Dublon Island. The large engine cowlings and propellers dwarf scuba divers exploring the wreckage. Aircraft instrument panels, in particular, hold fascination for divers who are able to scrape away some of the encrusting marine organisms and still read the heading on the sealed compass.

Looking at a map, it becomes immediately apparent why Truk's deep, sheltered lagoon was of strategic importance to the Japanese. These Eastern Caroline Islands are located just about in the mid-Pacific. The islands of Truk lie on an axis, some 565 nautical miles southeast of Guam, 1,842 nautical miles east-southeast of Tokyo, and 3,075 nautical miles southwest of Hawaii. Truk comprises some eleven larger uninhabited islands and many smaller inlets lying inside the protected shelter of a natural fringing reef. There is very limited access to the lagoon through passes in the reef, which the Japanese mined and could close with nets, yet it was deep enough for the largest warships to navigate and anchor. Thick cement bunkers built into rock caves and surrounding mountains stocked with artillery made a naval or land assault on Truk virtually impossible. Confident of their victory, the Japanese used Trukese forced labor gangs to clear the jungle and build roads and formidable stone and concrete structures, including the hospital on Dublon, now overgrown with tropical foliage.

Off the tip of Dublon Island a newly discovered shipwreck gives silent testimony to Japan's imperial dreams. At depths as great as 150 feet, a small Japanese freighter sits upright. It displaced only 3,763 tons, but the *Nippo Maru* is a self-contained memorial to war and warfare. In the eerie stillness below 130 feet scuba regulator sounds are muted. The demand valve labors to deliver more air to keep the diver's lungs at their normal volume against the pressure of this depth. The diver's wetsuit is compressed, only a thin and less buoyant layer, pressing against the body as shrouds and wires of the *Nippo's* masts and superstructure come into view.

More than the other wrecks, the *Nippo Maru* is a phantom ship. Its bridge is intact and in the clear water and subdued light of the lagoon at this depth, the *Nippo* appears to be emerging from a fog. Its slight list to port adds a dimension of realism to the silent ship. On deck a Japanese tank cants oddly, the massive iron treads overgrown with marine life. The gun port is protected by an iron plate, the tank's cannon and machine gun stowed, probably inside the iron chariot to be assembled for action when the tank was landed ashore, a secret destination, whose manifest was never unsealed.

On the forward deck a truck chassis lies thrown up on the rail, precariously balanced, deck cargo broken free of its fastenings as the *Nippo* went down. Aft, behind the bridge and superstructure amidships, Japanese artillery pieces sit on the deck. The guns, on their wheels and carriages, were dislodged and moved into disordered positions by the force of the explosion that destroyed the entire stern section of the ship. Barrels on the upright guns point into the air, making them appear ready to fire, save for sprigs of hard coral growing out of their muzzles, bright red under the diver's waterproof light.

In the *Nippo*'s holds, round shapes protrude from the silt. Mines lie helter-skelter in the forward hold, still live and unstable after their long immersion in the sea. On the flying bridge, ship's china has spilled out onto the deck. Inside the pilothouse, the ship's compass is intact; the telegraph remains, covered with bright marine sponge growth. The wheel housing is still in place, spokes rotted and only a frame remaining attached to the capstan. Looking forward out of the bridge, it is easy for a diver to imagine the ship under way, directing the ghost ship on a course heading nowhere.

The Imperial Navy pressed many civilian ships into service to aid the war effort. A passenger ship built in 1930 by the Osaka Iron Works was converted into a submarine supply ship. On its port side in about fifty feet of water, the ship's name, *Heian Maru,* meaning peace, is inscribed on the steel plate. The name was retained, although incongruous to the ship's last mission, and is written in large Japanese characters with its English translation underneath. Huge propellers loom up from the stern, each of their four blades dwarfing divers swimming down to inspect them.

Near the destroyed bridge areas live torpedo warheads lie where they were stored on deck. One of the curiosities on the *Heian Maru* are the many submarine periscopes, carried on deck along a companionway. The precision optics have been covered by sea life, new war material that never saw service. Looking up from the bottom, a sunburst on the surface glows over a tangle of iron stays, cable, and rigging. Huge masts protrude from the iron ship resting on its flank, dwarfing the divers who explore the 510-foot hulk.

One of the tankers whose oil polluted the lagoon for many years after the attack on Truk is now one of the most majestically overgrown ships in the lagoon. Lying off Param Island in about 132 feet of water to the sand and about 60 to 70 feet to the decks, the *Shinkoku Maru* is upright on the bottom. Displacing more than ten thousand tons with an overall length of 500 feet, the *Shinkoku* is a veritable city unto itself.

The ship's hospital is equipped with an operating table and instrument sterilizers. Lamp fixtures hang on bare wires over the operating room; the ceiling panels have collapsed, exposing iron girders and steel plate from the deck above. The bridge deck of the *Shinkoku* has fine ship's china in what must have been the officers' pantry and lounge area. The *Shinkoku* was built and operated by the Osaka Merchant Marine Company before the war, and the distinctive symbol on the ship's service is still in use today by Japan's "K Line" Container and Steamship Company. On the bridge large brass telegraphs are encrusted with algae and sponges. Small branches of soft coral grow out of the spokes. Divers can scratch away some of the growth on the ship's compass and still read the direction below its thick binnacle glass. In the engine rooms and crew compartments aft, bones and skeletons of the sailors who were trapped at their posts when the ship went down can he seen in the thick silt. The skulls and human remains are grim reminders of the consequences of war. Divers swimming between the engine spaces, ducking down through open skylights on the afterdeck, can imagine the frantic scrambling as crewmen tried to climb narrow iron ladders to escape the sinking ship.

A smaller transport ship that sank off Uman Island at a depth of hundred feet to the sea floor provides divers with one of the most beautiful encrusted areas in the lagoon. The mast and large iron crosspiece of the *Sankisan Maru* host a wide assortment of marine life, including hard and soft corals, sponges, algae, and fluted oysters. Bright red clown fish dart in and out of pure white sea anemones attached where the kingpost joins the mast. As a diver approaches, a small clownfish swims out, only to retreat rapidly behind the stinging tentacles of the anemone. Immune to their sting, clownfish live in a commensal relationship with the anemone, drawing fish within range of the stinging cells, in turn being afforded protection and the right to feed off morsels of captured prey. The mast and kingpost provide a panoply of form and color. Divers with an interest in underwater photography often spend hours observing and taking pictures of reef life that has overgrown the mast. Trucks stowed as deck cargo aboard the *Sankisan* are overgrown, their tires home to colorful attaching organisms. Trucks are also stowed inside the *Sankisan's* forward hold along with large airplane engines and bullets. The superstructure and after section of the *Sankisan* were destroyed in the bombing attack.

The cargo ship *Yamagiri Maru,* its name meaning Misty Mountain, is sunk in about 110 feet of water. The flank of this 435-foot, 6,440-ton freighter is at about 40 feet. When the *Yamagiri* went down it was carrying a cargo of 18-inch diameter shells. These were the largest naval artillery shells ever made. At the time, each of the projectiles had a range of twenty miles and cost the price of a Cadillac automobile to manufacture. In the annals of naval history, there were only two battleships in the world with guns capable of firing these immense projectiles: the legendary *Yamato* and *Musashi,* which for a time ruled the Pacific. The large projectiles intended for these ships lie scattered about *Yamagiri*'s holds. Massive shells still protrude from the accumulation of silt, framed by the eerie yellow of a diver's light. The shells are unstable after years underwater, and divers are warned not to disturb them. The hull and superstructure of *Yamagiri* give mute testimony to the courage and fury of the American attack. Gaping torpedo holes have peeled back the ship's thick iron plates. Bombs dropped on its deck destroyed much of the pilot house and superstructure. The *Yamagiri* was an armed cargo ship with 140-mm cannons on the prow and poop. The guns point off aimlessly, gray silhouettes that come to life with color when a diver's light illuminates the brilliant red and orange gorgonian coral that have overgrown them.

One of the Japanese oil tankers rolled over when it was hit and sank upside down. The 475-foot "Treasure Ocean," or *Hoyo Maru* in Japanese, was struck by torpedoes on the port side while it was anchored off Fefen Island. The torpedoes ripped gaping holes in the *Hoyo*'s side peeling back the steel plate like a banana skin. The body of the ship broke in two. Part of the hull sticks up just a few feet under the surface. To the snorkel diver the long flat keel of the tanker is an ideal artificial reef. Hard and soft coral have grown up on the hull, and many small reef fish dart in and out of the protection of the coral growth.

Diving on shipwrecks always requires special caution. In the case of an upside-down ship such as the *Hoyo,* the danger of diver disorientation is increased. Slipping under the ship forward, where the prow and superstructure have kept the vessel's forward rail area up off the sand, divers can enter the bow section and forward crew area. In the bow, signal lanterns lie in a heap in the silt. Small lobsters inhabit this signal room and dart about furiously when disturbed by the intrusion of a diver's light. A ship's safe lies in the thick accumulation of silt, rust red amid a tangle of gear and debris long since tumbled down.

The prow of another wreck points upward toward the surface. Snorkeling along the narrow deck divers discover an open area where the *Susuki Maru*'s funnel used to stand. The *Susuki* was used as a submarine chaser during the war, known as Patrol Boat 34. The wreck is upright in shallow water sunk off Dublon Island. Snorkel divers can swim under the remnants of a companionway that leads off from the bridge area.

The *Susuki* is a smaller ship, 235-feet long displacing just over a thousand tons, and it is relatively easy to swim over the ship, surfacing only once or twice for a breath of air. At first the cylindrical objects on the *Susuki*'s poop may not register, so fascinating and otherwise well disguised are the former armaments of war. Live depth charges remain mounted on the ship's after deck, unexploded when the stern settled in about thirty feet of water. Dropping down off the *Susuki*'s stern, a diver can swim around the propellers and rudder assembly.

In all, about sixty-five Japanese ships were sunk in Truk Lagoon. After the first raid in February, the U.S. Pacific Fleet launched another carrier-based air attack on 29 and 30 April 1944. The raiders were met with some air resistance. One dramatic aerial photograph taken at the time shows a Japanese "Jill" bomber in flames, shot down by gunners aboard the aircraft carrier *Yorktown*. U.S. Dauntless dive bombers devastated Japanese shipping at anchor resupplying land forces and then concentrated on destroying land fortifications and air fields on the islands. The thick reinforced concrete control towers and buildings remain standing. Long-range guns rust in their mountain caves and bunkers overlooking the lagoon. Kids play in caves that once served as air-raid shelters and war storage depots.

Ambassadors and officials from foreign nations dive over the remnants of war, exploring torpedoed ships like the *Gosei Maru,* a small 269-foot long cargo ship that sank on its port side off Uman Island. One foreign representative participated with Truk's governor and other officials to dedicate a new fisheries dock on Dublon Island. He took time to don scuba equipment and explore the *Gosei*'s hull and overgrown masts. "This is a good means of assuring peace. These are memorials. It is good that the Truk government is keeping them as reserves. Perhaps if more people would see firsthand the carnage of war it would he easier to keep peace in the world," the foreign ambassador said, awed by the ghostly ships where nature's balm has salved their wounds of war.

Japanese forces surrendered on Truk aboard the *Portland* on 2 September 1945.

Lt. Gen. Shunzaburo Magikure and Vice Adm. Chuicki Hara signed the surrender to American Vice Adm. George D. Murray. The inhabitants on the eleven larger islands inside Truk's ten-mile-wide lagoon went back to planting and fishing. The islands returned to obscurity, and a sleepy peacefulness settled in Micronesia. Slowly the oil, aviation fuel, and debris from the shipwrecks flushed out to sea and life began to encrust the steel hulks. The shipwrecks, substrate for artificial reefs, became quickly overgrown. The islands in Micronesia were eventually ceded in trust to the United States under the auspices of the United Nations. Truk, like the other districts, was governed by a high commissioner who officiated from the seat of government in Saipan, 590 nautical miles away. Truk is now one of the federated but independent States of Micronesia. Represented by the United States for defense and foreign affairs, the island state has a large degree of autonomy with an elected democratic government. The names of the islands in Micronesia have been changed in some cases to reflect original language and nomenclature.

Slowly, adventuresome tourists began discovering the charm of Micronesia. As Air Micronesia was joined with Continental Airlines and regular air service to the islands was instituted, divers began to explore the coral gardens that had taken up residence on Truk's shipwrecks. A law in Truk has set aside the shipwrecks in the lagoon as natural reserves. It is illegal for anyone to disturb the shipwrecks or remove artifacts from them.

The ghost fleet of Truk lagoon will not last forever. Eventually the iron and steel will erode, and the wrecks will collapse into the sand. For now, at least, the wrecks have become havens of life and cities unto themselves, serving as laboratories for biologists studying marine growth. "Their guns have turned to garlands," a cinematographer working for the National Geographic Society once remarked. Chronicled by historians and viewed by divers and explorers, Truk's navy remains unique in the world. A fleet of about sixty-five ships, some yet to be discovered, serve as time capsules of history and an underwater war museum. The largest navy in the world that never sails.

PEARL HARBOR: THE ARIZONA

"I ask that the Congress of the United States declare that since the dastardly and unprovoked attack by the Japanese on 7 December 1941, a state of war has existed between Japan and the United States," Franklin D. Roosevelt said carefully as he addressed the Congress of the United States gathered to declare war on Japan.

The first wave of 180 planes flew over Pearl Harbor early in the morning on 7 December 1941. A second wave of 168 planes was launched from Japanese aircraft carriers shortly afterward. By ten AM, in less than two hours, four U.S. battleships were sunk and thirteen other warships damaged or destroyed.

Aboard the battleship USS *Arizona* 1,100 men were killed, including Rear Admiral Kidd and the *Arizona*'s commander, Captain Von Valkenberg. In all 2,113 Americans were killed in the attack on Pearl Harbor and 980 were wounded.

The auditorium is hushed. The normally boisterous tourists in flowered print Hawaiian shirts are quiet. A ranger from the National Park Service introduces the film after collecting tickets at the door. The bustling and moving about stops as a solemn narrator describes the attack on Pearl Harbor. The documentary account comes to life on the large movie screen. The fury and horror of war bursts forth as the most dramatic segments of the attack are revealed on the screen. When the film is over, the exit doors are thrown open to the daylight and the auditorium empties abruptly as the tourists are shuttled to government launches waiting to take then to the Arizona Memorial. There is a knot of tension in stomachs, not quite recovered from the documentary violence portrayed as it was lived.

Unsmiling women in black uniforms escort tourists into the launches. As the boat pulls away from the dock heading for Ford Island, a white arch is visible across the harbor. It is difficult to associate the arch with anything in Pearl Harbor's anchorage of battle-gray navy ships and military buildings behind chain-link fence. As the Park Service launch lands at a ramp leading up to the entrance, a rust brown shape becomes visible on either side of the white structure. The huge archway was built amidships over the sunken hulk of the battleship *Arizona* about where the bridge would have been.

From the bridge way visitors can see the concrete moorings, cement pylons set out as permanent anchorages in what was known as "Battleship Row." A blue-purple plume of oil still seeps out of the Arizona's rusting fuel tanks. Huge round iron mounts protrude from the hull, thick steel emplacements where the guns were once mounted but long since salvaged from the sunken ship.

The *Arizona* rests in thirty-eight feet of water, lying parallel to the shore of Ford Island. One wall of the Arizona Memorial is inscribed with names of officers and crew who lost their lives on the ship. An opening in the memorial arch over the wreckage is often used by relatives or friends of the dead to drop flowers on the watery grave.

SUBMARINES: THE BOWFIN AND THE BLUEGILL

Near Pearl Harbor Memorial Park, the SS 287 is moored. The *Bowfin* submarine is operated by the Pacific Fleet Submarine Memorial Association as a living tribute to submariners who served during World War II. The submarine's huge twenty-one-inch diameter torpedoes, gleaming brass warheads reflecting the sun, lie in braces on the dock. The *Bowfin* carried twenty-four torpedoes into action, with ten torpedo tubes, six forward and four aft. Each of the submarine's torpedoes was a veritable maze of complicated machinery.

The torpedoes were fired by compressed air after being loaded into the tube through the breech. As in most submarines, a safety device on the *Bowfin's* torpedo tubes was designed to prevent the breech from opening if the muzzle door was not closed against the sea. The torpedo tube could be vented, equalizing the pressure inside the tube with that of surrounding sea water. A vent in the tube deflects the compressed air charge into the submarine preventing air bubbles from escaping into the water to be seen on the surface by enemy spotters. To reload the torpedo tube, the muzzle door would be closed, and the water that had accumulated inside the tube pumped into the torpedo tanks, which were used to flood the torpedo tubes after loading.

The most popular submarine torpedo of World War II was called the Mark 14, a 246-inch overall length cylinder weighing 3,073 pounds. The torpedo held a 660-pound charge of torpedo explosive and was propelled through the water by a 340-horsepower steam turbine engine. At high pressure, the Mark 14 torpedo could cut through the water at a speed of 46 knots with an effective range of 4,500 yards. The range could be increased to 9,000 yards if the torpedo was fired at low pressure speeds of 31.5 knots. Inside the body of the torpedo 28.5 pounds of fuel were stored along with 83 pounds of water and 24.4 pounds of oil. The U.S. Navy reported that about 5 million tons of enemy shipping was sunk by submarine torpedoes and as much as 2.5 million tons of shipping received damage during World War II.

Submarines were effective weapons during the war, to say the least. As torpedo technology was refined toward the end of the war, the weapons became increasingly reliable and deadly. The *Bowfin* or hull number SS 287 was built and launched from the Portsmouth Navy Yard on 7 December 1942. The sub had an overall length of 311 feet, eight inches and a beam that measured 27 feet, 3 inches. It was powered by four sixteen-cylinder diesel engines and could carry as much as 116,000 gallons of fuel. Its two four-bladed propellers each had an eight-foot diameter and turned at a shaft horsepower of 5,480. The submarine could achieve a surface speed of 20.25 knots and a submersed speed of 8.75 knots. The *Bowfin* was a fleet-type submarine of the Balao class, with a maximum submersed operating depth of 400 feet, although the pressure hull was designed to withstand sea pressure at depths of up to 600 feet. Significantly, in the Pacific, where the *Bowfin* operated, the maximum explosion setting of Japanese depth charges was approximately 300 feet. The depth capability gave this class of submarine an advantage in outmaneuvering subchasers and taking evasive action. Each of the two main batteries used to power the submarine's four 1,375 horsepower electric motors for submerged running consisted of 126 cells. To give some idea of the size of these storage batteries, each cell weighed 1,650 pounds and was 21.5 inches wide by 54 inches high and 15 inches long.

During the *Bowfin*'s nine war patrols in the Pacific it reported sinking thirty-eight ships for a total of 109,230 tons. Its war record is a chronicle of submarine warfare, a submarine typical of its class and different only in that the ship and crew survived the dangerous missions intact. The boat is now accessible to anyone who visits Pearl Harbor, an excellent way of gaining insight into submarine warfare and the hardship endured by the ten officers and seventy crewmen who made up the submarine's battle complement.

The *Bowfin* began its first voyage from Portsmouth through the Panama Canal to Brisbane, Australia, where the new sub went through training maneuvers. Sailing to Darwin, Australia, the *Bowfin* set out on 25 August 1943 on its first war patrol to the Mindanao Sea. A month later, the SS 287 had its first taste of combat, firing at a convoy of six ships. Through the periscope the captain of the *Bowfin* saw one of the cargo ships, the 8,120-ton *Kirishima Maru,* sinking slowly. Another cargo ship hit by the sub's torpedoes was sinking stern first while thick black smoke curled skyward from a tanker. The submarine was forced to submerge by enemy fire from the remaining ships in the convoy. The *Bowfin* chased the remaining ships in the convoy but had to abandon the hunt when a Japanese plane was detected by the sub's radar. A few days later the submarine spotted a small interisland steamboat and gave chase. The submarine fired three torpedoes at the ship but missed.

Cruising out of the Mindanao straits the *Bowfin* spotted a troop barge. Because the torpedoes were expensive and there were a limited number aboard, submarines often surfaced and fired on small targets with their deck guns. At a range of a little over two miles, the submarine surfaced and began to shell the troopship with its 4-inch cannon and 20-mm MK 10 rapid fire gun. The barge was quickly destroyed, and the *Bowfin* continued its patrol. Two days later the sub sighted a two-masted schooner sailing off Balikpapan and sank it with two rounds from the deck gun. The *Bowfin* returned to Freemantle, Australia, on 10 October 1943, having been at sea fifty-five days, logging 14,430 miles.

The submarine's remaining eight war patrols took the ship and crew to the South China Sea, the Celebes Sea, Midway, Saipan, Honshu-Hokkaido, and the Sea of Japan, where it torpedoed shipping off the Japanese home islands. On the *Bowfin's* sixth war patrol the crew spotted Japanese ships heading into the Minami Daito harbor. Firing several torpedoes the three ships were hit and two went down. One of the torpedoes missed its target hitting a dock. A crane and bus on the dock were destroyed, accounting for an unusual addition to the *Bowfin's* battle flag.

After a stint on training duty during the Korean War, the *Bowfin* was inactivated and officially stricken from action in 1971. The submarine was turned over to the Pacific Fleet Submarine Memorial Association, and remains on display for visitors to Pearl Harbor.

Across the channel from Oahu, where the *Bowfin* is moored, another World War II submarine lies underwater at a depth of 135 feet. Launched by the Electric Boat Company in Groton, Connecticut, on 8 August 1943, the SS 242 or *Bluegill* saw service in the Pacific from New Guinea to Formosa. During its six war patrols, the 312-foot submarine of the Gato class sank ten Japanese ships amounting to 46,212 tons, including the *Yuhari,* a light cruiser torpedoed on 27 April 1944. The *Bluegill* amassed an excellent war record. Its configuration and structure was much the same as the later-designed Balao-class submarines like the *Bowfin* except that the older pressure hulls used on the *Bluegill* and other Gato-class submarines limited their operating depth to three hundred feet, within the maximum explosion range of Japanese depth charges.

After decommissioning, the U.S. Navy scuttled the *Bluegill* in 1974 off Lahaina on the island of Maui. Navy divers used the sunken submarine to practice their salvage techniques and training procedures. At 135 feet a diver can spend very little time below without making long decompression stops on the way back to the surface.

The *Bluegill* is intact and sits upright in the sand. The conning tower and bridge area loom up, dwarfing divers in the warm Hawaiian water. Taking time to observe features on the museum ship *Bowfin* familiarizes and orients divers once below as they explore the sunken vessel. Schools of weke and other fish dart about around the *Bluegill*'s pressure hull. Its two large five-bladed propellers give an eerie appearance as divers drop down to examine the sub's after torpedo tubes. Along the hull, huge trim stabilizers flank the propellers and rudder. Moving forward to the bridge area and catwalk divers can observe the forward deck. A narrow walkway in front of the periscope housing served as a lookout's perch, and from here underwater explorers used to get a feeling of the submarine's size. The *Bluegill* has now been moved by the Navy into deep water, not accessible to sport divers.

THE ALOSE

Submarines and submarine warfare have always fascinated divers and armchair historians. One of the oldest submarines in existence in the world was recovered in the Mediterranean in 1977. The *Alose* was raised from a depth of 167 feet off the coast of Saint-Raphael. It was discovered by Dr. Jean-Pierre Jonchery in 1975 and is currently on display in the Comex diving complex in Marseille, France. It is one of the most interesting historic submarines in existence.

The *Alose* was designed by marine engineer Gaston Romazotti in 1886. It was manufactured for the Marine Nationale Française in their Naide series of boats. The ship measures only about eighty feet in length and displaced 68 tons. The little sub was powered by a motor fueled with Benzol, a mixture of benzine and toluene. *Alose* was able to attain an eight-knot surface speed and could dive to a depth of about one hundred feet, where its battery-powered motor enabled the submarine to advance at a speed of two knots, with an autonomy underwater of twenty-four hours.

Entering the tiny ship through a narrow cutaway section aft, one immediately senses the atmosphere in the small hull. It is difficult to walk past even the remaining machinery and impossible for a tall person to stand erect inside the hull. One can imagine the hardship the crew of thirteen must have felt, cramped into crowded spaces between the engines.

The *Alose* was decommissioned from the French Navy in 1913 and used as a target ship until it was sunk in 1918. The little submarine remains in fairly good condition on the outside. Only vestiges of its original machinery and equipment remain inside the hull.

YAP AND PALAU

Traveling across the Pacific to the legendary island of Yap, one is immediately caught up in the contradiction of progress and tradition. Stone money still remains the traditional means of barter, although its use today is largely symbolic. Inside a traditional house with stone money stacked grouped against the portal, residents may be seen watching color television while chewing beetle nuts and drinking Coca-Cola from aluminum cans. Yap was occupied by the Japanese during the war. Their memorial stones and small temple posts remain on the islands.

Steeped in island tradition is the legend of His Majesty O'Keefe. When his ship wrecked offshore in 1878, David Dean O'Keefe was the only survivor. Marooned on Yap, O'Keefe was nursed back to health by the friendly people. As he regained his strength O'Keefe saw the inherent wealth of the lush tropical island with stands of coconut palms and lagoons rich in fish and sea cucumbers. The islands had never been exploited because no one had yet succeeded in getting the Yapese people to work. Their only pursuit, apart from subsistence, was to voyage in their small sailing canoes to the island of Palau about 250 miles away where they would quarry stone and bring it back in the round forms with a hole in the center as their sacred stone money.

The voyage to Palau was perilous. Every family on Yap could recount tales of hardship and bravery as well as tragic disappearances in which sailing canoes were lost in storms in the open ocean. After he recovered, O'Keefe shipped out on a tramp steamer and found a partner in Hong Kong. He returned to the island with a large sailing ship and offered to take the Yapese to Palau and return them to Yap with all the stone money they wanted in return for their work in gathering the coconuts and sea cucumbers.

Returning to the island with the boatload of sacred stone money, O'Keefe was made king of the islands and proceeded to earn a fortune trading in copra and sea cucumbers, a delicacy in the Orient. His Majesty O'Keefe's good fortune lasted until the German occupation of the islands during the First World War. Never able to get along with the Germans, O'Keefe secretly left Yap in his sailing ship one night and was never heard from again, presumed lost at sea.

Snorkeling around what used to be the mansion on O'Keefe's island inside Yap's lagoon, artifacts can be found in the sand, clearly indicating the good life O'Keefe lived on the islands. Porcelain dishes from China, port wine bottles, fancy china, and assorted earthenware pottery depict a life of opulence at the turn of the century. The mansion is destroyed, but its grandeur can be imagined from the tall brick stairway that led up to it.

Not far from O'Keefe's island, in the principal settlement called Colonia, a shipwreck explorer who has found wrecks around Yap is willing to share his stories and wreck locations. His parents fled from the Russian Revolution traveling across Russia from Moscow, finally settling in Yap. Alex Tretnoff was born on the island and has lived there his entire life.

Diving outside Yap's lagoon for trumpet shells, Alex came across a U.S. destroyer sunk during the war. The destroyer had been captured by the Japanese when they invaded the Philippines and was pressed into war service. Diving on the ship, Alex recovered the compass the Japanese had installed on the bridge. The compass was marked "Saura Keiki Seisakusho Co. Ltd."

Many ships have struck upon Yap's fringing reef. A large modern vessel missed the pass through the reef trying to navigate into Yap's harbor. The ship remains thrown up on the coral, rusting and battered by the waves. Further along the reef an LST is exposed where it wrecked in 1948. While stories about Spanish ships and treasure circulate among the few divers that live on Yap, only cannon have been found to date and those apparently belonged to the wreck of a Spanish ship which has yet to be identified.

Rock islands and magnificent coral reefs lure divers to Palau. Palau's deep natural harbor, with access to the ocean through a narrow pass between the rocks, was an ideal anchorage and headquarters for the Japanese fleet during World War II, protected by big naval guns mounted in caves in the rocks facing the ocean—now ominous shapes subdued by guano from nesting sea birds and vines hanging down from trees.

Peleliu, one of a group of about one hundred islands and islets that make up Palau, was the site of one of the fiercest battles in the Pacific. The original Japanese dockways and barges remain rusted and abandoned. An old wooden boat is sunk in shallow water in a narrow channel leading in from the sea. The remains of half-tracks and tanks lie rusting on their sides, all but smothered by dense jungle growth.

Francis Toribiong, a diver on Palau, has discovered and explored many of the shipwrecks in Palau Harbor. A light cruiser, two tankers, a submarine chaser, and a small aircraft carrier are among the ships sunk by American air raids. Hulks of derelict ships also dot the harbor. Some wrecks cant at odd angles, resting on sand, abandoned; ghost ships soon to join the casualties of war, eventually to be reclaimed by the sea.

CHAPTER EIGHT

Scapa Flow: Graveyard of the North

A gentle breeze pushed across the knoll. Beyond the rolling hills, meadows eventually fell away and a green sea dominated the horizon. In an area of shaggy fields, long abandoned and overgrown bunkers, rusting fuel tanks, and rotting piers, the cemetery was freshly mowed. Pink flowers grew against tombstones, uniform military headstones rowed double, back to back. Humble plantings coming into bloom, intermittently illuminated by the fleeting summer sun.

The naval cemetery at Lyness on the island of Hoy in the Orkneys north of Scotland is as much a history book as any ever written. The tombstones mark the victims of war and tragedy, plaintively logging the annals of maritime events shaped by this vast deepwater anchorage known as Scapa Flow.

"Thurs. 21st 1918 2:55 PM CinC GF to Adm. von Reuter." The neat hand-writing was penciled on a yellowing Admiralty form used to make a record of ship's signals. The signalman dutifully recorded the message that his commander, the commander in chief of England's Grand Fleet, sent to Vice Adm. Ludwig von Reuter, the officer in charge of Germany's interned Imperial Fleet.

"The German Flag is to be hauled down at 1557 today Thursday and is not to be hoisted again without permission (1450) 21-11-18." The signal was terse. The German High Seas Fleet had not surrendered; they had not been defeated in battle; the ships were not under guard by British personnel. They were interned, an undetermined status while the winning powers in World War I hammered out the peace terms that would eventually be incorporated into the Treaty of Versailles.

The message issued at the outset of the Imperial Fleet's internment was but one of a series of humiliations that would eventually provoke one of the most bizarre events of the war, of any war, unique by its magnitude in naval history.

There are many shoals and skerries in the seventy odd islands that make up the Orkneys, most uninhabited, some just used as pasture for sheep left to graze the summer. It is believed that Orkney is derived from the Icelandic word "Orkin" for seal and "ey" meaning island. The Orcadians, numbering about eighteen thousand, live for the most part on the larger islands, principally in the towns of Kirkwall and Stromness on the island of Pomona or Mainland, as it is more frequently called. The Orkneys lie off the northeast tip of Scotland between the North Sea and the Atlantic Ocean. The closest spit of Scottish mainland is the hamlet of John O'Groats, across the Pentland Firth from the islands of Hoy and South Ronaldsay.

The natural deepwater anchorage of Scapa Flow is formed by a horseshoe of islands ringing Mainland Island southward. Porpoises abound, and seals cavort in the bays, basking in sunshine on the offshore rocks.

Stone Age peoples settled the Orkney Islands five thousand years ago leaving behind burial mounds, waterfront stone villages, and unusual rock formations. These archaeological sites are considered to be among the most important vestiges of ancient civilizations in Europe, and certainly in Britain. Viking exploration and settlement followed as evidenced by writings in the burial mound at Maeshowe Cairn that attest to the sacking of the tomb by Norsemen about 700 AD.

The Vikings recognized the importance of the Orkneys and plied the North Sea coast, sheltering within the many natural inlets and harbors. The cathedral in Kirkwall, built by Jarl Rognvald Kolson in honor of his victory over Paul in 1137, fulfilled a pledge given by Rognvald's uncle, Magnus of Norway. The tower and spire of St. Magnus Cathedral, completed around 1170, still dominate the town.

During the Napoleonic Wars, Longhope Bay off the island of Hoy was used as a convoy point where merchantmen trading with the Americas would gather and await navy ships to escort them across the Atlantic. Two stone Martello towers were built in 1813, mounted with 24-pounder guns to guard the entrance to Longhope Bay. The towers must have provided grim reminders to the German crews as they sailed into Scapa Flow in 1918 on what would be the last cruise of the Imperial Navy.

After the Franco-Prussian war of 1870, Germany emerged as a dominant power in Europe. The Prussian Army was a force to be reckoned with. As Germany watched, other European powers absorbed colonies in Africa and Asia. To enable competition in maritime commerce and colonial expansion, plans were laid to build a navy that would rival those of Britain and France. The architect of Germany's modern navy, Alfred von Tirpitz, was then a captain attached to the Baltic Fleet. Captain von Tirpitz advocated a strong navy, writing a thesis that eventually came to the attention of Kaiser Wilhelm II in 1894–95.

Relations with Britain became strained after the Prussians supported the Boers in their war with the English in South Africa. The Kaiser had also objected to Britain's construction of the Baghdad Railway across Turkey. To compete in colonial expansion and as a source of pride, the Kaiser appointed Tirpitz as head of the German Admiralty in June 1897. With lobbying support from the Krupp steel works, a Navy League was organized to drum up public support.

Shortly after the organization of the Navy League in 1898, Germany passed its first Fleet Law, launching a capital shipbuilding program that would eventually lead the world into the Great War. Looking back at the platitudes politicians used to justify this massive arms race, one is taken by the parallel arguments used today to justify military expansion. For while Kaiser Wilhelm II told Tirpitz, "With German battleship there was laid down a fresh pledge for peace," the seeds were sown for war.

As Germans passed their Naval Bill of 1900—with the preface that "Germany must have a battle fleet so strong that even the adversary possessed of the greatest sea power will attack it only with grave risk to herself"—the world then wondered if national self-restraint would prevail or whether these acts which triggered an arms race in Europe would inevitably lead to war. There were even those who predicted that the battleship would be obsolete with the development of advanced submarine-fired torpedoes and sea mines.

The race to build dreadnoughts and cruisers continued at an unprecedented pace. When a twenty-year-old Serbian student fired the shots that killed Austrian Archduke Franz Ferdinand and his wife Sophie, the Duchess von Hochenberg, at Sarajevo on 28 June 1914, accusations were hurled at Serbia by Austria. Russia, an ally of the Serbs, feared retaliation and mobilized troops, in turn provoking Austria's ally, Germany, to declare war on 1 August 1914.

A general mobilization occurred in Europe as Belgium and France called up their troops. On 3 August 1914, Germany declared war on France. When the Kaiser did not reply to a British ultimatum, the die was cast for World War I, a brutal conflict that would last five years and result in the death of approximately nine million people.

At the commencement of hostilities, Britain stood as the mightier naval power. In battleships, Britain had forty-three to Germany's thirty-one. England had about seventy heavy and light cruisers to Germany's thirty-eight, while in smaller destroyers or armed torpedo patrol ships England had 143 in service with thirty-six in shipyards under construction to Germany's 127 with twelve on the way.

World War I would mark the emergence of the submarine as a formidable weapon of war, used to great effect by the Kaiserliche Marine to attack merchant shipping. At the start of war, Germany had twenty-seven submarines in operation with another fourteen in the pipeline compared to England's thirty-seven serviceable submarines with a total of twenty-nine more slated for or in various stages of production.

The strategy of naval war was simple. Germany could pick off British ships weakening their fleets with submarine attacks and mines, while preventing resupply and harassing merchant shipping in the Atlantic and Mediterranean. It was the German submarine attack on the passenger liner *Lusitania* on 7 May 1915 with the loss of 1,198 civilians that turned American public opinion against Germany, influencing the eventual entry into the war.

In any event, at the outset of the war, Britain sent its Grand Fleet to Scapa Flow to cover the North Sea using the Channel Fleet to patrol between Dover and France, protecting troop carriers and resupply ships. Almost immediately, the Allies found a German master grid chart for the North Sea and signal code books on the dead body of a German warrant officer, floating in his life jacket after the sinking of his ship, the *Magdeburg,* in the Gulf of Finland. This piece of luck put the German navy at a great disadvantage. The Russians gave the codes to the British, and the information they contained was used to advantage during the entire war to predict German ship movements. Even with this momentous advantage, as we will see, there were no truly decisive naval battles in World War I.

The Germans adopted the strategy of saving their Imperial Fleet from direct conflict with the British unless the fleet could significantly inflict damage on the enemy. Instead, they would depend on predatory U-boat attacks to weaken the British fleet, always hoping to lure and destroy detached battle groups of English warships.

One skirmish occurred on 24 January 1915 off the Dogger Banks in the North Sea when the Germans ventured forth to harass and disperse the British fishing fleet. With the benefit of the code ciphers, the British were aware of the German plans. The German Imperial Fleet, engaged by the enemy, managed to escape with modest losses: the older battle cruiser *Blucher* was sunk, and damage was sustained by the battleships *Moltke* and *Seydlitz.* On the other side, the battle cruiser HMS *Lion* sustained heavy shelling damage.

While Germany was willing to sacrifice its fleet in battle so long as heavy casualties were inflicted on the British, the Royal Navy could not afford to lose supremacy of the seas. For Britain, a decisive loss of sea power would probably mean disaster because Germany's powerful armies retained supremacy on land. On their part, the Germans knew they could not win a face-to-face naval battle with the Royal Navy, and thus began a war of attrition with sorties and taunts, each side trying to tempt the other into a controlled battle situation. The Germans hoped to isolate a squadron of the Grand Fleet, the British to entrap the Imperial Fleet and cut them off from their home bases

Toward the end of May 1916, Adm. Reinhard Scheer, commander of the German High Seas Fleet, put a plan into operation that he hoped would draw the British into a trap set with U-boats lying in wait for British ships leaving their North Sea bases. The British decoded enough of the German signals to be certain that a ship movement of some proportions was under way. Orders came down from the Admiralty for the Grand Fleet and the battle cruiser fleet, under the over-all command of Adm. John R. Jellicoe, to mobilize. By 31 May 1916, the two great fleets were steaming toward each other. Only a chance encounter provoked what was to become the major sea battle of World War I. Destroyer screens of opposing sides sailed toward a neutral Danish merchant ship to investigate its pres-ence. The fleets were about seventy miles off the German coast as the destroyers reported contact and the battle cruisers closed. Both sides opened fire with salvos from their big guns. A German battle cruiser's gunnery control officer was quoted as saying: "The true sporting joy of battle woke in me and all my thoughts con-centrated on one desire, to hit, to hit rapidly and true, to go on hitting."

As barrage followed barrage, salvo after salvo, guns ranged and rapid-fired, and the smell of cordite permeated the ships. A British officer recalled his obser-vations from the bridge of the HMS *Tiger:* "I remember watching the shells com-ing at us. They appeared just like bluebottles flying straight towards you. Each time going to hit you in the eye; then they would fall, and the shell would either burst or else ricochet off the water and lollop away above and beyond you, turn-ing over and over in the air."

The shells were pitiless in their accuracy: the HMS *Indefatigable* was hit with two salvos. As an officer watched from a nearby ship, the *Indefatigable* burst into flame. "The main explosion started with sheets of flame, followed immediately afterwards by a dense, dark smoke, which obscured the ship from view. All sorts of stuff was blown high in the air, a fifty-foot steam picket boat for example, being blown up about 200 feet, apparently intact, though upside down," the officer reported.

These battle accounts hardly reveal the horror. The Battle of Jutland, or the Battle of Skagerrak as the Germans called it, will mark perhaps the last confronta-tion of great ships fighting in line, slugging it out. The HMS *Queen Mary* was lost after being struck by two German salvos. "As they hit I saw a dull, red glow amid-ships and then the ship seemed to open out like a puffball or one of those toad-stool things when one squeezes it," remarked an officer on the British flagship *Tiger.* Suddenly in the midst of battle between the cruisers, the column of German bat-tleships appeared, and the English ships turned to draw them northwest toward the main contingent of the Grand Fleet and into Admiral Jellicoe's waiting arms.

As the fleets collided, confusion, poor visibility, signaling errors, and incorrect position reports prevented the British from pressing home the advantage. The *Invincible* was destroyed. The German fleet sustained heavy shelling damage, eventually sending their destroyer flotilla and cruisers against the British fleet to buy time for the capital ships to get away.

As daylight ebbed the Battle of Jutland remained indecisive. Admiral Scheer cut across the British Grand Fleet's wake amid some skirmishing with enemy destroyers, and by the following morning Admiral Scheer had made good his tactical escape, and the Battle of Jutland was over. Each side claimed victory. The German High Seas Fleet returned to port where, with only minor sorties, it remained until the signing of the armistice.

In losses, the Germans had fourteen ships destroyed at Jutland, a battleship, a battle cruiser, four light cruisers, and eight destroyers with 2,551 men killed and more than 500 wounded. The British lost fourteen ships, including three battle cruisers, three cruisers, and eight destroyers, with 6,274 men killed, some 500 wounded, and about 200 taken prisoner. In tonnage, German losses amounted to 61,180 tons against British losses of 115,025 tons.

At the start of battle, Admiral Jellicoe had a capital fleet of twenty-eight battleships and eight battle cruisers; after the fighting twenty-four remained undamaged. The Germans entered the Battle of Jutland with twenty-two battleships and five battle cruisers; seventeen of them sustained damage.

Britain continued as master of the North Sea, effectively bottling up the German fleet for the duration of the war. Other tactics employed by Germany very nearly brought England to its knees, as submarines haunted merchant shipping and extracted a tremendous toll. The only major naval battle of World War I where the two great fleets collided was neither won nor lost by either side. Germany's High Seas Fleet would meet an ignominious fate only at war's end, while riding at anchor in Scapa Flow.

On 5 October 1918, an armistice was offered based on the famous Fourteen Points of President Wilson. Hoping to execute a final sortie that would enhance Germany's advantage at the peace table, the Imperial High Seas Fleet sailed out of their sheltered bases. Germany was in chaos. Mutiny in the services quickly spread. Committees of communist workers took over the dockyards, ratings refused to obey their officers, red flags were hung where once the proud ensign of the Imperial Navy flew.

The High Seas Fleet was reduced to impotence. When Kaiser Wilhelm abdicated to Holland on 9 November 1918, the armistice followed. The articles of the armistice provided for the surrender of the pride of Germany's navy, the intrepid fleet of U-boats, while the allies squabbled over what would be the eventual fate of the High Seas Fleet. It was decided by Lloyd George of England, President Wilson's representative to the Supreme War Council, Clemenceau of France, and the prime ministers that the German fleet was to be interned pending the outcome of the peace conference and the formal signing of a treaty.

It was also decided that seventy-four German warships, their best battleships, battle cruisers, cruisers, and destroyer-torpedo boats would be interned at Scapa Flow. The ships were to be disarmed and sailed across the North Sea by the Germans. The Allies threatened to invade Heligoland if the Germans did not comply.

The long gray line stretched for nineteen miles as the internment formation made for their appointed rendezvous in the Firth of Forth on 21 November 1919. Adm. Ludwig von Reuter managed, after a fashion, to get the mutinous crews to work at their posts. The once-gallant and disciplined High Seas Fleet was now a disheveled, ragtag, loutish mob. Officers no longer held sway, and Admiral von Reuter had to work through "The Soldiers' Council," a communist-inspired body of men. Fearing more trouble from the twenty thousand rebellious sailors who crewed the ships first to the Firth of Forth then to their place of internment in Scapa Flow, Admiral von Reuter sent many of the crewmen home. Their ranks were reduced to about five thousand officers and men and would he reduced still further as internment dragged on.

The British ordered that the German ships be inspected to ensure that they had been disarmed in accordance with terms of the armistice. The firing mechanisms of all of the big guns had been removed, as had their munitions and small arms. Yet because the German ships were not officially surrendered, no British guards were permitted on board. German caretaker crews had full responsibility for their ships, which had to be supplied food and material from Germany. It was on the day of internment that British Adm. David Beatty, now commander in chief of the Grand Fleet, ordered the German ensign to he hauled down and not to be flown again.

The austere winter in the Flow further depressed the morale of German officers and men. They felt an overriding sense of dishonor and disgrace, cheated of an opportunity to do battle. Admiral von Reuter would write in his report "*Wehrlos, Ehrlos.*" Disarmed, dishonored. From now on, he would wait and guess, as the powers debated the fate of the Imperial Fleet, arguing over how the spoils of war would he divided up. Bleak surroundings compounded dismal thoughts of the interned men. On some ships disorder reigned. Officers were threatened and their authority flouted. Admiral von Reuter himself could not find solitude to think as sailors roller-skated on the armor-plated decks. The men were not prisoners of war, but they were not permitted to set foot on land. What little news there was came late, and mail was censored by the British.

Eight British drifters patrolled the Flow, crewed generally by civilian captains and merchant seamen, but with a complement of armed sailors and an officer on board. Fraternization between the two sides was strictly forbidden, but often enough violated as sailors traded among themselves for soap, toilet articles, cigarettes, and other goods.

As hope began to fade for repatriation of the fleet, Admiral von Reuter began making secret plans in spite of an article in the armistice agreement that prohibited destruction of ships before their evacuation, delivery, or restoration.

The German capital ships had been anchored in Bring Deeps between Pomona and the island of Hoy and around Cava Island. For reasons of fuel economy, the destroyers were lashed together in groups of two or three. A dozen or so members of each caretaker crew lived aboard one of the series of rafted-together destroyers anchored between Fara Island and Hoy. About two hundred men were kept aboard each of the larger ships. In addition to the armed drifters which patrolled the waters, the British First Battle Squadron was stationed at Scapa Flow, as a precaution should any of the German ships try to break out and escape.

On the smaller ships the crews still respected their officers and a semblance of order and discipline prevailed. However, havoc and rowdiness prevailed on the battleships where some of the captains feared for their personal safety. Aboard the destroyers a plan was being hatched. Officers took their bedding and stayed aboard ships tied alongside, foregoing the accommodations aboard the headquarters' ship in the bunch rafted together. The destroyer men were preparing to sink their own ships to save the honor of Germany and prevent them from falling into enemy hands.

Connecting rods which went through the decks to control valves that could he opened inside the destroyers' watertight compartments were sabotaged. Destroyer officers put plans into readiness to smash water pipes and open sea cocks to flood the ships. Where possible, watertight hatchways were sabotaged and removed from their fittings. Compartment bulkheads were holed so that when the order to scuttle the ships was given, it would be impossible for the British to board the destroyers and stop the flooding.

All of this activity aboard the destroyers, including meetings as early as 13 May between the German commander Cordes and his destroyer officers, went on without Admiral von Reuter's knowledge until June. Von Reuter was a man of honor. He took the initiative and began implementing plans to scuttle his fleet only when it appeared that Germany would reject the terms of surrender and lose its interned ships to the enemy.

With his trusted officers, Admiral von Reuter ordered the preparation of all seventy-four ships for scuttling. Secretly, in order to prevent the information from leaking out to the British patrollers and to minimize the danger of betrayal from the worst elements of his crews, internal valves and joints were sabotaged and watertight doors and hatchways removed or fixed to remain open.

The British patrollers put a drifter at von Reuter's disposal and so communication of his orders to his captains was a simple matter. Detailed plans were ready by 17 June 1919. The admiral's order included prearranged signals that would order the sinking of the fleet. His instructions to his captains also warned that if the German government agreed to the terms of peace and surrendered the interned ships they were not to be sunk. Any attempt by the British to take the High Seas Fleet by force without the consent of the German government, von Reuter ordered, would be reason to scuttle.

Von Reuter was anxious to reduce the number of men aboard his ships still further. With the assent of the British, he had been regularly repatriating sailors that were unruly, sick, or chronic troublemakers. Von Reuter had been forced to transfer his flag from the *Friedrich der Grosse* to the *Emden* to get some peace from the noise and disorder. When the two regular German transport ships arrived on the seventeenth of June, von Reuter had his order dispatched to the other ships by the British drifter. Some 2,700 men were embarked on the transports returning for Germany, leaving von Reuter with about 1,700 men aboard his seventy-four ships. Some of the crews were already aware of the plans for scuttling, some were not, and von Reuter left it up to the individual captains whether or not to inform their crews.

Radio equipment had been removed from the German vessels as part of the armistice agreement. Because of English censoring procedures and delays in getting news to the Orkneys, there were always three- or four-day delays in getting newspapers. When Admiral von Reuter read an English newspaper which was dated 16 June, he saw a report that the Germans had only until 21 June to accept the terms of peace, threatening that war would resume. Von Reuter decided that he would have to act, assuming that since hostilities were to resume the next day it was necessary to scuttle his fleet to prevent the British from seizing the German ships.

Unknown to the men interned at Scapa Flow, on the very day that von Reuter was reading the four-day-old report in *The Times,* the German Reichstag voted to accept the peace terms and the armistice was extended until 23 June. Unable to signal or receive messages, acts prohibited under internment (the ships' radios had been disabled by the British), Admiral von Reuter acted, sealing the fate of the High Seas Fleet.

Historians record the fine sunny weather in Scapa Flow on 21 June 1919. Admiral von Reuter came onto the *Emden*'s bridge wearing his decorations. To his amazement, he was informed that the main contingent of the British First Battle Squadron, including their five battleships, had left Scapa Flow. He was also told that his chief of staff had read a report in an English newspaper dated 17 June 1919, calling for unconditional surrender and not simply the surrender of the High Seas Fleet in return for reparations concessions. For Admiral von Reuter, his duty and the honor of Germany demanded that he execute his plans. At 10:30 on the morning of 19 June 1919—while the British squadron was embarked on training exercises, having left only three destroyers, one in repair, and the patrol drifters in Scapa Flow—Admiral von Reuter ordered the signal to scuttle hoisted from the *Emden*'s mast. The flags went up, signal lamps blinked, and semaphores flashed: "Paragraph eleven. Confirm."

In an hour the signal was around the fleet. From the destroyer-torpedo boats the defiant battle flag "Z" was hoisted signaling "advance on the enemy." As the ships settled in the water, imperceptibly at first, the doleful sounding of the battleship's bell came across the Flow from the *Friedrich der Grosse*. German ensigns and battle flags were flying for the first time since they were ordered hoisted down at the start of internment on 21 November 1919. At 12:16 on the sunny afternoon of 21 June, the *Friedrich der Grosse* settled in the water and sank. Around Scapa Flow the rest of the Imperial High Seas Fleet was sinking— an entire navy of seventy-four ships was on its way to the bottom.

Tom Rich was born in 1909. There were only three crofts on Cava Island where the nine-year-old boy lived on 21 June 1919. Looking out on the Flow that day, Tom Rich related his eyewitness account of the scuttling. "I was living on the island of Cava and that was right in the middle of the German Fleet. I saw them all sinking. That's a long time ago. It was Saturday. They started sinking about twelvish. We were used to seeing them everyday, and I thought this one was leaning a bit to one side, and after that it became obvious because the Germans came off in rafts. It looked as though something really was happening. Then eventually, when they actually did sink, lots of stuff came floating ashore," Tom Rich explained.

From his vantage point in the middle of the anchorage, Tom described the scene. "The ones that were in deep enough water turned upside down. There's one or two in shallower water, the *Seydlitz* lay on its side, the *Hindenberg* sat down on its bottom. Water wasn't deep enough for it to turn over. The rest turned turtle completely. One or two drifted ashore. There's one that landed on Cava, a light cruiser. But all the big ones turned turtle, they were in deeper water," Tom said. The scuttling lasted until four or five in the afternoon. The German sailors hurriedly abandoned their sinking ships. "A few of them landed on the island and just stayed on the beach," Tom continued. "The patrol drifters picked them up. There was three marines on Cava at that time. That was all."

The people of the Orkneys were used to seeing fleets anchored in Scapa Flow. The Grand Fleet used it throughout the war, and the German ships had been at anchor through the winter and spring. Looking out that morning, Tom Rich saw the ships he had seen every day since internment. "Well the usual ones that we used to see were just in front of the island and that was [*sic*] the *Seydlitz, Moltke,* the *Hindenberg, Kaiser,* and *Kaiserin.* . . . We didn't pay much attention to them, that was an everyday scene there," he related.

In the confusion, British patrollers opened fire on the German ships. Some were sprayed with machine-gun fire to try and force the sailors back aboard and prevent their sinking. A signal went out to Admiral Freemantle, commander of the First Battle Squadron sailing on torpedo and firing practice. The admiral ordered his fleet to return to the Flow at full speed. By then it was too late. The Germans did their sabotage well, and it was impossible to close the watertight doors and stem the flow of seawater from broken valves and sea cocks.

The British patrollers boarded some of the ships to try and prevent their sinking. On the battleship *Markgraf,* the captain, Lt. Cdr. Walther Schumann, was shot in the head while holding a white flag. It was too late to save *Markgraf.* Like the other battleships, a system of twenty-four-inch-diameter pipes ran inside the ship's double bottoms. The pipes were designed to flood or empty watertight compartments for fire control. The pipes also permitted ballast control in the event of destruction of an opposite number requiring righting of the ship by addition of seawater and to empty the water out. It was a simple matter to open the sea cocks and flood the entire ship once the universal joints running up to the valve controls were sabotaged.

In the melee nine German sailors were shot to death by the British. The graves at Lyness provide the final resting place for eight of these sailors and a few others who died earlier during the internment. A few Germans were wounded, but none drowned as the men scrambled to escape from the sinking ships. By the time Admiral Freemantle's fastest destroyers returned to the Flow around 2:30 that afternoon, most of the capital ships had sunk. Two battleships and five cruisers remained afloat. Some of the destroyers were run aground or settled in shallow water and refused to sink.

The Germans were rounded up and made prisoners of war. Admiral von Reuter himself attempted to obtain the intervention of the British officer in command to prevent further firing on his men. After several attempts to find someone in authority, the British drifter that had been placed at his disposal ran aground.

The British were able to put a tow on the light cruiser *Emden,* which had been von Reuter's flagship, beaching it before it sank. The same technique had been tried on the light cruiser *Bremse,* but before the British could get the ship close enough into shore it capsized and sank. Eventually, von Reuter and his officers were taken aboard Admiral Freemantle's flagship, and the rest of the 1,774 Germans were dispersed among the British ships which sailed for Cromarty Firth on the Scottish mainland, where they would be transferred to prison camp.

Of the seventy-four interned ships, only one battleship, the *Baden,* three of the light cruisers, the *Emden, Frankfurt,* and *Nurnberg,* and eighteen of the destroyers were kept from going to the bottom of Scapa Flow. These ships, although flooded, ran aground or were towed inshore and beached to keep them from sinking. While the cruiser *Frankfurt* didn't sink, it finally capsized in shallow water. By sunset on 21 June 1919, fifty-two ships rested on the bottom of the Flow. When the count was in, twenty capital ships, the pride of modern ship-building, had sunk: ten were battleships, which displaced upwards of 25,000 tons each, five were battle cruisers, and five light cruisers, all scuttled, along with thirty-two of the destroyer-torpedo boats.

Admiral von Reuter was dressed down by the British who hoped to prove that he had carried out a plot hatched in Germany. Von Reuter insisted that he had acted entirely on his own initiative, unaware of the developments in the peace process, and that his actions were justified. At home, the German people found a modicum of triumph in the act—the last heroic demonstration of the German High Seas Fleet. The commander of the High Seas Fleet wrote in his report that "While I had to conclude that if the Peace Treaty were not signed by Saturday 21 June, a state of war would once more apply, judging by the tone of rejection of the final Note of the Entente, and by the speech of the Government spokesman in the German National Assembly and the attitude of the German Press, I was entitled to assume that the Treaty would not be signed, and therefore that a state of war would be resumed on the Saturday. In this context I should like to say that I received no information of any kind, either from the German or the English Governments, about the extension of the Armistice. . . . My only sources of information were the English newspapers, which I received as a rule four days after their publication. In the belief that the state of war had been resumed, I gave the order to sink the interned German Fleet on Saturday 21 June. I first learned of the extension of the Armistice period to Monday 23 June aboard the English flagship *Revenge* during the afternoon of 21 June, from the interpreter to Vice-Admiral Sir S. B. Freemantle."

The British put every effort into proving a conspiracy. In the end, Admiral von Reuter was never tried on any charge. The Treaty of Versailles was signed on 28 June 1919. The Allies exacted dock and shipbuilding equipment from the Germans as reparations for the scuttling. Eventually the German sailors, then Von Reuter and his officers, were repatriated to Germany on 29 January 1920, after Germany agreed to turn over additional ships left in Germany and the dock equipment. The admiral who scuttled Germany's fleet was received home a hero. A few months later von Reuter was released from the German navy. He died of a heart attack in 1943.

Officially, the British Admiralty declared the shipwrecks unsalvageable. Navy diving teams refloated the beached ships but declared the capital ships sunk in deeper water to be beyond salvage capability. In time oil slicks that bubbled out of their sunken hulls washed away. The flotsam, which was once widespread, ceased to interest Orkney residents, and Scapa Flow returned to peacetime obscurity.

Tom Rich remembered playing football with German black bread that washed up on shore. Anthony Duncan still has a German navy towel his grandmother picked up on the beach. "There were bloodstains on it," Anthony Duncan related. "It was a good towel, so my grandmother washed out the blood and used the towel."

As dramatic as the scuttling, the effort that would eventually be expended to salvage the sunken warships was equally unique in its complexity and magnitude. Probably the earliest efforts to salvage valuables off the ships occurred when locals boarded the more accessible ships and removed souvenirs and non-ferrous metals. The British Admiralty for the most part ignored the scuttled ships, not wanting to renew the embarrassing memories of having an entire interned fleet sunk right under their noses. The glut in scrap metal just after World War I made it unpractical to undertake salvage, where transportation and logistics would be difficult and expensive. Interisland steamers would run up on the sunken hulks, and many of the locals called the sunken ships a hazard to navigation. One destroyer that had been beached was bought by a local man who cut it up for scrap. He allegedly polished the ship's brass boiler tubes and sold them for curtain rods.

Four years after the scuttling, a salvage operator formed a company known as the Scapa Flow Salvage and Ship-breaking Company and brought up four of the German destroyers. The methods used to bring up the destroyers combined cranking them up between large concrete floating barges and attaching huge balloon-like bags, filled with compressed air, to aid in the lift.

About this time an ingenious entrepreneur, Ernest Cox, who had been breaking up old British battleships in Scotland, paid a visit to Stromness on the Orkney mainland. Cox surveyed the scene and decided he would buy the German wrecks from the British Admiralty. Moving his salvage operations to Lyness, the former Royal Navy headquarters on the island of Hoy, "The Man Who Bought a Navy" prepared for the task of raising and refloating it.

Cox bought some twenty-six of the sunken German destroyers from the Admiralty for 250 British pounds. He also purchased the battleships *Hindenberg* and *Seydlitz* and began salvage work under the firm name of Cox and Danks. In Cox, the British Admiralty found a ready market for all manner of odds and ends that they had reaped from the Germans as part of their share of Inter-Allied Reparations Committee collections.

Cox had already purchased a German floating three-thousand-ton lifting capacity dry dock for 24,000 pounds. There was a cylinder on the inside of the dry dock that the Germans had fabricated to test their submarine hulls. The dry dock was immense: the cylinder used for hull testing alone was some four hundred feet long and forty feet in diameter, big enough to fit an entire submarine inside, seal it off, and add pressure to test the sub's hull strength. Cox scrapped and sold the metal cylinder, loaded up his floating dry dock with salvage gear, and towed it about seven hundred miles from the mouth of the

Thames River to Lyness. Cox cut the dry dock in half, so he could lift his German navy ships with half the dry dock on each side of the sunken wrecks.

The tides in Orkney vary about twelve feet from high to low water. Cox moored his floating dry docks on either side of the destroyer and had his salvage divers attach cables to the wreck, slipping them under the hull. The cables were attached to shackles. Lifting tackles aboard the improvised dry dock were tightened to their maximum at low tide. When the tide came in, the floating dry dock sections on either side of the submerged wreck would rise, and the cables would thus lift the sunken ship up off the bottom. The dry docks with the sunken destroyer cradled between them would then be towed into shallower water until the submerged wreck touched bottom. The salvors would wait for low tide, taking up slack on the pulleys and shackles still connected to the wreck. With a new high tide they would float the ship again and beach it until it was eventually high and dry.

The salvors could then throw pumps on board and draw the water out of the hulk. While the process used to lift the destroyers is easily explained, it was a difficult undertaking, posing great danger for divers working in difficult conditions and for the workmen on the dry docks. On the first lifting of the German destroyer *V 70*, the chains being used were not strong enough to hold the weight and snapped. Luckily no one was injured.

In order to absorb a ship's weight, Cox obtained nine-inch-diameter steel cable which had to be reslung around the wreck. Using the new cables, Cox and Danks lifted their first destroyer from the bottom on 31 July 1924. When the destroyer was towed into the salvage base at Lyness, Cox found out to his dismay that pirates had already stripped the ship of much of the more valuable non-ferrous metal. The large torpedo tubes made of gun metal and used with great efficacy by the German torpedo boat destroyers during the war had already been taken as well.

Ernest Frank Cox and his firm succeeded in raising twenty-six of the German destroyers, winching them up between the two L's of his halved floating dry dock with the aid of tidal power. The destroyers that had been rafted together and those that sank together in groups of twos and threes presented difficult problems for Cox's divers. Divers had to work between the sunken hulks, cutting away the nests of cable and chain holding the wrecks together and disengaging the upper works that crashed together during sinking. Cox and his salvage divers had to respect the efficient job the Germans made of scuttling their ships, contributing as it did to the difficulty of salvage. Hatchways and watertight doors had been removed, toilet water connections pulled out so they would flood, all belowdecks valves to ammunition storage areas and boilers had been opened and, where possible, sabotaged.

Cox worked his crew long hours. When a tally was made after a year and a half, he had raised twenty-four of the twenty-six destroyers, ten of which had been patched and towed to Rosyth for breaking up, the rest either sold off or broken up as scrap at the salvage yard at Lyness. These German destroyers were about 270 to 320 feet long with 28-foot beams, displacing about a thousand tons. When Cox finished raising the destroyers in April 1926, he set his sights on the battleships and large cruisers.

The *Hindenberg* sank upright. The massive decks and superstructure were awash at low water. For all intents and purposes the *Hindenberg* seemed to present Cox with the most straightforward salvage of the bigger ships. Classed as a battle cruiser, the *Hindenberg* had an overall length of close to seven hundred feet displacing about twenty-eight thousand tons. It was a massive ship which took four years to build, armed with eight twelve-inch-diameter turret-mounted guns with plating that was at least a foot-thick overall. Obviously none of the techniques used in salvaging the destroyers could be employed with these larger ships. Cox and his principal salvage officer, Commo. T. McKenzie, decided to patch up the holes in *Hindenberg's* hull and pump the water out so the ship would rise on its own.

Divers were required to measure all of the holes with models from which patches were fabricated. In all more than eight hundred patches were required to seal up the *Hindenberg* so it could be refloated. It was discovered that many of the patches were being nibbled away by voracious fish attracted to the tallow used to make the patch watertight. When the technical problems were conquered, the patches replaced, and pumping began, a violent storm destroyed part of Cox's dry dock and wrecked a destroyer hulk he was using in the salvage operation. So many problems plagued the raising of the *Hindenberg* that

Cox decided to postpone raising the ship temporarily and went on with other salvage work.

Cox came back to the upright battle cruiser after the New Year in 1930. The tripod mast and turrets forward were removed to lighten the *Hindenberg.* Patches were repaired and all of the heavy steel above water was cut off the ship to make the lifting job easier. Huge pumps were brought in for the job. Massive concrete blocks were placed under the ship's stern to keep it from capsizing as the water was pumped out and the ship began to rise. By mid-summer 1930, the largest ship ever salvaged from the deep broke the surface. It was reported that the salvage of the *Hindenberg* alone cost Cox and Danks upwards of 30,000 pounds. The hulk was beached, made seaworthy, and towed to the breakers yard in Rosyth on the Firth of Forth.

The problems presented by the other capital ships, for the most part lying upside down in deeper water, were overcome by the ingenuity of Cox, McKenzie, and his stalwart Orcadian divers and salvage workers. Cox, after his preliminary failure in trying to raise the *Hindenberg,* had turned his efforts to the battleship *Moltke,* a 22,640-ton, 610-foot-long ship with a band of foot-thick armor around its sides. The *Moltke*'s turrets mounted ten large eleven-inch-diameter guns. The ship was so enormous that its bottom broke the surface when the tide went out, creating a danger to navigation in the Flow.

Cox and Danks divers sealed up the obvious holes along the bottom and sides of the overturned battleship, which lay on a muddy bottom, listing over on one side. The ship started up when massive amounts of compressed air were pumped into it, but was permitted to sink again when the salvors thought there was a danger that the ship would turn over on its side. The *Moltke* lay in water that was about eighty feet deep. Cox decided to mount an air lock on the bottom of the *Moltke.* The device, fastened to the overturned hull, was equipped with watertight doors, which permitted caisson and salvage workers to enter the outer lock, close it behind them, then enter the lower lock. This permitted entry through a hole cut in the ship's hull, onto which the air lock was attached with airtight and watertight seals. Compressed air inside the overturned hull drove the water out. The air lock system permitted workers to enter without losing pressure. Pressure to the air lock was controlled by valves operated on the same principle as modern two-lock decompression chambers. Once the pressure in the air lock equaled the pressure inside the ship, the inner air lock door could be opened, allowing the salvage worker to enter the ship.

The fixing of the four-foot-diameter air locks to the hull was an arduous task. Divers had to rig webs of cables and use great care in fixing the flanges to the ship's bottom. Cox first fabricated his air locks for the *Moltke* out of old discarded boilers, later improved by special fabrication. The Cox and Danks salvage men and divers worked under pressure created by pumping air inside the overturned hulk. They were also working inside the ship in extremely dangerous conditions. Inside the overturned ship, heavy equipment had broken free. Workers also risked danger from fittings breaking loose in the upside-down ship. The divers succeeded, however, in fitting patches on watertight doors, plugging and sealing holes and compartments so that they would hold the compressed air, which would be pumped into them.

It is difficult to imagine the arduous tasks imposed on the divers working inside a submerged upside-down battleship, having to cut and work their way through several decks of armor plate to seal sections off. Increasing the risk were bad weather conditions, gale-force winds, ice-cold water, and frequent storms.

As the work progressed several air locks were fixed to *Moltke*'s overturned hull. Section after section was sealed off while air hoses were connected. When all was in readiness, the pumps were attached and the salvors watched to see if their nine months of arduous labor would pay off.

Emily Chapman was in her early teens when work began on the *Moltke*. Her father, James Sinclair, was the captain of a salvage tug used by Cox and Danks. Emily vividly remembers the raising of the battleship. "I saw the first ship coming up, and, believe you me, water stood high, high in the air it came up and had to he put down again to bring it up even. It would have gone on its side. It was really a tricky operation to do," Chapman explained.

With the *Moltke* floating upside down in Scapa Flow, Cox had to arrive at a method of scrapping the huge battleship. Cox had the long air lock tubes removed and capped over the short locks he left attached to the hull for use during the towing. The ingenious salvor obtained an agreement from the British

Admiralty to allow him to float the upside-down battleship into one of the Admiralty dry docks. Divers blocked up the hulk's bottom. The water in the dry dock was evacuated, and the ship broken-up from the keel down. Reports of the salvage record that the *Moltke*'s huge guns got their muzzles stuck in the mud on the bottom of Scapa Flow as the crew started to tow the ship, requiring divers to go down underneath and blast them free. To lighten the *Moltke* prior to towing, Cox laid railroad tracks onto the hull and moved a crane out onto the hulk that he used to lift out metal from holes his workers had cut in the inverted hull.

"The German Fleet just sank really as it was. Everything was there—knives and forks, cutlery. There's souvenirs in this house belonging to those ships," Emily Chapman said, describing what salvage workers found once they got inside the raised German warships.

"There are glasses and plates and bed chambers," Chapman smiled as she continued to describe chamber pots found in the raised ships. "There were two different grades of bed chamber pots. One for officers and one for crew. The officers' bed chambers was bone china, the others was plain pottery," she said, showing off some of the souvenirs her father had collected from the German ships.

Among some of the most interesting artifacts found inside the scuttled ships was a handwritten logbook kept by one of the German sailors. The log is preserved under the supervision of Bryce Wilson, curator of the Stromness Museum, which translated the neat German script. The personal log, written in ink pen, is waterstained in places but quite legible. The inside front cover bears the owner's name, Hermann Heidemann and underneath the sailor's home port, Wilhelmshaven.

One entry describes the events on board his ship on the day the German fleet entered internment.

> At 1 o'clock we were to reach our goal. Rain started and it became windier so that staying on the upper deck was not pleasant. However, about 11 o'clock the cry went through the ship "Land in sight." Everyone rushed on deck. Through the windy weather land could be seen in the distance, and as we approached it proved to be bare and barren rock. It was the Orkney Islands. We sailed past several of these islands. They rise out of the sea quite bare of any trees and bushes and even without any green growing

on them. On some of them, snow-capped mountains rise. Hiding in the bays lay the English fleet, which had hardly dared to poke its nose out of its hiding place during the whole war. . . . At 1:30 we dropped anchor; we had reached our destination. There was much activity on board. A commission of foreign officers examined our ship thoroughly. It was plain that the English still had colossal distrust of us. In the evening we had a cozy celebration. We slaughtered a pig and broached a barrel of beer.

Commodore McKenzie, the chief of Cox's salvage operation, was well liked, by the men. He never hesitated to work alongside them, donning a diving helmet to inspect the wrecks and work underwater even in the most hazardous conditions. Emily Chapman remembers McKenzie vividly. "He was really a very nice man. Very tall. He looked like a farmer. He wasn't dressy. You seen an old farmer going, that's what he looked like . . . and every time he went around, every time he came on board the boat, he took his two Siamese cats with him," Chapman related with a warm smile, remembering some of the lighter moments during the long cold winters of the salvage operations.

The salvage operations didn't always run smoothly for Cox and Danks. No one had ever attempted a salvage project of such a scale as that presented by the German wrecks, and certainly not by refloating seven capital ships—including battleships sunk on the bottom upside down—then taking them in tow upside down across Pentland Firth into the North Sea and then 280 miles to the breakers yard at Rosyth on the Scottish mainland.

The men worked through the depression years, and the project provided vitally needed income to the people of Orkney. The cost of finally raising the *Hindenberg* alone was estimated at the time to have been in excess of thirty thousand pounds sterling, a fortune in those days. Undaunted by the problems, Cox bought the rights to additional German capital ships. The costs involved were enormous. Cox had salary rolls in excess of a thousand pounds per week with an equal amount going toward fuel and coal to work his machines.

An event in the summer of 1926 nearly sealed the fate of Cox and Danks. Strikes and the increase in the price of coal from one pound to nearly five pounds a ton would have bankrupted Cox's operation, which at the time was burning up two hundred tons of coal each week. Just as things seemed the bleakest, the ingenious Cox thought of using the coal inside the sunken German battle cruiser *Seydlitz*, which had sunk in about seventy feet of water to lay on its side. The *Seydlitz*, like the other battle cruisers, was an enormous ship, displacing 24,610 tons, 606 feet in length with a 94-foot beam. It stuck out of the water at about 22 feet.

The coal bunkers of the *Seydlitz* were full, and Cox dug into them to fuel his machines for the length of the strike by the miners and coal workers. Even today, divers bring up large chunks of coal that they use to fuel their homes in winter or break up the coal to use in stoves aboard their vessels. "There's still plenty of coal down there. We fill up bags with it on the bottom, tie them off, and haul it up. It saves quite a bit in the winter time," John Thornton, a local diver, said. John pounded huge thirty-pound chunks of coal into smaller lumps for the stove that heated his ship belowdecks.

Cox experienced failure in the first attempt to raise the *Seydlitz*. The ship was sealed, patched, and pumped up with compressed air. It would be brought up on its side and flipped upright. When the battle cruiser was almost up, the patches gave way and the ship turned over and sank. It was held at a forty-eight-degree angle underwater by the masts and funnels. Much of the salvage equipment was ruined, having gone over with the *Seydlitz*.

The nine months of labor in patching and preparing the battle cruiser for lifting was wasted. Cox decided to bring the *Seydlitz* to the surface upside down, which presented a momentous problem because of the ship's canting angle. After forty tests of raising and lowering the hulk, the boilers were filled with cement and sunk under one side of the wreck, which was lowered down on them, causing the *Seydlitz* now to sit directly upside down on the bottom. It was an amazing feat of salvage for the day, and Ernest Cox arranged for newsreel photographers to film the raising of the ship—with him prominently present. Cox was on vacation in Switzerland when the *Seydlitz* came up out of the water on its own after too much compressed air was let into the hulk by workmen. Cox's reputation for flamboyance increased by several dimensions when he sent a telegram back to Scapa Flow to sink the *Seydlitz* and to wait for him to come back before bringing it up again so he could be in the newsreel.

It worked. The *Seydlitz* obliged the salvors a second time. The wreck was raised and towed through a storm to Rosyth. It was a harrowing trip for the tugs and the men, including McKenzie, who camped on the overturned hulk manning the compressors. The tow took seven days.

Cox raised the battleship *Prinzregent Luitpold* in much the same manner as he had raised the other inverted giants. The *Prinzregent,* however, was sunk in 105 feet of water and listing to one side, with almost forty feet of water between the overturned hull and the surface. The ship was a record of sorts since no one had ever brought a ship of that size up from such a depth before upside down. It was 1932, and Cox and Danks had been working at raising the sunken German fleet for eight years. Ernest Frank Cox never really made any money at the salvage operation. His costs always seemed to overrun the gain they earned by breaking up the wrecks and selling the scrap.

Cox decided to call it quits with Scapa Flow. His company had salvaged twenty-six of the German destroyers, the battleships *Prinzregent Luitpold* and *Kaiser,* the battle cruisers *Seydlitz, Moltke, Von der Tann,* and *Hindenberg,* and the light cruiser *Bremse.* Cox sold his interests to the company that had been breaking up his wrecks at Rosyth, the Alloa Shipbreaking Company, which became Metal Industries Ltd.

Commodore McKenzie was kept on to direct the firm's salvage operations in Scapa Flow. There was a good spirit among the workers under McKenzie's direction. After every lifting, the men were paid a bonus and had a grand bash and banquet party. "When they was lifted, all lifted and away, they used to have big dinners for the men at Lyness. In them days it was a big bonus. If they got a thirty pound bonus, that was a lot of money in those days," Emily Chapman said, recalling the shindigs her dad attended. Emily preserved the invitation, a stylistically printed ticket, "Metal Industries Ltd., Friedrich der Grosse, Admit Bearer and Lady Friend to Dance, 28th May 1937."

Mrs. Chapman also kept the souvenir menus that her dad brought home from the dinners thrown by Metal Industries at the Lyness Recreation Hall, sporting a dapper picture of Commodore McKenzie on the cover. McKenzie himself was paid a five-thousand-pound bonus for every ship raised, and although the three hundred workmen were salaried at eleven pence halfpenny as an hourly wage, they were glad to get the income through the harsh depression and lean post-depression years.

Metal Industries paid a thousand pounds for the salvage rights to the battle-ship *Bayern,* but that figure was doubled by the Admiralty for the remaining bat-tleships. Metal Industries turned a good profit on their salvage operations, for while the ships were upside down and had to have air locks built on their hulls under-water—with all the perils of treacherous lifts and tows—the price of scrap metal increased significantly. On the twenty-eight-thousand-ton battleship *Bayern,* Metal Industries realized a total of 118,463 pounds from the sale of its scrap, turning a healthy 50,000 pound profit on the operation. Some of the high-grade steel was exported to Germany, where it was melted down and used in Hitler's new navy.

Work on the Imperial Fleet was halted when the Admiralty yards being used by Metal Industries to break up their ships were required for military use as a new war loomed on the horizon. The last ship salvaged by Metal Industries, the 26,180-ton, 689-foot-long battle cruiser *Derfflinger,* was raised but not broken up until after the war, some seven years later. Throughout that time caretakers kept pressure in the overturned hulk, maintaining the upside-down wreck afloat, moored in Scapa Flow.

After raising and salvaging five battleships and one battle cruiser, finally scrapping the *Derfflinger* in 1946, Metal Industries left Scapa Flow. The com-pany decided that the remaining ships, three battleships and four cruisers, were sunk in water too deep to make the salvage operations economically feasible. Eventually the remaining wrecks on the bottom of Scapa Flow were bought by Nundy Marine Metals Ltd., which sent divers down with explosives to blast away parts of the thick steel plate, attaching cables and hoisting the steel up to the surface.

After World War II, the thick steel had a greater scrap value because it was among the last steel manufactured before the atom bomb blasts. The A bombs had so contaminated the atmosphere that any post–World War II steel, smelted using air blown into the furnaces, contained traces of radioactivity. This radioac-tivity could be detected in sensitive instruments, and shielding for medical equipment and radioactivity detectors require uncontaminated steel.

Even with the specialized market for pre–World War II contamination-free steel, the depth of the remaining wrecks eventually caused the wreckers to aban-don their haphazard salvage attempts. Some wrecks were again sold, while others remaining in Admiralty hands were leased. Various plans for their salvage were considered. Four of the wrecks are owned by Shetland Islander Tommy Clark, whose lease on three others including the HMS *Vanguard,* a British ship that exploded in Scapa Flow in 1916, expired at the end of 1982.

There has been renewed interest in salvaging the wrecks, but according to John Thornton, a local dive charter operator in Scapa Flow who earns his living taking sport divers out to dive on the shipwrecks, "The Orkney Council has decided that since the wrecks are in harbor waters, persons who wish to salvage them must get a license." Thornton and other Orcadians are trying to have the last vestiges of the German Imperial Fleet declared nature reserves in the aim of promoting sport diving and tourism in Orkney. There is growing support for opposition to the issuance of salvage licenses.

Exploring the remaining seven ships of the ghost fleet of Scapa Flow is an exciting adventure. Because of the depth, exploratory dives on the wrecks usually last from twenty minutes to a half-hour.

Anyone who has ventured aboard an ocean liner for the first time, walking from deck to deck then fore and aft, trying to get oriented, can well imagine the difficulty a diver at 130 feet, in water where the visibility ranges from 15 to 30 feet, faces trying to get oriented on a twenty-six-thousand-ton, 660-foot-long battleship. The diver hardly has time on any single dive to explore small areas or to perhaps snap a few pictures before having to return to the surface.

Part of the excitement presented by the wrecks in Scapa Flow is the adventure of discovery. Divers can vicariously relive the historical events that were a prelude to Jutland. They can let their imagination wander to the shipyards at Kiel and Wilhelmshaven and explore the remnants of history that shaped the face of world events.

The three battleships that remain on the bottom are the *Konig, Markgraf,* and *Kronprinz Wilhelm.* Four cruisers remain: the *Koln, Brummer, Karlsruhe,* and *Dresden.* Bits and pieces of other ships lie scattered around the Flow as well, including gun turrets and tripod mast sections and unrecovered scrap that fell off or was blasted away when some of the other ships were salvaged, all of which make for an interesting dive environment.

The battleship *Konig,* launched from Wilhelmshaven in 1913, lies on a slope on its starboard side in about 125 feet of water. The 25,390-ton, 580-foot long *Konig* has been blasted amidships, and parts of the 97-foot-wide vessel are a tangled mass of steel. In places forward and aft, the *Konig* is intact, the solid fourteen-inch-thick armor plate overgrown with sea anemones and marine life. In the forward section, the ship's 12-inch guns lie in their turret, under the overturned hulk. "You can actually put your head into the barrel, even my head will fit," John Thornton joked, remarking that the sheer size of the turret often causes divers to miss seeing the guns, thinking that it is just another part of the massive hull.

The highest part of the *Konig's* overturned hull lies sixty feet below the surface. Swimming down off the hull, divers can observe a latticework of steel, part of the superstructure, hanging like so many bars between bulwarks, overgrown with a variety of attaching marine life. The *Konig* had been severely damaged in the Battle of Jutland, shipping some sixteen hundred tons of water in several flooded compartments. It eventually made it back to port for repairs, finally meeting its fate at the bottom of Scapa Flow.

The battleship *Markgraf* lies upside down in deep water. The depth is about eighty feet to the shallowest part of the inverted hull and about 145 feet to the deepest part, lodged in the sand. The *Markgraf* is sunk near the *Konig* off Cava Island. Bryce Wilson, curator of the Stromness Museum, has preserved an official German sailor's record book, obtained after the scuttling of the *Markgraf.* The German sailor, Johannes Allers, began serving on the SMS *Markgraf* in 1916 and saw action during the Battle of Jutland. The *Markgraf* was heavily damaged during Jutland, taking four direct hits from British heavy guns within the space of a couple of minutes. The *Markgraf* was struck in all with five enemy shells, compared with ten hits on the *Konig.* Both ships were repaired after Jutland, saved from battle, only to meet their end at the hands of their own crews in Scapa Flow.

The third battleship remaining on the bottom of Scapa Flow is *Kronprinz Wilhelm,* a *Konig*-class ship like the *Markgraf,* which was launched from the Kiel shipyards in 1914. "The *Kronprinz* sits in about 60 feet of water to the shallowest section and about 132 feet to the deepest. Remember there are 10- to 12-foot tides in the Flow, so it varies," John Thornton explained. "The *Kronprinz* lies well over on one side and has been quite well blasted. Some bits are quite well broken up. The crow's nest and spotting top can still be seen though," Thornton added.

Among the most accessible of the German cruisers on the bottom of Scapa Flow is the 4,400-ton displacement *Brummer*. Built in Stetting, Germany, in 1915, the *Brummer* was a *Bremse*-class light cruiser. The ship had a maximum speed of twenty-eight knots and was 461-feet long with a 44-foot beam. Unlike the battleships with armor plate more then a foot thick, the light cruisers were built for speed. Their armor plate averaged about an inch and a half for the lighter *Bremse*-class ships and two and a half inches for the larger, heavier, and later-built cruisers. The *Brummer* lies on its side in 55 feet of water to the shallowest part and 110 feet to the sand. The bridge has square windows and a relatively intact superstructure. The *Brummer*'s guns are overgrown with sea anemones that protrude into the green sea.

Swimming below the bridge, divers come across enameled medical pans, spilled out of the ship's hospital room, which itself is visible under and behind a mass of twisted steel. Two operating tables lie strewn about. Off the side of the hospital room are iron stairs leading back up to the bridge area. Forward on the *Brummer*, the bow is held up off the sand. Swimming under and inside the bow, divers can gain access to the forward section of the ship. Huge gears in the forward section hang precariously, still fixed to their steel rods, used to hoist the anchor chain. Lying about in the sand and silt are reminders of the German sailors who manned these ships: a sailor's boot, an empty medicine bottle, a champagne bottle, which somehow belies the notion of privation and hardship of the internees.

The light cruiser *Koln* lies on its starboard side in water 110 feet to the bottom. The 512-foot-long ship had a 47-foot beam. Divers reach the wreck starting at about 55 feet. The *Koln* was a *Dresden*-class cruiser that displaced 5,600 tons when work on it was completed at the Hamburg shipyards at the end of 1916. The *Koln* had eight 5.9-inch cannons and an armed battle bridge that became the control center when engaging the enemy. The battle bridge of the *Koln* is preserved, and rectangular viewing ports of the round structure give the bridge an odd appearance underwater. Mounted on the battle bridge is a long, cylindrical trajectory finder that was used by the gunnery officers to locate the range of enemy ships.

The *Karlsruhe* is in the shallowest water of all the warships still on the bottom of Scapa Flow. The *Karlsruhe* lies on its port side in 50 feet of water to the shallowest part of the wreck, 90 feet to the sand. The *Konigsberg*-class light cruiser had an overall length of 496 feet, a beam of 147 feet, and displaced 5,440 tons, armed with eight of the 5.9-inch guns. The *Karlsruhe* has been blasted, and the midsection has a lot of damage because of helter-skelter salvage attempts.

The last of the seven warships on the bottom of Scapa Flow is the *Dresden*, a 5,600-ton, 512-foot-long light cruiser. The *Dresden* had an operational maximum speed of twenty-nine knots when it left the shipyards at Kiel in 1917. The wreck now lies on a sloping seabed, on its port side. The depth varies from 60 feet at the top of the flank to 105 feet to the seabed, deeper at the stern section. The *Dresden*'s guns loom out of the darkness, their barrels overgrown with marine life, parts of the breach sections picked and chipped away by souvenir-hunting divers. A flap of twisted steel gives access to a room inside the ship, and a row of urinals remain, still fixed to the bulkhead but in an odd position, canting with the ship laying on its side.

Each of the shipwrecks is a veritable city unto itself. When the ships were in service they mounted crews of upwards of a thousand men. Today the wrecks attract adventurous divers who come to explore a bit of history and in the process contribute to the Orkneys economy. The wrecks provide an attaching substrate for marine organisms. Fish, crabs, and lobster abound around the hulks. Hopefully the Orkney Council will decide that these last ships of the Imperial High Seas Fleet should remain on the bottom of Scapa Flow to be enjoyed by visiting divers and enhance fishing by enlarging the ecosystem in the Flow.

HMS ROYAL OAK

Scapa Flow was Britain's Grand Fleet anchorage throughout World War I. The sheltered anchorage provided the fleet access to both the North Sea and the Atlantic. The Grand Fleet was protected from submarine attack by closely controlled antisubmarine nets, patrol boats, and shore watchers. Access to the flow from the Atlantic Ocean through Hoy Sound past the little island of Graemsay or around through the Pentland Firth south of the island of Hoy were the major routes for the warships and maritime traffic. Access from the North Sea, likewise, would have to be through the Pentland Firth south of the island of South Ronaldsay. Between Mainland (Pomona Island) and South Ronaldsay lie three smaller islands. While the British were aware that small boats could navigate between these islands into the Flow from the North Sea during high tides, they discounted the ability of submarines and larger ships to get through. As a precaution, they sank a few old ships between the islands, presuming that this would prevent access, especially through Kirk Sound. Patrols were then concentrated on the southern and western approaches, sealing Switha and Hoxa Sound and Hoy Sound with protective booms and anti-submarine nets.

Between the Mainland hamlet of St. Mary's and the island of South Ronaldsay lie first Lamb Holm Island, then Glimps Holm, and finally Burray, the larger of the three islets. As World War II loomed, Britain again fortified and equipped Scapa Flow as the home base for their Grand Fleet operations. Almost at once, mystery shrouded the events that took place in rapid succession almost immediately after the outbreak of war in September 1939.

A German submarine, U-47, had been prowling the sea, hunting British shipping. On 13 October 1939, Comdr. Gunther Prien surfaced in the clear moonlight at high tide and ordered his navigator to steer a course for Lamb Holm Island. Inside Scapa Flow only a few British warships remained, the Admiralty having ordered the main fighting force out to sea, fearing German air attack. At anchor in the Flow was the venerable HMS *Royal Oak,* a battleship veteran of World War I. Even with the high tides created by the moon, there would be little draft between the Mainland off St. Mary's and Lamb Holm Island through a ripping current that could attain a speed of ten knots during the height of its flow.

Whether Prien's raid was a daredevil unplanned surface raid or a carefully prepared attack with the aid of spies living on Orkney will probably never be known for sure. Longtime residents on Orkney have their own versions as to what happened. Emily Chapman was working at the Royal Dockyards when the *Oak* was sunk. "It wasn't sabotage," Chapman said. "It was a German sub, definitely. Because my father was on the boat and they put divers down. They came up with it—part of a torpedo that done it. And the men that was in that big a hurry to get it they knocked the diver back again, back in the water grabbing the piece. Poor diver went back again. It was definitely a German sub," she insisted. "My Dad was captaining the boat that brought the divers out to the *Royal Oak*," she continued. "Navy divers and some of Metal Industries divers as well. They went down and came up with [the torpedo piece]," Chapman asserted, negating equivocal British Admiralty information given at the time of the sinking.

Chapman related how she thought the German U-boat was helped by a spy living on the island. "I really couldn't visualize a German U-boat coming in. It came along the Ham and it was led by a man who used to live over in St. Mary's. He disappeared after it happened, and he was never seen again. The man who stayed in the last house in the village of Ham. Every night he went out with a wheelbarrow. This night he took a wheelbarrow and went out to Hoxa Head. He was seen that night but was never seen again. That man disappeared with that wheelbarrow. It was funny for that to stop immediately when the *Oak* was sunk. There was lights seen flashing right enough. The U-boat hid off before it came in," Chapman said, adding mystery to the tale of daring.

Commander Prien's U-boat log revealed that he ran into Scapa Flow, fired his torpedoes, and had a difficult time getting out again on the surface because of the fast tide running. The *Royal Oak* heeled over and sank with the loss of 833 officers and men. Some of the dead from the *Royal Oak* are buried in the Lyness Naval Cemetery. The ship's bell hangs in St. Magnus Cathedral in Kirkwall as a memorial to the men who lost their lives in the sinking, and the British Ministry of Defence has designated the *Royal Oak* a war grave. The wreck is visited once a year by Royal Navy divers who post a flag over the wreck and inspect it for damage. Diving is otherwise prohibited on the site in deference to the families of the war dead.

Survivors of the *Royal Oak* sinking have had a reunion with surviving members of the U-47's crew, the attack considered part of warfare, and as such respected for the courage reflected by the feat itself. Prien was killed in action later on during the war and the submarine lost. No one has ever proved or disproved the existence of a spy on the island who may have provided intelligence to the enemy U-boat or signaled them along the Ham through the narrow pass with lights.

OTHER GHOST SHIPS IN SCAPA FLOW

There are many mystery wrecks on the bottom of Scapa Flow. The cause of some sinkings remain shrouded in mystery, superstition, and suspicion. One of these ships, the HMS *Hampshire,* remains the subject of debate among many Orcadian and naval historians.

The *Hampshire,* a *County*-class cruiser, was on a special mission to Russia. The *Hampshire* was carrying emissary Lord Horatio Herbert Kitchener, who had emerged as a hero in Sudan but had lately become a thorn in the government's side. On 5 June 1916, the *Hampshire* sailed out of Scapa Flow when in the Atlantic, just off the headland, the ship exploded. It was reported that the *Hampshire* struck a mine and sank with the loss of more than seven hundred officers and men, including Lord Kitchener. Rumors spread that the ship was destroyed nefariously to prevent Kitchener's mission to Russia.

The wreck of the HMS *Hampshire* lies in close to two hundred feet of water down in the Atlantic. The depth and the cold water put the ship at the virtual limit of compressed air diving. John Thornton took a group of British divers to the *Hampshire* site; they had trained for the depth for a long time in England prior to making their descent but were able to make only one exploratory descent, although they still hope to eventually conduct a study of the shipwreck. For the most part, Thornton thinks the *Hampshire* will remain well beyond the range of average sport diving enthusiasts.

Another legendary shipwreck that sank in Scapa Flow is the HMS *Vanguard.* The 19,250-ton British battleship blew up in Scapa Flow on 9 July 1917. The *Vanguard* was 563 feet in length with an 84-foot beam. Like the *Royal Oak,* the British Admiralty declared the *Vanguard* to be a war grave, a designation local dive charter operators consider an attempt merely to appease the oil company whose North Sea pipeline comes into Scapa Flow and passes near where the *Vanguard* is sunk. The *Vanguard* has been blasted for salvage and now lies in pieces on the bottom. An Admiralty lease on the *Vanguard* expired at the end of 1982. Locals assert that the war grave status was only a ploy used by the

British to keep divers away from the oil pipeline underwater. Divers have reported that torpedo warheads and live shells carried aboard the *Vanguard* are still inside the intact stern area of the ship. Some have reported seeing cordite explosive on the bottom as well.

A World War II German destroyer escort, turned over to the British as part of the postwar division of German naval ships, sank at anchor in Scapa Flow on 30 December 1946. The destroyer F 2 displaced some 1,065 tons and had a length of 250 feet. Wreckage from the F 2 lies in 60 feet of water, blasted and ravaged by what appear to have been clumsy salvage attempts. Divers enjoy exploring the sunken ship, which served as a submarine support vessel in the Baltic Sea during the war. While much of the wreck is in a tangle of crumpled and torn steel, it has become a fish haven and is overgrown with a variety of marine life. Sinks and assorted ship's furnishings are scattered about on the bottom. A narrow opening in the hull permits penetration into one of the motor spaces.

Along the causeways that link the islands of Lamb Holm, Burray, and South Ronaldsay to the Orkney mainland one can view many remnants from both world wars. Historic documents and photographs in the comprehensive collection of the Orkney Library in Kirkwall chronicle the eventual creation of concrete barriers built between these islands, paved over on top to permit vehicle traffic.

After the sneak attack by the German submarine and the sinking of the *Royal Oak*, Winston Churchill determined that the use of old ships sunk in the channel to block passage between the islands did not provide enough security for the British fleet based inside Scapa Flow. Many of these old block ships dated from World War I. They had been sunk across Holm Sound and in the other passes from the Atlantic into the Flow. Some of the ships that had made it across in early convoy days, too decrepit to head back across the Atlantic, were sunk in shallow water between the islands. Old lifting barges used by Cox and Danks were also employed for this purpose. The block ships are clearly visible in the shallow water, masts and superstructure well above the high-water mark.

Infuriated by the German U-boat attack, Churchill ordered that permanent barriers be built across the four channels, thus connecting the islands and permanently sealing the eastern approaches to the Flow. In order to accomplish this massive building task, the British used forced labor, employing Italian prisoners of war captured during the campaigns in North Africa.

It was a massive undertaking. A total of about one and a half miles of barrier had to be laid, which in some places required dumping concrete blocks sufficient to fill an area where the water depth was sixty feet. To accomplish the task, the Italian prisoners were set up in a prison camp on Lamb Holm Island. Some 250,000 tons of stone and 66,000 cast concrete blocks weighing 10 tons each were used in the construction of the barriers, later called the Churchill Barriers.

Most of the prisoners of war happily threw themselves into the work. While life on the Orkneys was spartan, they were well treated and enjoyed a certain liberty their ill-fated Fascist experience had denied them. It seemed that it was a war they had not wanted. In any event, the prisoners of Camp 60 worked well and had contacts with the Orcadians, who also worked in the camps.

Emily Chapman worked as a cook in the camp and remembered with affection some of the nicer Italian prisoners. She recalled the psychological hardship they experienced. "We had Italian prisoners of war that came here to work and some of them was allowed out to work with us in the cook house. Some of them were really nice. . . . There was one especially, we had an interpreter, a Sergeant Brunner, and one day he came with a letter to Luigi. He had never heard from his people since he was taken prisoner of war in 1940. He never heard from them until that day in 1945, when the sergeant came with a letter to him. That's the first he knew whether his people were living or dead. And it broke his heart. He cried his eyes out, and he came and threw his arms around my neck and cried and cried. I really felt very, very sorry for him," Chapman related.

As work on the barriers progressed, the Italian prisoners felt the need for a house of worship. Gathering scraps of metal and bits and pieces of unused material, the men were able to fashion a magnificent chapel, ornately painted and decorated by a talented prisoner, artist Domenico Chiocehetti. The Italian chapel remains on Lamb Holm Island today, overlooking the barriers and block ships.

Many of the block ships remain as curiosities for divers who swim down to explore the hulks. A local Orkney resident, Robert Swanney, owns some of the wrecks. "Actually I bought them from Granny," Swanney explained. "She bought them off some fellows who had been salvaging them. I started taking scrap off them and one day I said 'Granny you're not getting anything from those wrecks, do you want to sell them?' She said how much, and I produced a hundred-pound note that I had just got from selling some of the scrap, and Granny sold them," Swanney said.

The block ships are photogenic, often inspiring local artists. One of the wrecks, the *Calndock,* sits right up on a beach, prow burrowed into the sand; its cemented-in bridge and rusting machinery serve as silent reminders of the role Scapa Flow played in war.

A number of German submarines have been sunk in and around the Orkneys. U-18 lies on the bottom of the Flow in an area called Panhope Bay, near the oil pipeline. Sunk in October 1914 in an attempt to attack the British fleet, U-18 had been accessible to divers until authorities designated it off-limits because of the proximity to the pipeline that comes into the Flow, carrying oil from North Sea rigs to Flotta Island inside Scapa Flow. "The submarine has been pretty much blasted apart," John Thornton said. "We used to dive it, but there really isn't very much there where you can recognize it as a submarine on the bottom," he added. Other sunken U-boats include U-15, rammed two months earlier than U-18, and U-116, which sank in an unknown location outside Scapa Flow when it struck a mine in October 1918.

The Orkneys and northern isles have been the site of many ship disasters and wreckings. The rocky shoals continue to claim not only ships and their crews but the men that go out to save them. In one single incident on 17 March 1969, eight men, the entire crew of the Longhope lifeboat, lost their lives while going to the aid of a stricken freighter.

The weather conditions were tempestuous: gale force winds had been blow-ing for many days, and the sea was whipped into a furious state. A Liberian reg-istered freighter, the *Irene,* sent out a radio message that it was out of control. The two-thousand-ton displacement freighter broadcast the alert, sending up distress flares at 8:25 PM. The ship was caught in a southeasterly force 9 gale.

Without cargo, it was being tossed about precariously. The captain and crew of seventeen had left Granton and were heading for the coast of Norway when the ship radioed for assistance off Halcro Head on the island of South Ronaldsay. The stricken vessel was drifting precariously toward the rocks.

When the distress call went out the Lifeboat service was informed and rescue boats were launched. The crew of the Longhope lifeboat on the island of Hoy put out from their station and headed into the Pentland Firth. By this time the storm had intensified. The forty-seven-foot Longhope lifeboat almost immediately experienced radio problems. Finally communication was lost with the lifeboat entirely as sixty-foot waves were reported in the area where the lifeboat had put to sea. In the meantime, the stricken freighter *Irene* was pushed toward shore by the wind, and the freighter was dashed upon the rocks of South Ronaldsay at Grimness.

Robert Swanney heard the report of the stricken freighter in his hotel in Kirkwall. A newspaper reporter visiting the islands to cover an infamous homicide case persuaded Swanney to drive him out to the site of the *Irene,* where it had dashed upon the rocks. Taking his vehicle from Kirkwall across the Churchill Barriers to South Ronaldsay, Robert Swanney reported what developed.

"We proceeded out of Kirkwall and down to the south islands, which are connected together by the four Churchill Barriers. The Barriers can be quite alarming in bad weather. The sea washes right over the top of them and the roadway can be fairly dangerous. On this occasion, on the second barrier, the stones were being flung up, and when I say stones, boulders from the beach were being flung up onto the top of the barrier. Apart from the spray and the broken water we also had to negotiate past these rocks and boulders, and we also favored the risk of the engine stopping with the amount of salt water that was going through the radiator. We crossed the barrier successfully and we came to the sight of the actual shipwreck, which was at Grimness Point in South Ronaldsay. When we arrived the ship had just came onto the shore and they were making attempts to put a breeches buoy across to take off the crew," Swanney related.

"At this time the captain of the ship had been down over the side of the ship on a rope ladder. We assume he was trying to make fast a rocket line when he was washed off the ladder and he ended up in the surf. The coast guard spotted the danger he was in and made a very brave and successful attempt in rescuing him and pulled him in through the surf with a rocket line. He was in a state of near collapse when he was taken ashore.

"The wreck was lying parallel to the shore. The seas were hitting it, and it was swinging alarmingly back and forth, although it turned out that there was no risk to the crew. Eventually, it did at that time take some alarming lurches as it slowly moved inshore across the rocks. The wind was so strong that there was great difficulty standing on the cliff face. The wind was making it just about impossible to keep a footing while this was going on. They secured a breeches buoy, and they started taking the crew across on this breeches buoy. The operation went very smoothly and successfully. In fact, as the crew came up over the top of the cliff, we had a very small local doctor there on the spot and he was getting them by the seat of the pants and firing them up over the cliff. The wind behind them was shooting them up over the top of the cliff and they were caught by local coast guards.

"The sea was in an absolute white turmoil breaking right over the ship. Between the ship and the beach it was a swirling mass of white foam, it certainly wouldn't support a swimmer. The Longhope lifeboat had been launched and had been last seen passing the Northern Light south of South Ronaldsay. It was going with the tide which was probably running at about nine knots, and the tide was running into the sea which was coming from the southeast. The sea conditions in that area were, to say the least, highly dangerous. Communications with the Longhope lifeboat had been lost, and the Coast Guard had asked everyone to keep a lookout for lights. Finally it was announced that the lifeboat was spotted floating upside down in the Pentland Firth, and then of course everyone's worst fears were realized. It was towed to Scrabster, where it was righted by a crane. The crew, all but one, were found to be inside. The crew were in the crew's cabin; the coxswain was in the wheelhouse; the engineer was missing presumably lost overboard. They were all dead," Robert Swanney said softly, describing a tragedy that resulted in the loss of eight men.

The crew were mostly from the village of Brims, Longhope, and for some families the tragedy was even more poignant. Three men, a father, and two brothers died from one family, and many of the others were related by blood or marriage.

The Royal National Lifeboat Institution exists throughout Britain, for the most part a voluntary sea rescue service. While bravery among lifeboat crews is commonplace, this tragedy in the Orkneys typifies the courage and endurance of the northern islanders who brave the harshest seas to render assistance to imperiled ships.

The Orkney tradition of quiet courage distinguishes the special sacrifice of the Longhope crew. Today some of the relatives of crewmen who perished when the lifeboat was lost man the new Longhope boat, viewing their service humbly. Ian McFadyen, whose older brother, Eric, at twenty-four years old the youngest crewman aboard the ill-fated lifeboat, serves as mechanic for the new boat. Lifeboat service is a tradition for the McFadyens and many other families in the hamlets and villages around Scapa Flow in the Orkneys. Ian McFadyen was only twenty years old when his brother lost his life in the Longhope lifeboat disaster. "I don't know. It's been in the family, I think, for years," Ian said, when asked why he went into the lifeboat service. "My grandfather was the second coxswain of the boat here and my grand uncle was coxswain. I had three uncles who were on the boat here, and my dad was on the boat and my brother, who was lost, and myself," Ian said, reflecting that tradition of the people of the northern isles of Scotland.

Scapa Flow and the skerries and shoals around the Orkneys have claimed countless ships over history. Treasure hunters and salvage divers continue to probe the depths hoping to locate shipwrecks that will make their fortunes. Some have found ships laden with treasure like the Dutch East India ship wrecked in the Shetland Islands north of Orkney in 1737, with a cargo of seventy-nine silver bars and thirty-one sacks of coins.

The islands also claimed the *Titanic*'s sister ship, the *Oceanic,* which hit a Shetland Island reef and sank on 8 September 1914. Myriad ships have struck the rocks between the Orkneys and the Shetland Islands on their passage from the North Sea and the Atlantic.

Davy Reid, who has explored the rocky reefs on Fair Isle north of the Orkney Islands claims that more than three hundred ships have been sunk on the treacherous rocks surrounding these islands. Reid lost his own fishing trawler on the rocks in Fair Isle, going back when the weather permitted to recover one of the ship's large propellers, which he has on display in a hotel he owned on the island of Burray.

There is much unaccounted legend and mystery in the folklore of Scapa Flow and the northern Scottish isles. While famous shipwrecks like the *Royal Oak,* *Hampshire,* and *Vanguard* captivate historians, the scuttling of the seventy-four ships of the German High Seas Fleet marks Scapa Flow as a most unique place in history. There is still a great deal to be discovered in this graveyard of the North, a place where the motto on the many medals for valor issued to Orcadians by the Royal National Lifeboat Service truly has meaning. For in this adventurous northland it is the mariner's prayer, "Let not the deep swallow me up."

CHAPTER NINE

Bermuda: Cemetery of Sunken Ships

The lines paid out behind the ship. Red balloon floats marked the end of the cord a few feet from where divers held on. It was exhausting work. The sun drilled down overhead. The ship pitched and rolled in the sea, making it better duty to be in the water dragged behind the ship at the end of a stout line than up on the flying bridge keeping a lookout, steering a course back and forth between two markers for what seemed to be endless hours. If the divers spotted anything below, any anomaly, a chunk of metal, a pottery shard, a cannon or anchor, or other evidence of a shipwreck, they would drop off the line and snorkel down to investigate the site. Once the captain was informed that one of the men in the water had dropped off the line the ship would begin a wide sweep circling around to pick the diver up.

It became routine. No one on board got excited anymore when a diver left the line to investigate something below. The diver would surface, explain that what was seen didn't warrant further investigation, be picked up, and the search would continue into the hot Bermuda afternoon.

There is treasure in these waters—and hundreds of shipwrecks. Some have been found but nothing near what remains hidden, encrusted by coral, on the ledges and shallows of the islands' reefs and shoals. The Bermuda Islands lie in the mid-Atlantic, the nearest land is about six hundred miles due west to Cape Hatteras, North Carolina. Yet, from the days of the first navigation to the New World, Bermuda's treacherous reefs have claimed a heavy toll of sailors and ships. No one knows exactly how many. In many cases information about where and how the ships have wrecked has been lost to time. For the handful of searchers who spend their lives looking for them, the shipwrecks hold a special fascination.

"Wait, hold on," a loud voice called out from behind the boat. Billy McCallan put over the helm as he stood up to look over the stern. The lookout had grown tired of watching and didn't see the diver drop off and swim down to investigate what he saw on the bottom. McCallan had to swing around carefully, maneuvering the ship so as not to tangle the lines dragging behind the boat or injure the divers in the water.

"It looks like something. Better mark it and take a look, Billy," Ernie Decouto called up from the water, no trace of emotion in his voice. There had been too many disappointments, too many false alarms, yet each site identified might hold a clue to the disappearance of a ship, a ship whose cargo of riches would stagger and bedazzle the imagination of the world. If the divers were excited, their emotions were well concealed for fear of giving in to what might prove to be another false alarm. McCallan positioned the boat and anchored. The divers came up on deck and described what they had seen.

"It looks like some iron and what could be wood. It's just to the side of the sand hole there," Robert Limes said pointing. McCallan donned his scuba tank and listened as the divers described what they had seen. In a minute he was over the side swimming down toward the area where the free divers had spotted what appeared to be evidence of a shipwreck. McCallan moved fast underwater, he didn't waste time looking at things instinct and experience told him were not important. He spent a few seconds at the iron object and chunk of wood on the bottom, half embedded in the coral. He paused to sense his direction then swam off over the reef.

In a moment he was peering into a coral hole, where more metal objects were concealed. He began fanning at the sand bottom with his hand, creating large clouds in the otherwise limpid water. It was off the northwest part of the island, about seven miles out. The submerged reef here jutted away from the island, ensnaring hapless mariners who never expected shallow water so far from land.

McCallan was joined by the other divers. They spread out over the reef, looking for more evidence of the shipwreck. Ernie Decouto found it. In a moment he was back signaling the divers to follow him further along the reef, where a large anchor remained wedged in where it caught years ago and held fast. What manner of storm or tragedy befell the sailors who dropped the anchor and the condition of their ship—which must have dragged over the shallows and shoals, perhaps with a bottom staved in and taking water—one can only guess.

The position of the anchor was evidence that it held and was pulled by a heavy ship. McCallan examined the anchor. The wooden stock crosspiece had long since rotted away, its iron bindings had fallen down on the shank now grown over by coral. The crown and fluke were well embedded into the coral, the anchor shank leading off to the west. Billy raised his two hands and motioned as Decouto and Robert Limes swam off in the direction the ship must have been in when the line tautened and the anchor caught. They found nothing. The men returned to the boat.

"It could be anywhere. The line could have parted, the ship could have drifted off. It's not that old," McCallan said, mentally making a note of the position of the site. Stock anchors were employed on ships from the fifteenth century up to the mid-seventeenth, so the anchor alone wasn't enough evidence to go on. He decided to continue searching, still hoping to find an early Spanish shipwreck. Divers went over the side again, holding on as the lines paid out. McCallan resumed the search pattern.

It would be easy to overlook a visual trace of a shipwreck on the bottom. The boat pulled the divers along at the end of the lines so they could scan the bottom, which ranged from fifteen to forty feet deep. "Nothing is straight in nature. Anything you see that's straight or even is foreign to the reef," Decouto said. Saying it didn't make it any easier to locate evidence from the surface as one was being pulled behind a ship. "Your legs will get tired, so you'll have to switch legs," Decouto said, showing how he put his foot in a loop in the line to take the strain off the arms when dragging.

"That looks like a scrub mark there," McCallan would say. "Yeah, that's where the ship came across the reef. See that scrub mark? See there—where that sand is? A ship lay there on the bottom," he affirmed, putting over the helm and looking back at the two red balls floating in the water behind the boat, marking the divers. McCallan steered his ship across the site he spotted from the flying bridge.

As the divers reached it, one of them called out, signaling with his hand. "Stay there," McCallan yelled from the bridge. "Let me go a little further along, see if there is anything else." He dragged back and forth, endlessly patient, unwilling to break off the search to anchor over the site where the divers had seen something on the bottom. McCallan wanted to be sure that he did not miss some area of the site where the ship may have broken up or spilled cargo or ballast or cannons. Finally he returned to the place where the most promising sighting was made. The second probable shipwreck location of the day.

He used no navigation equipment to get back to the place; McCallan had told the divers simply, "I can find this again. Let's see if we can spot any more of the wreck." True to his word, he found the place again, in an ocean of sameness with only vague, hardly visible landmarks seven miles away on the islands of Bermuda. Billy McCallan recognized the bottom, the pattern of the reefs, things only a fisherman born on Bermuda and who worked these waters since childhood would recognize.

He dropped anchor and the divers prepared to go to work. Billy geared up first, taking a hatchet from its hook in the cockpit. He disappeared over side as the other divers readied their equipment. Unlike the first site, there was ample evidence of a shipwreck here. Pottery was welded into the coral, almost unrecognizable except to the trained eye. A sand hole ran through the middle of the site where McCallan set to fanning with his hand. On each side of the sand hole, artifacts were enmeshed in the coral: tiles and pottery, cannonballs and fused masses of metal. It was an ancient shipwreck and this was the first time anyone explored it. This time there was no disguising the divers' excitement as the methodical search continued, and they attempted to piece together the history and chronology of the wreck. The work went on underwater until all of the divers ran out of air. Then they surfaced, gobbled down a quick snack, turned over pieces of pottery that had been brought up in their hands, put on another tank, and went down again.

Underwater McCallan was just as methodical as he was at the helm, navigating among the coral, stopping here and there to break an object free, getting the lay of the wreck, slowly trying to make sense of what had been found. He soon spotted a cylindrical object almost entirely encrusted by coral. He tapped the coral around it, but the object was almost entirely fused into the reef which had grown around it. With the hatchet, McCallan chopped deftly at the coral, using care not to mark or damage the object. As he chopped it free the outline became unmistakable. It was a ship's sounding lead, about eighteen inches long with a hollow base into which the early navigators would pour wax so that the lead would bring up samples of the bottom.

Using a sounding weight, early navigators could not only determine depth for their ship's safe passage but, sailing usually within sight of land as much as possible, observing the consistency of the bottom would often be part of their instructions. Sailing directions might read: "Run north along the coast until the bottom turns to brown sand," one example of the sort of notes appended to early navigational charts.

McCallan held up the sounding weight and struggled to transfer the heavy object back to the boat. It was a good find, as were some of the pottery artifacts. As night began to fall and wisps of red streaked the Bermuda's sky, the tired divers surfaced and weighed anchor. McCallan left no marker over the site. He would come back again, navigating by that special sense unique to men of the sea.

The islands that make up Bermuda form a fishhook, with the point curving around at the westernmost end. How it came to be that so many ships wrecked on Bermuda is explained by inveterate shipwreck diver, Harry Cox. "What happened was that because of the navigation limitations, the very limited knowledge, and the superstitions of the age, these ships sailed south from Portugal and Spain down the known coast, which was Africa. When they reached a certain latitude, which came to be known as the Horse Latitudes, they turned right and sailed west. They encountered first the West Indies then encountered a vast hulk of land which was South America," he said, describing the route from the Old World to the New World.

"The galleons went to Cartagena and to Vera Cruz, and it was at this point that they were confronted with a great problem of navigation, namely how to return home safely. What they did was they steered a course north and east, until they gained a latitude of 32 degrees north. At 32 degrees north, once again the galleons turned right and began their lumbering return back to Spain. . . . As they approached the island of Bermuda, which hopefully they would miss if they saw it at all, they had to make a decision—whether to pass below the island and proceed home or pass above the island. If they were to pass below the island, and that is to say along our south shore, they were in deep water, where our barrier reef is very close to shore. If they elected to go north of the island, the reefs extend seven miles from the shore. Being Europeans they scarcely expected to find so shallow water so far from the land. If they miscalculated or turned too soon, their fate was sealed, and they became one of Bermuda's three or four hundred ships that have been wrecked here over almost five centuries of Bermuda's history . . . there are ships here spanning the maritime history of five centuries and of every nation that had business in the sea," Cox said, as he described the geographic peculiarities that caused so many ships to wreck on the treacherous shoals and offshore reefs.

Cox made some spectacular shipwreck finds diving Bermuda's reefs. Cox relied on instinct and experience rather than gadgetry when he searched for shipwrecks. Like Billy McCallan, Cox dove Bermuda waters for more than thirty years. He had that special sense of the oceans. "I don't own a magnetometer. They're very expensive, and everything I do is visual. The disciplines of visual search are tedious and physically exhausting. In one sense it also evidences the innate reluctance to cede human experience and knowledge to the enigmatical functioning of advanced technologies," Cox said. Every day off he'd be found aboard his boat, the *Shearwater,* with a group of friends searching the reefs offshore, looking for shipwrecks. Cox hoped to discover evidence of his family's own ships, three of which wrecked off Bermuda in the early days of settlement.

The flags stood out straight on their staffs when Cox brought the diving cylinders out and left them on the cement dock next to his boat. "The weather is marginal," he said. "The wind has to be blowing at fifteen knots to make a flag stand out like that," he pointed with his chin, the perennial pipe clenched between his teeth. "Well, give it a try. We may have to turn back, but we'll see what it's like once we get out there," Harry added, stepping down on the *Shearwater* to turn on the marine radio to get an update on the weather forecast. With the dive equipment loaded, he cast off. The *Shearwater* eased away from the dock out into the harbor. Cox and his friends had found three important shipwreck sites during their diving experiences in Bermuda. There was great enthusiasm among the crew of the *Shearwater,* convinced that they had just found the fourth and perhaps most exciting shipwreck.

As the *Shearwater* made its way across Hamilton Harbor out into Bermuda's Great Sound, the wind and water picked up. "It's protected in here," Cox said. "Out on the reef it's open ocean, but we'll see what it's like." He continued steering from atop the flying bridge as the boat heaved and rolled. The sea caught on the bow and an occasional wave sent water up over the deckhouse and cowlings. Once the *Shearwater* cleared the sound and was out in the ocean, Cox had to keep a sharp lookout to steer between the coral. The wind and water were up, and the ship heaved so that the equipment had to be secured on the after deck. High water or not, the crew was energized. The *Shearwater's* log described one find on the site that encouraged the divers. The log reads, "Found $3\,{}^{1}/_{2}$ foot long cannon, bronze, marked on first reinforce 6 on cascabel reinforce is the letter J and the numeral 2, date it to first quarter of 1600s (manufactured in early 1500s and were rare by early 1600s) and none known to have been made after 1700."

It is difficult to date a shipwreck simply from one artifact. The gun could have been carried as decorative armor; it was a swivel gun and could have been mounted on the poop for its bronze decor. Cox and his divers were fascinated by their find. Near the gun the divers located seven breech blocks, convincing them that more of these early breech-loading bronze cannons must be nearby.

"This is the only pass through the reef," Cox said, pointing off at the ocean as he steered his ship over a patch of sand that was only slightly wider than the boat and between two darker coral reefs looming up near the surface on either side. "The reef here extends nine miles out," he added, concentrating, knowing well that it was these reefs that claimed so many ships over the centuries as the early navigators turned and thought they had ample deep water on their way back to Europe. Thirty years of navigation in treacherous waters had taught Harry Cox caution. Within an hour and a half, the *Shearwater* was over the newly discovered wreck site.

"There's the boot," Cox declared, pointing to a patch of sandy bottom that formed an outline underwater resembling a boot, surrounded by dark reef and coral growth. "The shipwreck site should be here," he said, looking back toward the land. A squall had come up and with the rain and bad weather it was difficult to see land. "My eyesight is not as good since I lost the vision in one eye." He strained to see as waves broke over the bow. He held the *Shearwater*'s head to the wind and sea. A rope end had struck Harry Cox in one eye while he was readying gear aboard the *Shearwater* some time back, impairing the sight in his left eye.

One of the divers donned a mask and snorkel and jumped over side to be sure they were in the right position. In a minute he came back on board and put the anchor over. "We'd better use two anchors. Put the Danforth in with plenty of extra line. Let the weight hold on the mushroom. If that gives then the Danforth will pick up the strain," Cox said. He preferred to anchor with the mushroom anchor and use the Danforth only as a security measure since the hooks on the Danforth would make it difficult to pull up once it caught in the reef and took the strain of the ship.

In a few minutes the divers were geared up and in the water. Waves came in large rollers. In the six-foot seas, it was precarious going to get over the transom with the heavy scuba gear as the boat rocked sometimes violently. Nevertheless, the water was very clear. A school of curious chub circled the divers who prepared their tools and set up on the site. Cox had found another breech block in a crevice in the coral. He and Reeve Trott set about trying to break the coral that covered it to get the block free. Apart from a sand hole nearby, the entire site was overgrown with coral. The reef had formed over and around everything. The divers had to poke into narrow spaces to locate pieces of the wreckage.

In one narrow hole objects glistened, reflecting the light from an underwater lantern. They were square, dark glass bottles. It was difficult to reach the bottles. They had to be eased out of the hole with a pole and hook. Nearby under another piece of coral lay an iron piece of wreckage, for the time being impossible to identify. A large lignum vitae log was found. The dense, heavy wood was usually carried aboard early sailing ships so the carpenter could fashion blocks and dead eyes when needed.

"It probably means the ship is not as old as I thought," Cox said when the square glass bottles were brought aboard the *Shearwater*. The bottles were hand blown of heavy glass with large pontil marks. They could be dated from their shape and form, later identified as to origin. The bottles would provide more evidence that would enable Cox and his team to trace the history of this shipwreck.

As the day wore on the storm worsened. Driving rain and wind came in from the sea. One of the anchor lines parted, and the *Shearwater* was only held by the second anchor put down as a precaution. "We can't leave even if we wanted to," Cox said. "It's better to ride it out if it gets bad," he added looking off at the advancing squall. As the brunt of the storm approached the divers made for the cabin. "I used to dive out here in a double-ended lifeboat," Harry said. "It was all open. You come to appreciate the cabin," he declared, dipping a fork into a jar of peanut butter, eating large scoops.

Reeve Trott was wolfing down canned oysters. As the driving rain pelted down, a woman diver who had accompanied the excursion excused herself from the cabin and made a trip to the rail. Whether it was the heaving boat or the oysters and peanut butter, she didn't say, probably having second thoughts about throwing in her lot with these shipwreck hunters in rough weather. Cox, however, was in a good humor. He had planted a fake gold cross on the bottom, leaving it just slightly exposed. It had been happened upon, providing momentary excitement as the divers recovered it, then realized the joke Harry had played. "Once you touch gold underwater, you can't he fooled," Harry said, smiling, as the crew enjoyed his good natured prank.

In these rough seas, the divers had a chance to contemplate Cox's description of a shipwreck and appreciate his reverence for what these underwater time capsules represent. "A shipwreck represents a terrible moment of tragedy and loss of life," Cox said, adding that the wrecks are "the preservation in an instant of time not only of shipbuilding but the artifacts of people and their daily life. When a man goes to sea he takes with him a compression of his life. Even as a traveler today boards a modern aircraft and takes in their suitcases what could be regarded as a cross section of their home, these ships provide a remarkable insight into a given period."

In that spirit, Cox rejects the term treasure hunter for what he does, declaring that one would do "a great disservice to call me a treasure hunter. I am not a treasure hunter." Cox has found treasure, surely, some of the most beautiful and valuable things recovered from the waters around Bermuda, but Harry Cox and the crew of the *Shearwater* are driven by their quest for history, hoping some day to find one of the Cox family ships.

"Someone very wisely pointed out that there is no one in the world—and this is certainly true up till now—who has become rich seeking treasure underneath the sea. It is very expensive, it is very dangerous, and very often those who have discovered treasure have met with nothing but sadness, and I think this is a great tragedy and reality of treasure diving, and I'm happy to tell you that the greatest single insult that you can give to me and my friends and my family is that we are treasure hunters. Our treasures are measured in discovery and in the enjoyment of the real measure of diving. . . . The real treasure is not gold. If you're fortunate to find gold, which we did, were you to measure the value of that gold against the cost and the time that was required to find it, we've found nothing," Cox declared.

Indeed, Cox's most exciting find did involve the discovery of gold. He remembered the incident vividly. "It was a perfect day, July the 26th, 1968, we were on the *Shearwater* together, there was no one there save men and women who were friends. We'd spent three quarters of the day diving on a ship looking for some bottles. We decided to make a return to the island, watching casually the bottom that passed underneath us on the return. As we went home we found some ballast stones. Nothing else, ballast stones. We put a marker buoy down and we circled the area for an hour or so. We found no evidence of the ship except some lignum vitae logs. We dived on the lignum vitae logs and there was nothing, so then we went back to pick up the buoy. Whether it was tenacity bred by a hundred broken ships that I'd seen, whether it was the injunction of providence, whatever it was, something made me go to the bottom for one last look at these pitiful ballast stones, which were strewn about this lonely reef. While I was there a piece of eight rolled into my hand. This piece of eight had a cross on it, I remember, and the name of Philip the Second of Spain and his royal coat of arms. I recognized it instantly. I'd read about these things, and then there twinkled into view the gold coins which were as perfect as they were the day they were minted. I rushed to the surface having found a gold bracelet which was unceremoniously flung into my boat by a lady who didn't know much about such things. She threw this piece of gold into the boat, and one of the divers said 'What's that?' and she said 'I don't know what it is. It's a piece of brass that Harry's found on the bottom, and the diver picked it up and his

exact words were, 'Brass. Brass my ass—this is gold!' and that was the instant
of the beginning of the most thrilling discovery in our lives," Cox recounted,
describing what has been called the most valuable package of sixteenth-century
maritime treasure thus far recovered in the western hemisphere.

"The intrinsic value of that find is not what renders it sublime. What renders
it sublime is the fact that it happened to us, and in my hand at the end of that
day I held a sixteenth-century maritime astrolabe. The experts were able to tell
me that it was made by a man called Lorenzo Caldo. Its date was 1531. Lorenzo
Caldo put into the hands of men an astrolabe— it's the earliest form of navigational instrument in the world to be used in opening the New World, and
we found one," Cox affirmed, his voice dramatic, remembering the moment of
discovery vividly and emotionally.

It was the fulfillment of a dream of discovery in that first instant as Cox held
history in his hands, rare and beautiful objects last touched by humans hundreds
of years ago. Among the artifacts discovered by Harry Cox was a fifteen-and-
a-half-foot length of gold chain. On the chain was a grooming tool or mani-
cure set still in perfect condition, the gold as bright as when it was made. The
pieces of eight were made in Spain, bearing the marks of Philip II, minted in
1578, according to Cox. Olive oil jars and pottery was also discovered at the
site, dating the shipwreck to the days of Spanish conquest of the New World.

Cox and his diving companions have found other very interesting and
important shipwrecks diving off Bermuda's coast. One of the shipwrecks may
have been a Portuguese vessel that Cox believes antedated Columbus's voyages
of discovery in 1492. "I think that we discovered the oldest-known wreck perhaps in the western hemisphere," Cox declared. "For any diver to use superla-
tives like the oldest or the deepest or the biggest is obviously a very great mis-
take. I have no idea whether the ship is the oldest one known now, but certainly
she antedated the time of Columbus's voyage in 1492," Cox continued, going
on to explain his discovery. "From a very unencouraging beginning we were able
to recover from that wreck a deck mortar made out of iron hoops or iron bars
bound together by iron hoops, a very primitive gun indeed which could have
been made in the middle of the 1400s. We recovered half a dozen very beautiful but very deteriorated iron breech-loading swivel guns," Cox recalled, adding,

"The prize find on that wreck was a bronze cannon I believe cast in Denmark and I think it is dated prior to Columbus's voyage in 1492. It's a small gun, an interesting piece of course, but we did find a most amazing number of Portuguese pots off this vessel or off her remains, and these pots I saw their likeness in Portugal. I believe this wreck very probably was a Portuguese ship," Harry Cox said. He described one of his first discoveries in the early 1960s.

The persistence of Cox and his divers paid off, for they were to be rewarded for their relentless searching again in 1977, while diving off Bermuda's northeast reefs. The wreck was called the Manila Wreck by the divers. "She was called the Manila Wreck because we recovered a vast number of manilas. Manilas are bronze half-closed bracelets which were used in the slave trade, I believe principally in Nigeria. They were introduced into the African continent by the Portuguese. Out of this vessel we brought an interesting cross section of eighteenth-century artifacts. The vessel was unidentified, was of indeterminate age but probably in the early part of the 1700s, but the wonderful find that this ship afforded us was a bronze cannon which was cast in Groningen in Holland, and the date on this gun is 1631. It was a gun of the Dutch West Indies Trading Company," Cox explained. The gun proved to be an exciting discovery.

Charlie Reed, a close friend and one of the men who dives regularly with the *Shearwater* crew, described how a sailor in a single-handed race crashed right onto North Rock. "That proves that even modern vessels with all the modern means they have are still crashing on Bermuda," Reed said. "What happened was the ship sunk, a small vessel, a sailing yacht. The keel is very heavy, and the motion of the water out there finally rocked the boat clear of the keel, left the keel there. They found the rest of the ship sixty miles to the north. It floated off; that has happened I'm sure to other larger vessels that wrecked in fifteen hundred, sixteen hundred. Must have, because very often you'll find ballast and nothing else, or you'll find an anchor and nothing else. So they must have either cut it free or it got torn free. The Manila Wreck was out on the northeast. With a westerly wind, if a ship struck that reef, which it did, it knocked the cargo out, which was twenty-four cannons and heavy, heavy ballast. The ship got more buoyant, even though it was broken in half, perhaps," Reed explained. He described how a wreck site can be spread over many miles of ocean.

"What happened, it was apparently around the early seventeen hundreds and nobody ever knew the ship wrecked until we came upon it," Reed explained. The direction of the wind and the position of the reef could have blown the thing to Africa from there—it would have missed the end of the island. People, debris, everything would have gone off to sea so people on the island wouldn't have known there was a wreck out there. If it washed ashore, people would have said 'Ah ha, that came in from there, and we'll look.' Surely didn't because they left a bronze cannon out there, which they wouldn't have left," Reed added, showing off a Manila bracelet and various artifacts he and Cox recovered from the wreckage.

With their recent discovery of the bronze breech-loading swivel gun, Harry Cox has embarked on a new, and perhaps his most exciting, discovery. "In actual diving hours I have spent some two to three years underneath the water seeking ships which belonged to my family and seeking ships which will yield some increase in knowledge not only to this island and its history but perhaps even to the knowledge and history of underwater archaeology," Cox said, declaring his motives and aspirations. Born on Bermuda, Cox remains proud of the island's heritage and history. "All the Coxes have been born on Bermuda for three and a half centuries," he asserted, also pointing out that he introduced all three of his children to diving at an early age.

One of Bermuda's most famous shipwreck divers is Teddy Tucker. Living in Somerset with his wife, Edna, Tucker is renowned for his many adventures, having found what is still regarded as the single most valuable artifact ever recovered under the sea. The story of Tucker's Bermuda Cross is like a detective mystery: full of intrigue, daring, and a clever heist of the real cross from a carefully guarded museum collection, detected just minutes before the Queen of England was slated to inspect it.

Teddy Tucker was born on Bermuda. While his mother was from Virginia, Tucker's father's family traces its history back to the very early settlement on Bermuda, to Bermuda's third governor, Daniel Tucker, who held office in the early part of the seventeenth century. Teddy Tucker's account of his diving career began when he was a youngster growing up on the island. "I always had an interest in diving," Tucker said. "As a kid, I worked at the aquarium in Flatts. They used to put tourists down in a diving helmet for a dollar. I was the little kid who pulled the pump. I took turns diving," he continued. "When I got old enough and big enough to wear a suit, [the divers working around the piers] used to like to have a kid go down, so they could take it easy," he continued.

Tucker's diving career continued during the war when he was attached to the Royal Navy's Special Services section. Tucker came back to Bermuda in 1947, after the war. "I've been fishing and diving ever since, and I'm still going," he declared, pointing off with his chin toward his treasure hunting work boat, the *Miss Wendy,* at anchor in Mangrove Bay near his house.

"He can stay down all day long," one of Tucker's friends remarked, describing his tenacity underwater. Born in 1924, there is absolutely no sign that Tucker intends to slow down. One of his best-known finds occurred in April 1950. Tucker was diving in the North Channel when he found several cannons on the bottom. Searching around the site, Tucker found more cannons, musket balls, pewter ware, and other artifacts. Tucker brought his artifacts to the authorities at Bermuda's Trust who decided to purchase them, offering Tucker $100 for everything. The deal concluded, and Tucker went on to other things, not bothering to return to the North Channel wreck site for five years.

Eventually Tucker dove the North Channel wreck again. This time, an amazing treasure horde was uncovered. In short order, Tucker discovered silver pieces of eight, gold bars, and gold ingots as he dug into this old Spanish nao which went down around 1595. It was on this wreck site that Tucker found the magnificent gold-and-emerald-studded cross. In all his diving adventures, Tucker considers that the "most interesting thing was that cross."

The gold cross measured two-and-three-quarter by one-and-five-eighth inches with five large emeralds on the vertical and one matching emerald on each horizontal arm. The stones were perfectly matched, making the cross a priceless treasure. Tucker identified the shipwreck as the *San Pedro,* which was on its voyage back to Cadiz, Spain, from Cartagena, Colombia, when it wrecked in November 1595 off Bermuda.

Tucker hid out the loot for a while. Rumors of his find were spreading, so he finally revealed his discovery, which earned him international fame. The government of Bermuda bought Tucker's treasure, including the famous emerald-and-gold cross for $100,000. The treasure was displayed at Bermuda's

Aquarium but transferred to the Maritime Museum when the museum was to be officially opened and dedicated by Queen Elizabeth II on 17 February 1975. Just minutes before the queen was to arrive at the Maritime Museum to look at the treasure, it was discovered that the famous cross had been stolen. "Somebody got it out of the safe and put a plastic one in. It was only discovered when the queen came in and they were opening the Maritime Museum," Teddy Tucker said.

Sgt. John Instone of the Bermuda Police described the incident. "I was actually there when the counterfeit was discovered," Sergeant Instone said. "I was at the Maritime Museum providing security for the queen. Twenty minutes before she was to arrive they came up to me and put this in my hand and said, look at this. It felt like nothing. Of course inside a case nobody would really notice." The counterfeit cross was made of plastic and closely resembled the original. The case is still unsolved. "We have notified Interpol. It's probably in the hands of a private collector," Sergeant Instone declared, looking at the plastic replica at Hamilton Police Headquarters. The theft of the cross remains one of the most famous crimes in Bermuda's history.

The dock at Tucker's Somerset house is crowded with gear and items he has recovered from Bermuda's shipwrecks. "Some cannons over there," he said, pointing. "We leave them in the water until we can preserve them," he added, motioning with his chin to the shallows near the dock. Piles of grindstones were stacked that Tucker had recovered from the *Caesar,* an English brigantine sailing vessel en route to Baltimore, Maryland, from Newcastle, England. The *Caesar* wrecked on Bermuda's West End reef on 18 May 1818. Some very interesting and rare bottles were found on the *Caesar,* including Masonic flasks traced to Henry Schoolcraft of Boston, who made them in about 1800. The Masonic flasks bear the emblem of the Freemasons on one side and an eagle on the other. Rarer still, oblong melon flasks were found on the site by Tucker, who sold examples of the unusual bottles for upwards of $2,000 each.

Not far from the site of the wrecked *Caesar,* Tucker discovered the remains of another Spanish galleon that wrecked on Bermuda's West End reefs on 12 September 1621. The navigational charts that trace the reef configuration where the *San Antonio* struck is marked "No passage over these flats." The irregular line of coral stretches in a large arc out from the West End of Bermuda around to where it arches far offshore. It was near a place known as Little Bar that the *San Antonio* struck. The ship's captain, Fernandino Da Vera, was heading back to Spain from their port of call at Cartagena with treasure and general cargo collected in the New World. Indigo dye was found by Tucker and his divers, along with tobacco remnants still on sticks that were used to wrap the leaves for shipping, hides, and items of everyday shipboard life.

Teddy Tucker is as enthusiastic about relatively modern shipwrecks as he is describing some of his more spectacular treasure finds. "There are two small locomotives on deck, one with the coal tender," Tucker said. "The *Admiral Durham* went down in thirty-two fathoms. I loosened one of the trunion pins on the bell; that's when I spent three hours hanging on the cord decompressing and the boat was drifting," Tucker smiled, describing the difficulty of working such a deep shipwreck. "She has as cargo two guns made in Philadelphia, big ones, they must weigh two hundred tons and be about the size of the *Miss Wendy*—about sixty-three feet. They were the answer to the big German guns. The Allies were going to load them on railroad cars and shoot them at the Germans," he added describing war material that never reached Europe when the cargo ship sank.

The settlement of Bermuda itself began with the wrecking of an English ship en route to the British colonies. Bermuda comprises about 140 separate islands with a land area totaling some twenty-one square miles. It was formed out of lava from an extinct volcano. The islands were discovered by Juan de Bermudez, a Spanish explorer who landed on the islands in 1503. The Bermudas have long enjoyed a reputation for danger, called the "Isle of Devils" by English mariners for the many ships which were lost on the islands' treacherous reefs.

It was the wrecking of the *Sea Venture* that actually precipitated settlement on the islands. En route to Jamestown, Virginia, from Plymouth, England, the *Sea Venture,* commanded by Adm. George Somers, was caught in a gale and became separated from the nine-vessel fleet. The *Sea Venture* was pushed off course by the tempest. Battling fierce winds and sea for five days, barely able to keep their ship afloat, the crew spotted Bermuda on 28 July 1609. Landing on the island in their longboats, the crew found food in abundance.

The shipwrecked sailors set up a settlement camp on the island and began building ships that would enable them to continue their voyage. Wood and fittings were salvaged from the waterlogged *Sea Venture*. Eventually the crew constructed two small ships which they christened *Deliverance* and *Patience*. One of the original party aboard the *Sea Venture* was John Rolfe, whose wife bore two children while they were marooned on Bermuda. Rolfe's second marriage later in Virginia is perhaps better known because of his bride, the famous Indian princess Pocahontas.

One year after they landed with their sodden, sinking ship, the crew of the *Sea Venture* set sail in their two ships for Virginia. Admiral Somers left behind three men, who led a solitary existence until a ship returned for them two years later. Admiral Somers himself returned to Bermuda where he died in 1610, lending the islands their British name, Somers Island. Two years after Somers's death, settlers colonized Bermuda at St. George's town and began importing slaves in 1616. The mid-1700s Manila Wreck found by Harry Cox, with its cargo of slave bracelets and trade beads, bears mute testimony to the slave trade that existed on the islands until its abolition in 1834.

The wreckage of what is believed to be the *Sea Venture* was discovered in The Narrows off the tip of St. David's Island on Bermuda's east end near the landing for St. George's town. The remains of the ship, its broken keel in thirty feet of water and timbers from below the orlop are all that mark the site that experts believe are the last remains of the ship whose wrecking marked the colonization of the islands. The wreck is the subject of a salvage and preservation effort by local officials.

Jane Downing, whose father discovered the wreckage of the *Sea Venture* in 1958, serves as curator of Bermuda's Maritime Museum. The museum has preserved one of the iron cannons recovered from the *Sea Venture* and has a collection of fine artifacts. Some of the artifacts were recovered by Edmund Downing, including a number of Rhenish stoneware jugs. The jugs bear the image of Cardinal Bellarmine at the mouth, trailing beard and hair, rounding off below the neck. Discussing the *Sea Venture* finds, Downing said, "We have a group of shipwrecks here unique in the world and we in Bermuda have little to show for it." Her comment was directed at the concern that "every day people go out and take things off wrecks and there is nothing you can do about it."

While the Maritime Museum has a fine collection of artifacts and treasure recovered from some of Bermuda's shipwrecks, Downing has underscored the controversy that has been raging between shipwreck divers and strict preservationists, who express the concern that important historical knowledge will be lost if the wrecks are left to excavation by untrained divers. Bermuda's Maritime Museum's caretaker, Doug Little, is an accomplished poet, whose wit and enthusiasm are widely known on the island. Hobbling along on his peg-leg, Doug described the wrecking of a famous ship. "The *Kate* struck on Long Bar and ripped herself full of holes," Doug said, prompting him to pen the lines,

When Fate preferr'd her lie in state full seven fathoms down—
  Old rusty 'KATE' with crumpled plate
Pick's rustic Tucker's Town.
  From Texas, near The Rio Grande
Over-stuff'd—with cotton!
  She'd veer Bermuda's verdant land
When water, stores, went rotten.
  'Twas wild December, '78—
Stupendous hundred years
  Since Simpson stood the watch on 'KATE'
Help'd shoulder, too, her wares.
  Gibb's Light! Did you these times but lend
Besides your brilliant flash
  All-piercing blast, to reach-transcent—
T' avert—that fatal crash!
  Had you loud-hailed "Your course is wrong,
Veer off—show swiftest, Green!
  Your Ruby Light does not belong
Where 'tis, at present, seen!"

Doug Little's research in Bermuda's library archives turned up a great deal of information about the *Kate* and other shipwrecks, anecdotes about their crews and cargo and often violent wrecking told in his poetic tales.

One of Bermuda's foremost authorities on shipwrecks and local history is Dr. Edward Harris, director of the Maritime Museum. From his office in one of the old stone ammunition storage buildings on the grounds of the former Royal Dockyard complex, which houses the museum and its collection of boats, artwork, glass bottles, and treasure along with displays of maritime craft and local history, Dr. Harris has hopes of making the Bermuda Maritime Museum one of the finest in the hemisphere.

"I think in time our collections will reflect the significant role Bermuda has played in development and discovery and trade, particularly between the United Kingdom, the United States, Canada, and the West Indies. We obviously want to develop the research side, there is not that much active historical research being done in Bermuda. We think that the Maritime Museum can be the logical body to expand the scope of that work in maritime history and archaeology," Dr. Harris said.

"It's my view that shipwrecks are ancient monuments," Dr. Harris declared, putting forth the argument for the preservation of shipwreck finds. "And while it is no longer permissible for an individual to walk into a cornfield and tear up ancient monuments, I think the same should be true of shipwrecks. I look at these things as ancient remains, and I believe they should he protected," he added. Donations from local divers and artifacts purchased by the Bermuda government from treasure divers have provided the Maritime Museum with a beautiful collection.

The keep yard and buildings inside the old fortress that house the exhibits are unique, a most beautiful setting for the Maritime Museum. The old fort's keep yard is separated from the bay by a narrow passage through the walls. "It was originally a cave through the rocks," Jane Downing explained. "They caved in the top in building the fort, left the passage to row the ammunition and stores through the wall into the lagoon from the supply ships anchored in the bay," she added.

It is in this anchorage that local divers like Robert Limes spend time hunting up old bottles and other artifacts dropped, tossed, or lost overboard when the supply vessels unloaded. "It's a regular trash dive," Limes said, "but you find a lot of old handblown glass bottles, some rare dark glass as well," he smiled. The Maritime Museum's fine collection of handblown glass bottles is displayed in one of the powder magazines. The collection was donated to the museum by diver Peter Bromby, who collected them from the relatively shallow areas around Bermuda. The Royal Dockyard with its historic stone buildings, including a commissioner's house overlooking the ramparts of this sea fortress, commands a view of the ocean and sky.

The museum has a number of restored vessels on display and preserves the tradition of shipbuilding using skilled shipwrights to restore some of the wooden vessels found, in some cases, abandoned and forgotten in the back bays around the islands. The museum collection includes the pilot cutter *St. George,* Bermuda dinghies, small sailboats, and a fitted-out whaling boat, a remnant of the trade that dwindled and then disappeared altogether in the islands.

Responding to the allure shipwrecks hold for divers, Limes developed a dive charter business to explore many of the ships that wrecked on Bermuda's southwestern reefs. A cannon and anchor from the *Virginia Merchant* are on the beach in a cove where Limes moored his charter boat. The ship, owned by the Virginia Company, was en route from Plymouth to Jamestown, Virginia, when it wrecked on 26 March 1551. The *Virginia Merchant's* cargo was salvaged by locals. The reefs are now protected by the famous Gibbs Hill Lighthouse, a century-old structure that dominates the West End from its promontory on a hill overlooking the Atlantic to the south and Little Sound to the north. It was Gibbs Hill light that was eulogized in Doug Little's poem.

The reefs in the West End are littered with shipwrecks. "I wouldn't go around hitting the projectiles with a hammer," Robert Limes told his divers, who responded with laughter, as they prepared to descend on the wreck of the *Pollockshields.* The ship was out of Cardiff, Wales, with ammunition for Bermuda's garrison when it struck the reef in September 1915 during a hurricane and was torn apart on the shoal.

Although the divers joked about the live ammunition still aboard, the cordite explosive, contained in sealed brass canisters, is still very much alive. Projectiles strewn about the wreckage still look ominous even after years of immersion in the sea. Taking a small stick of cordite recovered from the wreck and lighting it with a match, Robert Limes demonstrated how the explosive still burned with a bright flame. "They mixed these small lengths in with the thicker sticks of cordite, which provided the explosion to fire the shell," Limes said, watching the intense flame.

Underwater, the wreckage of the *Pollockshields* is strewn over several hundred feet. Locals salvaged much of the ship's cargo and bravely carried a longboat down the cliffs and across the beach to help bring the crew off. The ship's iron propeller shaft looms out of the wreckage from the after section. The ship is torn apart amidships, its boiler and machinery strewn about. Aft, the rudder assembly frames divers as they explore the wreck. In the mid-ships sections, remnants of wooden ammunition crates are buried in the sand that covers the hull. Fanning away the debris, Limes exposed cordite canisters, ammunition, and war material that never found its way to the garrison arsenal.

Not far from the *Pollockshields,* another English steamer, the *Minnie Breslauer,* wrecked on the reef on its maiden voyage. The *Breslauer* was carrying a cargo of lead ingots, cork, and dried fruit when it struck on 1 January 1873, en route to New York from Europe. The lead was salvaged by local divers, and much of the wreck is broken up and scattered over a large area of the reef comprising acres of coral, with steel plate and girders so grown over that they appear to be part of the reef itself. The ship's aft section with part of the superstructure remains, with the boiler works and machinery amidships offering home to corals and fish. "There's nothing to find on this wreck," Limes smiled. "The lead was salvaged, the cork floated away, and the fish ate the dried fruit."

Almost directly in front of Sinky Bay lies the wreck of a Civil War paddle steamer. The Confederate ship, *Mari Celeste,* was one of the blockade runners that ran between Bermuda and the southern ports with cargoes of food and munitions to supply Rebel forces. The *Mari Celeste* had rifles and corned beef aboard when it struck the reef on 26 September 1864. The wreck lies in about sixty feet of water, its huge side wheel looms out of the sand, the spokes resembling some immense underwater Ferris wheel. The ship's pistons and engine gears are about all that remain after the wooden superstructure rotted away. Pieces of the wreckage lie in the sand away from the main boiler area, and the iron is overgrown with coral where it is wedged into the sand. The *Mari Celeste* was extensively salvaged by Bermudians after it sank, but the machinery and immense paddle wheel make the wreck an enduring example of one of the many swift Confederate blockade runners that plied Bermuda waters carrying supplies to the South.

Bermuda became a center for Confederate intelligence activity and a trans-shipping point for supplies and war material. A Confederate museum is maintained by the Bermuda National Trust, which has preserved old photographs and mementos from the days when chivalrous captains ventured out to run the Union blockade and the Confederate navy attacked northern shipping.

The swift but small Confederate blockade runners were not large enough to be practical for transatlantic shipping, thus goods were brought to Bermuda on conventional English cargo vessels, off-loaded, and transferred to the smaller steam-powered ships. As Abraham Lincoln's blockade was tightening its grip, blockade runners came under increasing fire from U.S. Navy ships. The port of Wilmington, North Carolina, was a favorite landing site, protected by Confederate gunners at Fort Fisher until its capture in 1865, just about forcing an end to the lucrative blockade running trade.

The seat of Confederate government activity on Bermuda was in the old Globe Hotel, which had been taken over by Maj. Norman Walker, the Confederate agent. The hotel, located in the port area of St. George's, was acquired by the Bermuda Trust and now houses the Confederate Museum.

The islands saw a great deal of intrigue and excitement during the Civil War. In 1864, Confederate navy Capt. John Brame hijacked the *Roanoke*. He came to Bermuda for coal, but held offshore fearing treachery if he put into port, insisting on having the coal brought out in lighters. Bad weather prevented the offshore coaling of Brame's prize, so he finally decided to run the *Roanoke* onto the reef and set it on fire.

The use of Bermuda by southern agents and the blockade-running traffic very nearly brought Britain into the war. U.S. Navy Adm. Charles Wilkes seized two Rebel agents who were passengers aboard an English vessel. Admiral Wilkes then steamed into the harbor of St. George's with his warships to enforce a blockade of Bermuda. Britain protested, sentiment ran strong against the provocation by Admiral Wilkes who refused to let the blockade-runners sail out of port, dubbing Bermuda a "nest of secessionists."

Ships for the Confederacy were built in England. The raider CSS *Alabama* was only designated Hull 290 when it was under construction in England. Raiding Union merchant shipping, the *Alabama*, along with the Confederate navy ships the

Florida, Sumter, Georgia, Tallahassee, and *Shenandoah,* gravely disrupted the U.S. merchant fleet. Insurance rates on U.S. bottoms soared as the Confederate raiders attacked Union shipping. The CSS *Florida,* like the *Alabama,* was built in England. The *Florida* was commissioned at sea in the Bahamas on 8 August 1862. The *Florida,* a 191-foot-long vessel, was a fast propeller-driven ship, assisted by sails, and able to make twelve knots. When the *Florida* first visited St. George's in July 1863, the ship was saluted by the British forts. (This was the only time that the British saluted the Confederate flag; the fort commander was reprimanded as a result.) A silver cup and hinges from the *Florida* were given to a Bermuda resident by Capt. John Newland during the time the *Florida* was in port. The souvenirs are now on display in the Confederate Museum on the island.

The *Florida* went on to have an exciting history. On 7 October 1864, while anchored in Bahia, Brazil, a neutral port, the *Florida* was attacked by the U.S. Navy ship *Wachusett* and captured while most of the *Florida's* crew was enjoying Brazilian shore leave. The event prompted Brazil to lodge a formal protest. The *Florida* was ordered returned to Brazil. In a mysterious event, which the U.S. Navy dubbed a collision, the CSS *Florida* sank while en route back to Brazil on 29 November 1864.

A list of the *Florida's* prizes along with documentary photographs are recorded by archivists at the Bermuda Confederate Museum. Not only did the *Florida* capture thirty-seven prize ships for the South, but two of its prizes, the *Tacony* and the *Clarence,* earned fame on their own merit once pressed into Confederate navy service, capturing between them twenty-three Union ships.

One of the more famous Confederate blockade runners, the *Presto,* is displayed as a scale model in the old Globe Hotel Museum. Typical of the blockade-running ships, the *Presto* was 210-feet long, with a twenty-three-foot beam. The *Presto* drew nine and a half feet of water and could attain a maximum speed of 21.5 knots. Museum records reveal that the *Presto* ran the Union blockade successfully twenty-four times. On 21 February 1864, the *Presto* was engaged by the USS *Connecticut* and chased for fifteen hours. The *Presto* finally ran onto the wreck of another ship off Charleston and was destroyed by Union naval gunfire.

An interesting aside to the history of Confederate naval activity in Bermuda involved the secret shipment of the official Seal of the Confederacy. In February

1861 the Confederate Provisional Congress passed a resolution approving an official seal that would "consist of a device representing an equestrian portrait of Washington . . . surrounded with a wreath composed of principal agricultural products of the Confederacy," along with the motto "Deo Vindice." With God as Defender.

A London sculptor was commissioned to execute the seal. When the seal and a large seal press were ready, an officer in the Confederate intelligence service, Lt. R. T. Chapman, was instructed to take the seal from England to Richmond. Lieutenant Chapman embarked with his secret cargo on an English ship and traveled first to Halifax, then to Bermuda. In Bermuda, plans were made for his final journey across the remaining stretch of Atlantic Ocean to Wilmington, North Carolina.

Fearing capture, Chapman decided to leave the large seal press on Bermuda in the charge of Confederate Consul Bourne. He embarked on a blockade runner for the final leg of his sea journey with only the seal itself in his pocket. Chapman figured he could easily throw the seal overboard if his capture was imminent. The seal made it to Richmond and was put in the hands of Confederate Secretary of State Benjamin. Without the seal press, however, the seal was useless and never used. The seal press remained in Consul Bourne's custody until his death in 1867, when it was sold at auction. Eventually relatives of the buyer loaned the press to the Confederate Museum. Visitors to the island can strike their own impression of the seal of the Confederacy on the replica displayed there.

Bermudians tell many amusing tales about their ancestral reputation as an island of salvors and wreckers. "You know there's an old church on the island. You can still see it, sitting out on Church Bay," diver Ernie Decouto said. "Word of a shipwreck filtered through the congregation one Sunday. The preacher looked up when he heard the church emptying out, asking what was going on. When he found out a ship had wrecked, the minister called out to his parishioners, 'Let me give the blessing, then we'll all have an equal start.'" Decouto smiled, recounting a bit of folklore that was probably true of an era when most everybody on Bermuda eked out a living as a wrecker, even the clergy.

"The Bermudians would light fires to lure ships onto the reefs. When a ship wrecked they'd go out. That's how most people earned their living," a Bermuda diver related. Tales of the history of Bermudian involvement in salvage and wrecking began with the *Warwick,* which sank off Castle Point in 1619. "It was the ship that brought the first governor here. Within a year after that shipwreck they were salvaging it. So we're looking at salvaging shipwrecks in the Bermuda area fairly early." Billy McCallan said. "The *San Antonio,* a treasure ship, shipwrecked in the west of Bermuda. Governor Butler had crews that he would select from the various parishes that would take a barge out there and they would stay on the wreck site for a week at a time or longer. Of course their methods were pretty primitive by today's standards, but they did recover a tremendous amount of stuff that was never recorded. So as far as wrecking is concerned, it goes back quite a way," McCallan continued, describing an island tradition.

"It's a rare breed of people who dive for shipwrecks. They really sacrifice an awful lot in reference to expense, time, and effort, and very rarely can you say one gets reimbursed. It's what one selects in life to do. . . . It's an education. It is history, and if we were to lose this rare breed of people or take their interest away from them, who is going to find these things? In my opinion if you were to take this globally, I don't think we've really scratched the surface discovering shipwrecks. Those that are known wrecks today, who were they found by? They have been found by individuals such as myself. We would have a stagnation really if we were stopped. You might say a great deal of history would come to a standstill, wouldn't it?" McCallan theorized, touching on an issue widely debated that has some academics opting for laws that would prevent shipwreck finders and divers from exploiting their finds.

"There's areas where the ship can sit and become completely buried and preserved, and there are areas where the ship can sit on top of coral and, particularly in tropical waters, be completely eaten away by teredo worms. There are fragments and so forth that can be traced, and one gets a general idea this is, or could be, such and such a ship. This in itself is a fulfillment of the past in history," McCallan said, explaining some of the issues involved in treasure diving.

The early Bermudians voiced no such refinements. "On St. David's the Bermudians spotted a ship imperiled by the rocks. A local man went out and told the captain, 'I can guide you in.' The captain let him, and he drove the ship right up on the rocks. His mates came around and they raided him for their salvage," Decouto laughed, going back to describe the early wrecking history as he, McCallan, and Robert Limes sat around over coffee, sharing tales of shipwrecks and diving.

"If you go to the archives, you will find pages and pages of protests. In one they had taken a lot of the gold and silver off the wreck, lodging the crew ashore, charging them exorbitant prices for rent and food, really making Bermudians look bad. That of course was not us, the old timers," Decouto laughed, describing the well-deserved reputation early wreckers on the island enjoyed. "It was like a candy ship coming in," McCallan elaborated. "Maybe once every three months a candy ship arrived. Wrecking was a means of survival," he added.

Early shipwrecked sailors on Bermuda found wild hogs on the island, but how the hogs got there is still a mystery. "There's a lot of assumption that they must have come from a Spanish ship that got wrecked here. Although we know that hogs can swim, it is highly unlikely. I just can't believe that two hogs, a male and a female, came just from a ship going by. It becomes a challenge—that's where the work begins. One could spend years to find out the origins and identity of shipwrecks, even the history of the island itself," McCallan said, alluding to some of the puzzles yet to he solved by the analysis of Bermuda's shipwreck history.

The law that applies to shipwrecks in Bermuda is a unique one, a statute that divers like Harry Cox find equitable. The issue of who has a right to a shipwreck of historical or archaeological importance is hotly debated. Some, disdaining the work of divers, argue that treasure hunters will destroy valuable artifacts in their quest for the gold and silver. Divers like Billy McCallan, Harry Cox, and Teddy Tucker, who have been responsible for discovering many of the shipwrecks, disagree.

The care and concern the divers have for the history of their island makes it clear that they approach their work in a professional manner. What they discover is declared to the Receiver of Wrecks, and detailed records are kept of their finds. In Bermuda, what is found then belongs to the Crown. The Bermuda Government has first option to buy the artifacts recovered at a price agreed upon by the diver and a government representative.

In discussing the issue, which has been debated worldwide, Harry Cox said, "The law says when you dive, what you find belongs to government. Here in Bermuda it says the title resides in the Crown. The Crown may not deprive the finder unless they pay to him a price mutually agreed between them. If government does not exercise its option, then title reverts absolutely to the finder. Now this seems to me eminently to be the fair basis of a relationship between government and its citizens. If the divers feel they are going to get a fair shake from government, government will get a fair shake from divers. The other possibility of confrontation and of mutual hostility will result in all the evils which we have more than ample example of, and I refer to the black markets which beset the classical world of Greece and Rome. Here in Bermuda we have a law which, I would like to think, while it may not be perfect, will give guidance to those who are entrusted with legislation in this area . . . let there be a partnership rather than a position of mutual antagonism, because government will lose, without a question."

The artifacts these divers have recovered parallels human history in the New World. Even in little, seemingly insignificant things, as described by Robert Limes, the artifacts reflect historical events that can he pieced together by these shipwreck detectives. "Take the clay smoking pipes," Limes said. "The bowl got smaller when the price of tobacco went up," he continued. McCallan showed off some of the pipes found on various wreck sites. "In the 1800s the style of pipes changed. Pipes were built for particular people. When the clay pipe was small, the price of tobacco was high," McCallan said, reflecting on how the artifacts recovered from shipwrecks mirrored social and economic trends of the day. "I found a pipe with two fellows on it with a ball between them. It shows that rugby was not only a sport, but popular in those days," Limes added.

The wreck of *L'Herminie* lies off the western ledge. The French frigate mounted sixty cannons, some of which are still visible in the clear water surrounding the wreck. All of *L'Herminie's* 495 officers and crew were saved when the ship sank on 3 December 1838, en route from Havana to Brest. Divers fanning the wreckage still find French navy buttons and glassware. One of Bermuda's favorite wrecks for souvenirs is the *Constellation*. A 187-foot American four-masted schooner, the *Constellation* wrecked on 31 July 1943, off the West End near a spot in the reef called the Western Blue Cut. Bound for Venezuela from New York, the *Constellation* had a cargo of morphine ampoules which provided the plot for a popular novel. Red glassware carried as cargo is found in abundance in the wreckage, along with assorted wares. The spot where the *Constellation* went down is littered with the remains of other ships which struck in about the same place.

While the lure of gold may attract divers to the quiet of sunken ships, many important historic finds are far more valuable. Describing an early navigational instrument that he found on top of a breaker near the site of an unidentified wreck, Harry Cox said, "The octant we discovered is a comparatively rare example of Halley's Octant and only used and carried for a very short period of the 1740s. It was very soon superseded by the sextant. This example is of interest because it is all bronze."

Some of the cannons Cox and his divers have recovered may prove or disprove theories of early discovery in the Americas. "The cannon I described that antedates Columbus is a brass gun and thought to have been cast in the Moss works of Copenhagen. It has a raised and embellished fleur-de-lis on the touchhole," Cox emphasized again. An early example of a musquetoon made by John Skinner of London in 1651 was recovered by Cox from the wreckage of the merchant vessel *True Love* out of Bristol, which wrecked in the early 1700s.

Besides the Books of Protest, all Bermuda records were kept at Williamsburg, Virginia (Bermuda was part of the Virginia Company); some of these records were destroyed in a fire in 1775. The first newspaper was published in Bermuda in 1778, and Harry Cox points out a humorous commentary about what wasn't covered in newspaper accounts: "I asked my father why there were no articles in the newspaper about these ships wrecking. You would find just a little note. He said a shipwreck was not news. Everyone knew about it. When a shipwreck hit a reef, in an hour everyone knew about it." Cox could well have added that not only did all of the early Bermuda settlers know about a ship wrecking, but more often than not they were down on the beach or out in their boats taking what they could get.

The lure of Bermuda's shipwrecks have inspired seekers of fortune as well as poets and authors. It is a cemetery of sunken ships, a witness to tragedy at sea, at the same time an ocean spring of coral beauty.

O, I have suffered
    With those that I saw suffer! a brave vessel
(Who had no doubt some noble creature in her)
    Dashed all to pieces! O, the cry did knock
Against my very heart! Poor souls, they perished!

William Shakespeare wrote in *The Tempest,* a play inspired by the wrecking of the *Sea Venture* upon Bermuda's reefs in 1609. An event in maritime history unique only in that it resulted in the colonization of these magical islands, the haunt of ghostly ships and shipwrecked sailors who perished in the sea.

CHAPTER TEN
Ships Lost to Time

For as long as ships have put to sea, the sea has swallowed them up. Terms like "the cruel sea" imply that there is a vengeance in nature, a spirit that must not be invaded by human-made leviathans for to do so would result in tragedy. The perils of seafaring have fostered superstitious beliefs among mariners who stand in harm's way in violent waters, in calm far-off places at the corners of the world, or in crowded harbors called home port. The register of shipping is also a chronicle of lost ships, vessels that have disappeared, crews that have perished, ships lost to time.

VILLEFRANCHE

"It is not that I am taking up the relay from Jules Verne. He died in 1905, and I was born in 1905. I do not assign any value to that, other than it is amusing. But we are here, my dear friend, in the house of Jules Verne. That is a remarkable coincidence," Philippe Tailliez said in the garden of Nautilus, the family estate of Jules Verne in Toulon on France's Côte d'Azur.

Tailliez is the father of modern diving, the man who introduced Jacques Cousteau to the sport when the young naval officer was assigned to his ship after he had been seriously injured in an automobile accident. Tailliez remained active in maritime affairs. After his retirement from the French navy, he served as president of GRAN, a French marine archaeology research organization. From an office in Jules Verne's former family residence, Tailliez wrote, planned, and discussed excavation of a shipwreck at Villefranche, near Nice. The shipwreck was dated to within twenty years of the famous nao, the *Santa Maria* of Christopher Columbus.

The shipwreck in the bay of Villefranche was discovered by a diver in April 1979. His find was made on a day when a local man decided to dive without his video camera, which he had been using to search the bay systematically and record the images for study. On the day of discovery, the diver left his camera on the surface because of bad visibility, coming upon the wreck entirely by chance in sixty feet of water. Law required the diver to declare his discovery, and GRAN obtained French government authorization to make a sonar search of the area and begin excavation of the shipwreck. Several campaigns by divers under the auspices of GRAN carefully excavated the wreck. Preliminary operations removed nine to ten feet of sand and silt that covered the main wreckage. Many artifacts were recovered, including coins, ceramics, armaments, cannons, and ship's accouterments. Portions of the vessel's wooden hull, buried under the sand, were also in a good state of preservation.

"I dove the Villefranche wreck. We saw it was a ship from the time of François the First. In my opinion it resembles a nao and probably dates in construction to twenty years or so of the building of Columbus's ship, the *Santa Maria*," Tailliez said.

Very little is known about naval operations in the Villefranche area during the first quarter of the sixteenth century, a period during the reigns of Henry VIII of England (1491–1547) and François I of France (1494–1547). According to Tailliez, the ship was apparently sunk in combat because it lies in the middle of the anchorage and human remains have been found in the wreckage. At the time in question, Italy was at war. Villefranche was part of the Duchy of Savoy, and French ships put into port there. Adm. Andrea Doria of Genoa and other foreign commanders were often put in charge of French flotillas during this period.

Tailliez and the divers feel that the shipwreck holds the key to several mysteries. It was sunk when the winds of war brought Ottoman marauders onto the coast to attack shipping. The wreck itself measures about ninety feet long by twenty-four to twenty-eight feet wide. The keel to hull height was about twenty-five feet. Among the coins found on the wreck site were several trade pieces struck in Nuremberg dated to between 1480 and 1500. A silver coin struck with the effigy of Galeas Marie Sforza has been dated between 1474 and 1476, and a Louis XII silver coin found by the divers was struck between 1500 and 1510.

Various ceramic wares and armaments recovered from the shipwreck site have confirmed the approximate date of the ship as a vessel made in the early 1500s. The wooden structures under the sand are on a forty-five-degree tilt, which allow researchers to study the ship from the keel up to about twenty-six feet in height along the flank. The wooden vestiges show that the vessel was constructed with two or three decks, thus the cross section remaining underwater should enable a definitive study of the ship once excavation is completed. A carrack akin to the ships that brought Columbus to the New World is a rare and important find, and the divers are using care to cover over the wooden wreckage with sand after each season's dig to prevent deterioration before a complete excavation can be made.

LEPANTO

One of the world's foremost experts on ships of the Columbus era is Dr. Jose Martinez-Hidalgo. Dr. Martinez-Hildago served as director of the Maritime Museum of Barcelona. "For me, the discovery of America is the most important subject in maritime history," Dr. Martinez-Hidalgo said. He described his more than ten years of study of the era which resulted in his publication of books and papers on the subject and his supervision of the construction of several replicas of Columbus's ships.

Enthusiasm for the Villefranche project was evident as Dr. Martinez-Hidalgo and Philippe Tailliez discussed the project. "Besides new models for the museum, we built a full-size replica of the *Santa Maria* in 1964 for the New York World's Fair. We built another one in 1968 for the government of Venice. The replica in the port, also, follows the original plans of Christopher Columbus's flagship," Dr. Martinez-Hidalgo said, gesturing in the direction of the wharf.

Across the street from Barcelona's Maritime Museum building at Puerta de la Paz, a full-size replica of the *Santa Maria* is moored. Part of the museum's displays, the replica is about eighty-five feet in overall length with a sixty-foot keel and a beam of twenty-five feet. The little 120-ton vessel, whose mast rises almost ninety-five feet into the air, attests to early feats of seamanship and bold daring as mariners charted unknown waters in search of discovery.

In the same period, the Royal Shipyards, which have been converted to house the Maritime Museum, saw unprecedented growth in shipbuilding. The history of the shipyards at Barcelona provides a fascinating insight into the history of this maritime city. "The construction of Reales Atarazanas, these Royal Shipyards, was begun in the thirteenth century, enlarged until the eighteenth. The first document we have found which tells about the building is dated 1243. We believe that the shipyards were constructed a little earlier because King Jaime I built a big navy for the conquest of Mallorca in 1229. We believe that this fleet could have been built here," Laureano Carbonell, curator of Barcelona's Maritime Museum said, describing the context and activity of the yards. While water no longer comes up into the shipyard buildings as it once did, the configuration of the port has changed, and the slipway remains preserved as it was when the original mooring rings were used to tie ships fast.

"Galleys were built in this shipyard," the curator explained. "They were the ships of war used in the Mediterranean Sea. Huge fleets for successions of Spanish kings were built in the shipyards; archive records reflect shipbuilding activity here until 1748," he added, gesturing to one of the most unusual maritime displays in the world, an actual and exact replica of the *Galley Real*. The replica was constructed in the museum shipyard building exactly as it was when the original was built there, commissioned to serve as the flagship of Don Juan of Austria, commander in chief of the Holy League's fleet during the Battle of Lepanto in 1571.

A galley was powered by slaves, chained to their oars. The *Real,* while sporting sails, was equipped with thirty oars per side, each manned by four rowers. The length of each oar measured thirty-seven feet. Recalling anecdotes of the plight of the slaves, a museum historian illustrated how the rowers were chained to their places, living at their stations and having to attend to all of their physical needs chained to the benches where they sat. A soldier would man one position at each oar, able to take battle stations to board or repel boarders when required.

A Maritime Museum spokesman recalled the physical condition of the galleys in battle, the stink of the men, the slave masters compelled to throw buckets of water over the slaves to wash away the mess. Ship's officers who walked the deck above the slaves would smear perfume on themselves to surmount the foul odor emanating from the ship.

The reconstruction of the flagship followed two important plans. "The construction consisted of the ship itself, its hull, structure, and design and the decoration. The galley was built according to all the plans and designs in the shipyards of Europe. Accuracy in decoration was made possible using a book written by a man who directed the original work on Don Juan's flagship," the curator said.

The decoration for the *Real* was conceived by Juan de Mal-Larga, born in Seville in 1527, the son of a distinguished painter Diego Mal-Larga. His original handwritten manuscript, reprinted in 1876, provided Dr. Martinez-Hidalgo with accurate information about the conceptions and purpose for the intricate and ornate decor of the galley. Inlaid wood panels and mythological figures and scenes all had meaning to Mal-Larga and were faithfully reproduced for the museum's replica.

"The idea of Mal-Larga was to use decoration of people of mythological antiquity." The idea behind the artwork was that it could help Don Juan of Austria in the event he was stymied in coming to a decision in battle. "He could look at the representations and they would help him find a solution to the problem," a museum historian said, describing how Mal-Larga's book not only showed his plans and designs but also explained the mythology.

Don Juan's galley with a rakish prow sported a gilded wood effigy of Neptune holding a trident. The galley measured some two hundred feet in overall length with a deck that stretched about eighty-five feet. This one ship provides visible proportion in understanding the scope of the Battle of Lepanto, which took place on 7 October 1571, when the Armada of the Holy League met the Islamic flotilla off Scropha Point at the extreme northern entrance to the Gulf of Patras, between the Ionian Sea and the Gulf of Corinth.

The collective forces of the Holy League consisted of some 207 galleys, six smaller fighting ships called galeazas, and numerous support vessels mounting a total of 1,815 cannons. The armada was manned by 84,420 men, divided, according to Dr. Martinez-Hidalgo's research, into 28,000 soldiers, 12,920 marines and 43,500 rowers. Twenty thousand of the solders were Spanish. The Ottoman naval forces consisted of 208 galleys, sixty-six smaller ships with 25,000 soldiers, and 2,500 special troops armed with guns and bows.

The Armada of the Holy League engaged the Islamic ships at eleven o'clock in the morning. In battle, Don Juan of Austria's ships engaged those of the Ali Pacha. Adm. Juan Andrea Doria engaged Uluch Ali. Mehemet Siroco confronted the ships of Agostino Barbarigo. The fierce battle raged throughout the day culminating at four PM.

When the smoke of battle cleared, the Christian losses amounted to fifteen galleys sunk, with 7,650 dead and 7,784 wounded. The Turkish forces tallied fifteen galleys sunk, 190 captured, 30,000 dead, and 8,000 taken prisoner. Don Juan of Austria, half-brother of the Spanish King Philip II, claimed a decisive victory over the Turks in what was to be the end of an era wherein galleys manned by enslaved oarsmen chained to their benches were the main ships of war. The Battle of Lepanto is considered by historians to be the culmination of the Holy Wars, one of the most important naval engagements of all time, although not necessarily decisive in the war.

Dr. Martinez-Hidalgo has considered the ghost fleets whose remains lie off the coast of Cephalonia in the Gulf of Patras. When asked whether any expedition had been mounted to search for the shipwrecks of Lepanto, Dr. Martinez-Hidalgo replied that he could not recall any, voicing the hope that someday the vessels of this historic fleet would be discovered and studied.

COLUMBUS'S SHIPS

The voyages of discovery of the famed Genoese navigator Christopher Columbus have evoked tales of adventure and daring since he persuaded Queen Isabella of Spain to finance his voyage across new and uncharted reaches of the ocean in three small ships. Sailing from Palos on 3 August 1492, Columbus and his crews sighted land on 12 October 1492. They discovered the Bahamas island of San Salvador and then Cuba and Haiti, which was named Hispaniola.

The three small ships of Columbus's flotilla are recalled by every school child, but what became of the *Niña, Pinta,* and *Santa Maria* has been shrouded in mystery or lost with the passage of time. Two American explorers, one a veteran diver the other a pioneer filmmaker and skilled aviator, set about on an adventure to locate the flagship of Columbus's little fleet, which wrecked in the New World on Christmas Eve, 1492, during the first voyage of discovery.

One of the explorers, Fred Dixon, lost his life on the expedition in a bizarre diving accident before they were able to prove with absolute certainty that the shipwreck they had found off the coast of old Hispaniola was indeed the sunken remains of the *Santa Maria*. The evidence recovered by the divers strongly suggests that they indeed found the last resting place of the fabled ship. The narrative of their discovery is told by Herman Kitchen, who made a film of the exploits and described their adventure.

"The search began with reprints of Columbus's journals. The original journals had been lost, and I don't believe ever located, though there had been some transcripts made of them by some early Spanish historians as well as Columbus's son. Fred Dixon had examined those and had studied other historical accounts around the middle sixties. He decided that we would go down and make a preliminary search of the area," Kitchen related. The two explorers set off in Kitchen's airplane intending to overfly the offshore reefs and take pictures, using infrared photography so that anomalies would show up on the film. "We went to Cap Haitien and got permission from the Haitian government. There we met a pilot who flew for a missionary located in the interior of Haiti. He said, 'I've been flying over those reefs for quite a number of years, and I keep seeing something out there which looks very strange on the reef.' Outside Cap Haitien there are a number of reefs; there is one long one about fourteen to seventeen miles long and it is about seven miles out of the town of Cap Haitien. We flew over that reef, and, sure enough, looking down on it from seven, eight hundred feet, on this bare narrow sand reef was a boat-shaped obstacle, and we could see immediately that it was a small coral growth, closer to the inside of the sandy reef than to the outside. We knew that coral had to start on a hard surface, not from sand, therefore something had to be there for the coral to start on and that could easily be an old boat or ship," Kitchen said, going on to describe the account of the loss of the *Santa Maria*.

"Columbus's journal, or the transcripts of it, indicated that the three ships, the *Niña, Pinta,* and *Santa Maria,* were sailing together on Christmas Eve. Sometime before midnight, one ship following the other, Columbus being in the *Santa Maria,* third in line, turned in. The captain of the ship turned in, and the helmsman turned in. The ship was turned over to a young fourteen-year-old boy trainee who was told to follow the light on the stern of the ship ahead. That he did, but he apparently did not compensate for the onshore current. The other two ships went outside of the long reef whereas the *Santa Maria* went through a break in the reef apparently, and the boy kept guiding on the light of the ship ahead of him. They ran gently aground on a sandy bottom. The other two ships, not knowing that they were in trouble, went on out of sight. The tide went out, and the *Santa Maria* turned on its stern. The water level dropped, and the ship broached.

"The weight of it just broke it open. They couldn't salvage it. They couldn't get it to float again. Columbus decided to take the crew ashore, about seven miles in, at the confluence of a small stream that ran into this bay. Over the next few days, they unloaded everything they could get off the ship and put it ashore. One of the other ships came back and helped with this. They could not take all of the crew with them, so they left thirty-nine sailors behind at the fort they had built. They took most of the superstructure off the ship to use in building the fort. There wasn't much left of the ship except the keel, the ribs, and the ballast. Columbus returned nine months later and could still see part of the ship on the reef.

"All thirty-nine of the seamen had been killed by the local Indians. That's what we were looking for. Some years earlier, Ed Link had been down there looking for the *Santa Maria.* He did come up with an anchor that's still in Port au Prince, that they call Columbus's anchor, but it has never been proven," Herman Kitchen said. He described the events leading up to the loss of the *Santa Maria,* confirmed by their research. The reef Dixon and Kitchen overflew was just out of the water at mean low tide, about 10- to 12-feet high above the sand, measuring 120 by about 40 feet. Convinced they were on the right track, the divers acquired a work boat and began their salvage in earnest.

"We figured that following Columbus's account of [the *Santa Maria*] having gone aground and then turned about on the stern with the tide change that this particular end was where the rudder was. We started there. After a lot of hammering, getting our air lift going, and putting a flange on the boat to deflect the propeller wash, we moored our boat right over the site, and we began working the area. We worked away there for months and months and finally we came up with wood, apparently from the rudder, some lead sheathing, a brass bolt which was threaded—we could never compromise that. It was questioned whether they had threaded bolts at that time or not. We were not sure that that was something new for history or whether something else had come along and just happened to have lost a rudder on that reef. Not far from there we came across a couple of other wrecks, which we didn't go into very deeply. The material was sent to the museum at the University of Pennsylvania and was carbon-dated to plus or minus a hundred years of the right period. "Then we came up with some pieces of pottery which were sent to the university. The pottery was dated plus or minus forty years of Columbus's era. Pictures of this material were sent to experts who were convinced it was Columbus's ship. That's where it should have been, although other researchers, namely Link, read the logs differently.

"The bearings taken by Columbus at the time were at Point Picilet, which became the site of Pauline's Palace and the fortifications that General Leclerc, who was Napoleon's brother-in-law and Pauline's husband, built during French armed occupation of Haiti. So there were pretty good points from Point Picilet. Then there had been the fort left behind by Columbus. There had been change there over the years and a great deal of silting over. The original mouth of the river had been lost. So we never located the site of Columbus's fort to use as a bearing for the location of the shipwreck," Kitchen related.

"Finally the thing that really ended it all, Fred was injured on the dive site. He died three weeks later in Cap Haitien. Fred had jumped into the water to put a line onto a buoy and apparently he had fractured a septum in his sinus somewhere, and he just hemorrhaged to death," Kitchen said. This expedition most probably discovered the last resting place for Columbus's flagship. The artifacts recovered by the expedition have been placed in the Flagler Museum in West Palm Beach, Florida.

Columbus made four separate voyages of discovery to the New World. After the discovery of San Salvador, Cuba, and Haiti in 1492, Columbus returned to Spain in March 1493. By September of that year he had refitted and set out on his second voyage of discovery. This voyage lasted three years as he and his expedition explored the islands of Guadeloupe, Jamaica, Puerto Rico, and the south-west coastal areas of Cuba.

In 1498, during his third voyage, Columbus discovered Central America and the Orinoco River, venturing as far as what is now Caracas, Venezuela. From 1502 to 1504, Columbus's fourth and last voyage to the New World took the explorers to Central America again, where they ventured along the coast of modern-day Honduras. But the navigator who discovered a continent died in disfavor. King Ferdinand rejected Columbus's intercession on behalf of the indigenous Indian peoples against the Spanish domination that resulted in centuries of slavery and exploitation.

What became of Columbus's original ships and the ships used in his subsequent exploration of the New World is a question posed by generations of adventurers. While Fred Dixon and Herman Kitchen may have determined the whereabouts of the grounded *Santa Maria,* the eventual fate of the other two ships was less clear.

Sailing with Columbus on that first voyage were two brothers, Martín and Vicente Pinzón. Sons of a famed Spanish shipbuilding family, the Pinzóns raised capital for the voyage and captained the other ships: Martín the *Pinta,* and Vicente Yanez the *Niña.* Vicente returned to the New World in 1499, sailing in four caravels. His expedition discovered the Amazon River, found pearls in the Margarita Islands, and discovered animal and plant life unknown in the Old World.

The Pinzóns were seeking gold and slaves. They sailed to Haiti then set off for islands known as the Seven Islands of Baneque. Rumors of a person called the Hombre d'Oro, a golden man, and Indians who could be captured as slaves were said to await them. They anchored in a place called by the explorers Ojos de Babulaca. On 6 July 1500, a violent hurricane struck, sinking two of the Pinzóns' ships with their crews and badly damaging another.

Researchers at the Archivo de las Indias in Seville discovered a reference to the *Pinta* in a tax report dated 1499, when the Pinzóns' ships were being out-fitted in Spain prior to their voyage. Thus, it appeared that the *Pinta,* originally fitted out by the Pinzóns for Columbus's first voyage, was used by them in 1499. The three other ships of the Pinzóns' 1499 fleet were the *Frailia, Gordo,* and *Capitana.* The *Pinta* and the *Frailia* were sunk in the bay at the Seven Islands of the Baneque. The *Gordo* and the *Capitana* were repaired and returned to Spain. Of the three original ships then, the *Santa Maria* went aground during the first voyage and was dismantled to construct a fort on the island of Haiti; the *Pinta* was lost during a subsequent voyage by Vicente Pinzón; and references to the *Niña* appear throughout Columbus's voyages into the 1500s, probably meeting its end rotting in a Spanish port.

Salvage divers operating a company known as Caribbean Ventures claimed that the Seven Islands of the Baneque were actually the Turks and Caicos Islands north of Haiti and the Dominican Republic. Mounting a major expedition, Olin Frick and John Gasque discovered skeletal remains of a ship they believed to be the *Pinta* in the area thought to be the Bajos de Babulaca, indicated in the Pinzóns' expedition's logs. The salvors discovered an iron Lombard cannon and a breech-loading cannon made in the latter part of the 1400s. They found lead cannon balls, ballast stones of irregular shape—said to come from southwestern Spain where Pinzón assembled and fitted out his fleet, and anchors dated to around the right period.

Frick and Gasque discovered another shipwreck that they claimed was the wreckage of the *Frailia*. The *Frailia,* smaller than the *Pinta,* sank nearby during the storm in 1500. Thus expeditions of modern-day salvage divers may have indeed answered the questions remaining about Columbus's original ships.

The romance and adventure of potentially finding the vestiges of a ship that brought discovery of the New World has attracted divers for generations. Bob Marx, known for his Atlantic crossing in a replica of the *Niña* in 1962, undertook a project to discover the whereabouts of ships from Columbus's last voyage of discovery in April 1502.

Columbus was looking for a passage across Central America, hoping to find a route to the Orient. His ill-fated fleet of four small ships cruised the coast, taking water as the wooden ships deteriorated. Saltwater teredo worms ate into the wooden hulls, causing Columbus to eventually abandon two vessels. His two remaining ships, the *Capitana* and the *Santiago,* were filling with water.

Marx found Ferdinand Columbus's journal, which described their plight as the two ships tried to make Santo Domingo for repairs. "Day and night we never ceased working three pumps in each ship, and if any broke down, we had to supply its place by bailing with kettles while it was being patched up," Ferdinand wrote of their ordeal.

Finally the two ships reached Santa Gloria on the island of Jamaica on 25 June 1503. The sinking ships were run up on the sand. Columbus purchased a canoe from the Indians and sent word to Santo Domingo, but aid was delayed and Columbus and his 116 crewmen spent more than a year on the northern coast of Jamaica in a place known now as St. Anne's Bay.

Columbus and his men were finally taken off Jamaica on 29 June 1504. They returned to Spain, where the navigator died. King Ferdinand ordered a settlement at the site of Columbus's last bivouac on Jamaica, and in 1509 Spanish settlers founded New Seville near the vestiges of Columbus's rotting ships. The settlement was later moved. Using information gathered by author Samuel Morison and Jamaican Charles Cotter, who traced the location of New Seville and located the area of Columbus's wrecked ships, Marx began to dive on the site, probing under several feet of accumulated sand and silt.

Taking core samples, Marx found glass, ceramics, wood, and other items that enabled confirmation of the period of the wreck. Once verified, the divers began a full-scale excavation of the site, recovering timbers, ceramics, and many important artifacts from the last ships of Columbus's voyages of discovery in the New World.

LORD NELSON IN EGYPT

He was probably the first Egyptian to dive on the shipwrecks of Aboukir. A rather extraordinary person whose courage and inventiveness have earned him not only the highest military and civilian decorations of his own country, but the French Legion of Honor and the American Legion of Merit presented by Pres. Harry S. Truman. His invention of a sun compass enabled Allied armored vehicles to navigate in the desert and his reinvention of the papyrus papermaking process has earned him the plaudits of the world. A diver who founded the Sea Scouts at Aboukir, Dr. Hassan Ragab described his recovery of artifacts from Napoleon's sunken fleet.

"We found a bomb made of cast iron with a wooden peg. They would fill it with black powder. To use it they would take out the plug and put in a fuse.

When it arrives it explodes," Dr. Ragab said, describing one of the more curious artifacts he discovered while exploring the sunken ships. "One of those bombs, I took out that peg, and I discovered the powder was still usable. I was able to burn it," Dr. Ragab continued.

"We found three anchors from Napoleon's fleet. Each weighs five tons, we were able to get some cannonballs and some brass objects," he recounted. "It has been said that the French payroll in gold was aboard those ships," Dr. Ragab smiled, a bright glint came into his eyes. "I don't believe it. They also say that Napoleon, on his way to Egypt, stopped and ordered the silver gates taken off the Knights Cathedral in Malta," Dr. Ragab added. He described the lure that brought many explorers to the Bay of Aboukir on Egypt's Mediterranean coast near Alexandria.

One of the first divers to explore the sunken French fleet in Aboukir Bay was a Greek diver. "In 1956, he was looking for copper plates that covered the body of the battleships. He didn't find any. There are major parts of the ships still lying there. It is not very deep. The depth does not exceed four to five fathoms. The French, to be safe, tried to keep to the shallow side of the bay. Most of the sailors were on leave when Lord Horatio Nelson surprised them on 1 August 1798," Dr. Ragab said, describing the famous Battle of Aboukir.

"The day is long then. They started the battle in the afternoon, finished at night. Apart from the small ones, the French had thirteen ships. Nine sank, but four were able to escape," Dr. Ragab explained. He put a foot on one of the five-ton anchors he recovered. The anchor is part of a permanent display of the Pharaoh Village Ragab has constructed on an island in the Nile at Cairo. The last time this senior Egyptian inventor and diving pioneer explored the French shipwrecks on the bottom of Aboukir Bay was in 1958. Since then a number of projects have surfaced, all dedicated to eventually recovering the legendary lost payroll in gold and the silver gates of Malta.

The story of Nelson in Egypt and his surprise attack on the French fleet began in early 1798, when he was ordered to the Mediterranean to gather intelligence about Napoleon's fleet being readied in Toulon. A naval force to be reckoned with was being fitted out by the French. It consisted of thirteen large ships of the line, supported by two hundred transport vessels with armed escorts of seven frigates each mounting forty guns and twenty-four other small warships.

The British knew Napoleon was preparing to attack Malta and then Egypt. With a small squadron of eight ships, Nelson sailed out of Gibraltar to encounter the French ships. Ten days later a fierce gale dismasted Nelson's flagship the *Vanguard*. Separated from his escort of frigates, Nelson's flagship was taken in tow by one of the squadron and put into Sardinia for repairs. Luckily the disabled and poorly matched English squadron narrowly missed the French naval force that was sailing out of Toulon. Outgunned, the British would have lost the battle had they encountered the French fleet at sea.

Repaired and reinforced by ships dispatched from the Earl of St. Vincent's contingent on station near Cadiz, Nelson hoped to surprise the French who had successfully attacked Malta. But the French were a step ahead of him; thus Nelson set off for Egypt where intelligence reported the French fleet was heading. Without his fast frigates, lost in the tempest, and unaware of Napoleon's position, Nelson could not obtain accurate data on the whereabouts of the French fleet. When Nelson reached Alexandria on 28 June 1798, the French were not to be seen.

The city was making preparations for a presumed French attack after reports of the sacking of Malta reached the city. The ambitious Lord Nelson dreamed of capturing the French fleet with Napoleon on board. The French fleet, however, was not to be found, so Nelson returned to Sicily where he wrote, "I cannot to this moment learn, beyond vague conjecture, where the French fleet are gone to; and having gone a round of 600 leagues at this season of the year, with an expedition incredible, here I am, as ignorant of the situation of the enemy as I was twenty-seven days ago."

After reprovisioning his ships, Nelson sailed out of Syracuse on 25 July 1798, coming back into Alexandria on 1 August. The French fleet had been unable to use Alexandria's port, which was in poor condition. The French moored in Aboukir Bay, the first ship nearly on the shoal in the northwest, the rest in a semicircle. The fleet was anchored much as Dr. Ragab described it, keeping to shallow water so as not to be flanked. The force under French Adm. Francois Paul Brueys mounted 1,196 guns, with 11,230 men aboard the thirteen ships of the line and four frigates. The English squadron had thirteen 74-gun ships of the line and one smaller ship with a total complement of 8,068 men. The vessels mounted 1,012 cannons. The French had mounted guns on shore, where they had set up defenses.

In the fierce naval battle that ensued, the English sailed inside the anchored French fleet. Nelson's flagship the *Vanguard* was heavily damaged forward. Nelson was wounded in the head causing profuse bleeding. Admiral Brueys's flagship, the *Orient*, had cannons on three decks, sporting massive firepower from 120 guns. The *Orient* inflicted heavy damage on the English ship *Bellerophon*. As the battle continued to wage into the night, the wounded Nelson refused medical care until it was his turn at the surgeon. He believed, because of the profuse blood loss, that he was dying. The wound tore a chunk of flesh out of Nelson's forehead but did not touch the skull.

As the Battle of Aboukir Bay raged, the *Orient* caught fire. The French admiral courageously remained at his post although wounded three times, finally receiving a fatal shot. His flagship was consumed in flames. A rendering explosion destroyed the *Orient* at ten o'clock and the ship, carrying the plunder of Malta worth an estimated six hundred thousand pounds, burned into the night. By morning only two French ships of the line and their two frigates were spared by the fighting. They hoisted sail and escaped to sea.

With his characteristic flourish, Lord Nelson proclaimed, "Victory is not a name strong enough for such a scene." The scene when the smoke cleared left two French ships of the line and one frigate burned, nine captured, and one destroyed by its own crew. French losses amounted to 5,225; the British had 895 casualties.

Bodies of the dead floated up on the beaches. Some of the dead were buried on Bekier Island in an effort to prevent disease from spreading, a task that continued for years as bodies of the dead floated up as did pieces of the broken ships. From the mainmast of the *Orient,* found floating in the debris, one of Nelson's officers had carpenters fashion a coffin for Lord Nelson when he would finally take leave of the world, a fate Nelson escaped in the battle.

Nelson ordered the French ships that could be sailed across to Gibraltar with prize crews repaired for the voyage. Three French ships were burned, since refitting was practically impossible in time because of their damage. The burned hulks and shattered wreckage from this famous battle littered the shallow sand bottom, poked at occasionally by divers like Hassan Ragab.

From his office near the Champs Elysée, a French explorer, fresh from his quest for the legendary Dutch East India Company shipwrecks in Mauritius, began laying plans to make a film about the Aboukir wrecks. Jacques Dumas thought to interest the last living heir of Napoleon Bonaparte in the project, sure that Prince Napoleon's participation would attract public attention. Prince Napoleon readily agreed to participate with Dumas in the exploration of the Aboukir shipwrecks, and with French navy divers and a French navy vessel, the explorers set out for Aboukir Bay. Soundings and surveys revealed wreckage in the sand. Dumas and his divers discovered numerous artifacts from the sunken French ships and continued their surveys.

With the cooperation of Egyptian authorities, the divers planned to excavate the underwater sites, hoping perhaps to discover the famed silver gates of Malta, pillaged by the French in 1798. Sadly, Jacques Dumas died suddenly of a heart attack before his project could be realized. Eventually the relay was picked up and the sunken French fleet explored, with excavated remnants including military accouterments, the *Orient*'s rudder support bearing the ship's former name before the French Revolution—*Le Dauphin Royal*, and coins and navigational instruments. Philippe Tailliez led a major underwater archaeological project to explore Napoleon's scientific ship, *Le Patriote*, which grounded and sank in the approach to Alexandria Harbor. Cannons were raised along with equipment and supplies to create hydrogen gas to fuel Napoleon's aerial reconnaissance balloons.

Napoleon was trapped in Egypt for a year by the British blockade. Lord Nelson took a year to recover from his wound. When Napoleon finally escaped on a fast ship and returned to France, history was to be made in a different way. The Battle of Aboukir left England masters of the sea and ocean realm.

THE SHIPS AROUND CAPE HORN

It is a graveyard of old ships. Obscure islands at the crossroads where ships wore around Cape Horn, the Falklands provided bare subsistence for the few British inhabitants whisked into the focus of world attention in the conflict over the islands, possession. Indeed prior to the armed conflict in 1982 over the Falklands between Britain and Argentina, the islands were almost unheard of— a region of windswept knolls that overlook bays and harbors where ships put in, crippled by storms that raged where the two oceans met, and where winter is a perennial foe.

A handful of maritime historians visited the Falkland Islands to survey the wooden hulks, beached or abandoned ships whose day had come and gone but whose place in the history of the world was as glorious as the Pony Express. They were the clipper ships, the refinement of master shipbuilders' invention and craftsmanship. Remnants of a bygone era which pitted men against the sea in the twilight of sail.

In the South Atlantic some four hundred miles from the Argentine coast, the Falklands, lying northeast of Cape Horn, received the battered voyagers limping back from their battles with the storm-tossed cape. It is a region of moors, without trees, a somber land of cottages and sheep farmers, a port of call for vessels supporting Antarctic research stations.

Port Stanley, the capital of the Falklands, is the largest settlement with approximately twelve hundred inhabitants. From the old wooden hulks, islanders have extracted firewood and material for building supplies, storage warehouses, and breakwaters. Wrecks like the *Snow Squall,* once the pride of builders at Cape Elizabeth, Maine, when launched in 1851, or the *Jhelum* built in Liverpool in 1849, or the packet *Charles Cooper* built in Black Rock, Connecticut, in 1856 are the last surviving vestiges of an age when ships and men were worked to their limits to earn their captains' reputation and owners' dividends in the Gold Rush days of booming California.

The ships that could not be repaired at Stanley after their unsuccessful bout with the raging waters of the cape were condemned by marine inspectors for the insurance companies and sold to the islanders. Even today some of the old hulks are used for storage. One of the ships, used in Port Stanley as a warehouse, is the *Charles Cooper.* Purchased in 1968 for the South Street Seaport Museum in New York, the hulk remained in the Falklands awaiting funding to make it seaworthy so that it could be brought to New York.

When the *Charles Cooper* was first studied by the South Street Seaport's ship historian Norman Brouwer and the late marine archaeologist Peter Throckmorton they found that the transom was decorated with magnificent hand-carved leaves and rope work surrounding circular American shields of stars and stripes. The experts found that the *Charles Cooper* had a huge area cut out of its side when the ship was connected to the land by a pier and used as a warehouse, although much of the wooden hull and inner structures remain in remarkable condition.

The ship, which measures 165 feet in length with a 35-foot beam, was poetically described when visited by Peter Throckmorton as it lay in the mud in Stanley harbor. The *Charles Cooper,* he said: "is the most complicated piece of American nineteenth-century craftsmanship in wood that exists today—and probably the most beautiful. . . . Here then is the elegant eye of the Yankee craftsman, laying out traditional shapes in a traditional way. The beauty of the shapes created by the broad-axe and the adze, spile, and batten and a dozen kinds of planes pulls at the heart of the onlooker." Remarkably preserved knees and bulkheads between the decks of the *Cooper* demonstrated workmanship designed for the comfort of its passengers, immigrants on their way to the United States. The *Cooper* was preserved by the shedding built over it when the hull was used for storage until about 1970, having been condemned in Port Stanley in 1866.

Of great interest to the maritime researchers as they surveyed and chronicled abandoned sailing ships in the Falklands was the wooden square-rigged *Vicar of Bray.* Built in the Hardy shipyard in England in 1841, the *Vicar of Bray* was originally designed as an ore carrier. The *Vicar* carried coal from England around the Horn to the western coast of South America, where a return cargo of copper ore was taken aboard. But, in particular, the *Vicar*'s place in the annals of the California Gold Rush, having called on San Francisco in November 1849, preserves the ship's place in the history of American westward development, one of the last vestiges of some 777 ships that were part of the golden era.

The San Francisco Maritime Museum will eventually preserve the *Vicar,* restored to its full beauty. The ship was lengthened from its original 97 feet when built in 1841 to 120 feet in 1859. The 24-foot-wide *Vicar,* when surveyed at the shipyards in 1841 by Lloyds of London, was found to be a ship "as good as can be made—built of the best materials with excellent workmanship." When Peter Throckmorton inspected the *Vicar*—some 125 years after the original survey—he was equally impressed with the old wooden wind ship. The sturdy African hardwoods and English oak weathered the harsh ocean as well as years in the mud at Goose Green, where the hulk has been used as a breakwater. A cargo of coal is still in its holds. With fallen-in decks and a bow with missing timber, the *Vicar* bravely cants in the bay, an intact hull sheathed in copper awaiting appreciation and imbued with the romance and imagination of San Franciscans willing to restore and preserve it.

As the bombs and missiles were fired and dropped by Argentine jets during the battle for the Falkland Islands and modern British war ships exploded and burned, marine historians pondered the fate of these older gallant ships. Their mission had been not war but commerce, braving heavy seas and the fierce storms at the Tierra del Fuego to negotiate around the tip of South America. They remain silent witnesses to fierce land and sea battles, and, fortunately, reports from the Falklands indicate that these grand old ships were left undamaged by the war.

Grounded and disabled in an attempt to round the cape, the U.S. clipper ship *Snow Squall* was towed into Port Stanley where the insurance inspector condemned and sold the ship in 1864. The hulk was beached in the shallows and served with other hulks as a pier support for the Falkland Islands Company ships. When a permanent pier was built on the site, pilings were driven through the *Snow Squall*'s hull. Parts of the wooden wreckage were torn out until the ship was reduced to a skeletal wreck, ingloriously abandoned under the pier head, with a bow riddled by gaping holes where the sea has taken its toll and its stern buried in sand and silt, mute testimony to the grand era of American shipbuilding.

The Falklands are littered with shipwrecks. Some grounded, some sunk, left in most cases where they were condemned or put to use as storage containers by the islanders. The water is cold and visibility limited and the rather remote area has left the ships to the devices of nature. Dead eyes are cast up on shore; wooden breastworks remain intact; in some cases the paneling from staterooms and masters' cabins is still in place. Ships called downeasters from Maine, such as the square-rigged *St. Mary,* launched in Phippsburg in 1890, lie partly submerged, partly scattered upon remote beaches where it wrecked. The *St. Mary* limped toward Port Stanley after a collision on its maiden voyage to San Francisco from New York.

For the lover of old sailing ships, the solemn reaches of the Falklands are strewn with them. The voyage around Cape Horn from Tierra del Fuego around the rocks through Drake's Passage was identified with hardship for mariners sailing before the mast, marked throughout history by the skeletons of both men and ships.

From the Juan Fernández islands, early mariners navigated with the Southern Cross and the nebulae of Magellan's clouds, avoiding floating ice and treacherous rocks. They labored watch upon watch in freezing cold, icy rigging aloft, taking in and letting out sail as the ship, a hundred and more feet below, was stirred and contorted by the waves. Richard Henry Dana the author of *Two Years before the Mast,* described the voyage around Cape Horn in 1836.

"Tumble up here, men. Tumble up. Don't stop for your clothes—before we're upon it. . . ." Slowly, with the stiff ropes and iced rigging, we swung the yards round, everything coming hard and with a creaking and rending sound, like pulling up a plank which had been frozen into the ice. The ship wore round fairly . . . directly under our larboard quarter, a large ice island, peering out of the mist, and reaching high above our tops; while astern, and on either side of the island, large tracts of field ice were dimly seen, heaving and rolling in the sea. We were now safe, and standing to the northward; but, in a few minutes more, had it not been for the sharp lookout of the watch, we should have been fairly upon the ice, and left our ship's old bones adrift in the Southern Ocean.

Perhaps preserving some of the remains in this cemetery of old ships will rekindle the lore of the maritime trade that was at its height in the days of clipper ships rounding Cape Horn. It was a time of courage, daring, and enterprise, and of cruelty when men in the fo'c'sle were at the mercy of greedy captains and owners, living daily on the verge of calamity and adversity in ships worked to the limits of endurance. Ships later wrecked and condemned in the Falklands, graveyard of the South Atlantic.

THE GALLANT LADIES OF NEW YORK HARBOR

Looking back, the archaeologists' tracks left a trail in the gray-black ooze as they slogged ankle deep in muck across the marshland and then the mud flats to the listing wooden derelicts, cast up in the shallows, abandoned to time and the crabs. A once-grand, old wind ship—its name long forgotten—lies with its bows turned up in the mud, timbers broken and rotting, waiting for an inglorious end by fire or the wrecker's crane, representing the last remnants of

American shipbuilding existing in the world. Hulks of old ships lay abandoned in New York Harbor, almost completely forgotten until the U.S. Army Corps of Engineers and the State of New Jersey began a project to reclaim the marshland on Liberty Island for the establishment of a state recreational park.

Known internationally for his discovery of early Greek shipwrecks in the Mediterranean and a long association with the Department of Archaeology at the University of Pennsylvania, the late archaeologist Peter Throckmorton was first lured to take on the job of assessing, documenting, and then, if possible, preserving selected ships of historical importance by Dr. Simeon Hook, chief of the environmental and economics branch of the New York District Army Corps of Engineers.

"It's like the old group from Penn getting together again," Throckmorton said, glowing with excitement, as he pointed to two watermelon barges that he had come to Liberty Island to save from imminent destruction by the wrecking crane working nearby. "Believe me, there's a lot to do." Throckmorton walked back and forth on the shaky dock, which vibrated from the blows of a thirty-ton crane nearby. "There are thousands of wrecks around New York Harbor," he continued, between discussions with Dr. Hook and Ira Abrams, the principal archaeologist Throckmorton had brought on board to help supervise the project. "It's a bootstraps thing. We have the chance to set it up on the Mediterranean model. What we have to do is get an amateur volunteer project organized," Throckmorton said almost to himself as he poked around some bits of timber, eyes ever alert for a piece from an old sailing ship.

There were scores of derelict ships of every make, shape, and description: tugs, barges, schooners, lighters, steamers, and canal boats. Some sunk, others just rotting in the mud, awaiting discovery by this team of eager archaeologists and volunteers recruited through sponsoring organizations such as the South Street Seaport Museum and the National Maritime Historical Society in Brooklyn. The Army Corps of Engineers only became involved when the State of New Jersey took advantage of a cost-sharing program operated by the federal government. Work was begun under a grant that provided two-thirds of the funds with the state putting up the rest for projects aimed at removing the sources of debris in New York Harbor. Approximately $1 million was allocated to clean up the first zone outlined by the Liberty State Park Project.

"As part of our environmental impact study, we do a cultural resources evaluation to determine the impact the project has on any cultural or historical resources. This is where the work involving the ships comes in," explained Dr. Hook with a quiet enthusiasm for the project that couldn't help but spill over into his professional and businesslike approach. "We commissioned an overall study—an archaeological study of the area. Every vessel and derelict was marked and located. The original contractor used side-scan sonar to do a readout of the wrecks underwater. They made eleven recommendations. Ninety-eight percent of the vessels were of no value. They were mostly post–World War II barges. Throckmorton was recommended to evaluate and identify the ships," Hook smiled.

South Street Seaport representatives, Throckmorton, and Norman Brouwer, the museum's ship historian, came out and they went through the eleven wreck recommendations, narrowing them to three derelict vessels above water and four underwater. Throckmorton made eleven dives and found no value or significance to the underwater wrecks. They were pilings mostly. According to Dr. Hook: "Two of the wrecks are watermelon barges. Not because they carried watermelons, but because they are shaped like them. They were made in the 1850s and reconstructed from another type of vessel. The third ship we think is the *Newton,* a World War I wooden cargo steamer used as a navy training vessel. The *Newton* is the last of its class of vessel existing."

An interesting event helped to mold the fate of the Liberty Island marshlands. In 1916, an explosion shook the entire area with the sabotage of a munitions depot by a German spy. The Black Tom explosion and subsequent fire destroyed many vessels along the shore and created the marshland that is now part of the state park area. Other events in New York Harbor added intrigue to the archaeology project. Maritime records revealed the fact that the *Hussar,* a twenty-eight-gun British frigate laden with $4 million in silver, the payroll for British troops in the New World fighting the rebellious Americans, sank off Hell Gate on 23 November 1780. Parts of the *Hussar* were found in 1811, but no one has yet succeeded in locating its treasure. If indeed there was treasure on the ship, its shallow-water grave would have been plundered by intrepid salvagers.

Rumors abounded that the renewed interest in New York's nautical past would spur new ventures to turn up gold doubloons, guilders, and Spanish gold. Gold or not, there is plenty of history beneath the fouled, murky waters in the countless bays, lagoons and back canals off New York Harbor.

"It's not really that bad diving in here," Peter Throckmorton said. "You can't see, so you can't see. It's enough to feel around," he added. Regardless, the dank waters of the harbor had their unsettling effect. When Throckmorton was preparing a publicity stunt staged for newspaper reporters scheduled to photograph him jumping into the harbor off a boat in a symbolic first dive over the submerged wrecks, he wanted everything to go just right.

In order not to disappoint the reporters, Throckmorton carefully positioned artifacts underwater beforehand. This way he knew he could bring something up for the cameras. The trouble was, the water was so dark and murky when he dove down in full view of a dozen press photographers that Throckmorton couldn't even find what he had bunked out. As a consequence, and not to be upstaged, he located some other junk and hoisted it aboard the reporters' launch anyway. Despite the poor visibility in the contaminated water, a beneficial side effect of pollution in the harbor is the fact that the teredo worm, a small mollusk that bores into the submerged wood of a ship's planking, cannot live there. As a consequence, hulls underwater are preserved almost intact.

There is ample evidence of America's history among the reeds and shallows of many of the canals and bays. When Lake Erie was connected with the Hudson waterway by a forty-foot wide, four-foot deep ditch, 362 miles long, on 25 October 1825, the city burgeoned with midwestern grain that plunged in price from $100 to $6 a ton. Travel time from New York to Buffalo on the Erie Canal took only ten days instead of six weeks.

The seaport and harbor of New York boomed as ample stocks of cheap grain surged across the ocean to European ports. As part of this great commerce, canal boats were built, more than four thousand of them, of all shapes and sizes.

These barges tied up at Coenties Slip at the end of South Street in Manhattan. The canal trade flourished in the mid- and latter 1800s. Eventually steam-powered boats and the New York Central Railroad took over from the wooden canal barges. Most were burned to salvage their iron fittings or abandoned to rot, such as the 1923-built *Gertrude L. Dailey,* lying peacefully in the reeds at Tottenville, Staten Island. Other canal boats lie about New York and New Jersey shores—forgotten hulks, abandoned pieces of American history.

It was only about a hundred years ago that harbor records reveal that the Port of New York was visited by 1,074 steamers, 1,451 schooners, 1,076 brigs, 2,234 barks, and 389 full-rigged ships on the fourth of July. New York's bustling maritime trade is not surprising to those who witness the annual gala parade of old wind ships under sail up the Hudson to commemorate Independence Day. Images of the glory of New York Harbor in the days of sailing ships.

"I don't know who would remember her now. All the old-timers I knew that would know when she was left there are dead," a man recalled, sitting in a car with his son. "They used to break out the planking and sell it back to the barge builders. The wood under the water is in good shape, but you guys know that," the man continued, eating his lunch. He was working on the Liberty Park project with his son, remembering the waterfront and the boatbuilding activities on the Jersey flats. "About that ship, gee, I don't know who could tell you," the elderly resident added as Throckmorton and Ira Abrams left, trying to positively identify the old wooden ship once believed to be the *Newton,* the last remaining example of 560 wooden steamers made in America.

John Russo, a man who ran a small boat club on a rickety dock nailed together with flotsam on the borders of the Liberty State Park project, laughed when Abrams asked him about the *Newton.* "Now I'm old, but I ain't that old to tell you when she was brought in here. I been running this boat club here twenty years and she was here before that. She was here in 1933–34. I know that. We used to go crabbing over there then; that's how I know she was there," Russo said, pointing to the old wooden steamer. "There used to be a work house on her and decking you could walk around. We could go out there and throw our nets in," he reflected, pointing to the after section of the hulk, now only a shell of staves. "The kids set fires on there. Once we put one out, but one night she burned. When we came by in the morning it was all burned. It was beautiful here up until five years ago. I used to chase the kids off her, but what could you do," Russo continued reflectively, to the visitors from the Corps of Engineers and Throckmorton's group.

"He said she was there in 1933 or 1934. It can't be the *Newton* if that's true. The Navy says they abandoned the *Newton* in 1946," Ira Abrams grumbled to Throckmorton as they left the site. "Well we'll see. Anyway, what we've got here is a fine old wooden steamer," Throckmorton said, his enthusiasm for the old ship undaunted.

While the New York Harbor Archaeology Project barely scratched the surface in locating and documenting all of the derelict ships abandoned around the great city's waterways, it did demonstrate that many important cultural and historical relics lie forgotten almost everywhere, awaiting discovery by curious shipwreck historians in every port city in the world.

THE MONITOR

The hearing room grew quiet and conversations stopped as the experts who had just testified about shipwrecks gathered around the television monitor set up in the stately formal room that served the U.S. Congress, the Merchant Marine, and the Fisheries and Oceanography committees. As the television picture flickered then cleared, the viewers saw the distinct shape of the ship's iron turret.

The shipwreck was that of the *Monitor,* most famous of the Civil War ironclads, the subject of a major survey effort by agencies of the State of North Carolina, the U.S. government, and private enterprise. From the screen, viewers watched divers lock out of their submarine and swim along the flank of the overturned wreck. They examined the condition of the ship, its overturned hull and turret partially buried in the sand.

The *Monitor* signaled the advent of a new era in naval warfare. Iron-hulled warships had come of age and the impregnability of thick armor plating proved its worth in battle. The *Monitor* was built in response to the Confederate ironclad *Merrimack,* which was originally a wooden sailing ship captured by Confederate forces just nine days after the firing on Fort Sumter and the capture of Norfolk's Gosport Navy Yard by Virginia State Militia forces.

Retreating Union troops burned or sank most of the American navy ships at Gosport, including the USS *Merrimack,* which burned until the flames reached the waterline. The Confederates decided to rebuild the *Merrimack,* keeping the original hull but adding a superstructure of two-inch-thick armor plate, a submerged ramming device, and six 9-inch cannons. On the ways in July 1861, the newly commissioned Confederate ironclad was renamed the CSS *Virginia*.

To meet the threat of the Confederate ironclad, Union Secretary of the Navy Gideon Welles obtained Congressional approval to build ironclads. Engineer John Ericsson conceived a ship that presented no freeboard as a target, only a revolutionary revolving turret plated with eight-inch-thick iron.

The new ship was dubbed a cheese box. Its odd shape made it ungainly in the water with hardly more than eighteen inches of freeboard, decks awash, and all engine spaces, quarters, and storage areas below the waterline. Protruding like a large, round cheese box was the iron turret. The 120-ton turret measured twenty-one feet in diameter and stood nine feet high off the deck. It was mounted with two 11-inch cannons that could be brought to bear by rotating the turret.

Only a hundred days after commissioning, on 25 February 1862, the *Monitor* was launched from the naval yards in Brooklyn, New York. The ship was immediately towed south to intervene off Hampton Roads, Virginia, where the Confederate ironclad was wreaking havoc with Union wooden warships. The *Monitor* could steam on its own, but the design made it ungainly in the water as it laboriously slashed through the waves without any freeboard.

The *Merrimack,* renamed the *Virginia,* had sunk the Union frigates *Cumberland* and *Congress* and badly damaged the *Minnesota.* In the wake of the destruction, the *Monitor* steamed into the fracas on 9 March 1862. For four hours, the ironclads fired at each other, their cannons being brought to bear at point-blank range. The battle of the ironclads was a standoff, although the course of history in naval warfare was changed forever. Sustaining very little damage, save the dents from cannonballs, the ironclads withdrew. The CSS *Virginia* was eventually destroyed by its own crew. The *Monitor,* while being towed to South Carolina to join in the assault on Charleston's defenses, sank in a storm off Cape Hatteras, with sixteen of the crew aboard on 31 December 1862.

Scientists from Duke University researched the sinking of the *Monitor* and began acoustic and magnetometer surveys of the area where the Union ironclad was reported to have gone down. In 1974 the Duke University scientists located and photographed the wreckage of the *Monitor,* and in September 1974 the National Oceanic and Atmospheric Administration of the U.S. Department of Commerce declared the site of the wreckage the United States' first marine sanctuary, protecting the historic shipwreck.

Researchers and NOAA scientists located the *Monitor* about sixteen miles south of Cape Hatteras, North Carolina. The shipwreck lay upside down at a depth of 210 feet in an area where sea conditions are often difficult. The ironclad rested on the sandy bottom, its round turret propping up the hulk, partially wedged in the sand.

Divers probed the wreckage and ventured away from the site in the direction where they assumed the *Monitor's* large anchor would be found. As the cameras recorded the feat, a lift bag was attached to the massive four-pronged thirteen-hundred-pound anchor and slowly it began to rise off the bottom.

In addition to the iron anchor, which is being conserved so that it can be stabilized to prevent deterioration after being submerged in seawater for so long, a brass signal lantern with a red lens was recovered. The lantern is thought by the researchers to be the distress signal last hoisted by the stricken ship.

Submarines and support vessels from the Harbor Branch Foundation in Ft. Pierce, Florida, were used to survey and dive on the *Monitor,* enabling scientists to piece together photographic mosaics and films of the wreckage. The researchers believe that the ironclad cannot be brought up intact and have plans to raise the turret for preservation and display, an interesting aside to the naval history of the war between the states.

GRAVEYARD OF THE ATLANTIC

The Carolina coast is littered with shipwrecks. At a place called Nags Head, history is not far exaggerated by legendary tales of wreckers riding along the beach with a lantern strung around a horse's neck, luring unsuspecting ships to wreck and then setting upon them for the plunder. Coves and creeks, rivers, and sheltered pirates' lairs provide the Atlantic coast with a share of adventurous wrecking tales.

The skeletons of ships litter the bottom, left by the ravages of war, storms, or the deliberate acts of wreckers. Marine archaeologists like Lee Spence have devoted many years to locating, diving on, and chronicling these shipwrecks, which he calculates number more than three thousand in South Carolina alone.

Dr. Spence is probably best known for his discovery of the most powerful Confederate cruiser, the *Georgiana,* sunk in shallow water near the Isle of Palms, South Carolina, on 19 March 1863. According to Dr. Spence, the *Georgiana* was built in Glasgow for the Confederate navy. The construction of the ship, although veiled in secrecy, was discovered by the American consul who unsuccessfully attempted to have the ship seized.

Sailing with its guns stowed in the hold and a cargo including half a million dollars in gold bullion at today's value, medicine, ten thousand Enfield rifles, three hundred cases of bourbon whiskey, and china wares, the *Georgiana* made it safely to Nassau in the Bahamas. Spies alerted the Union's South Atlantic Blockading Squadron, and when the *Georgiana* sailed into the channel past the Isle of Palms, north of Charleston, the Union ship *America* fired on it, joined by the Federal steamer *Wissahicken.* Ten-inch-diameter cannonballs tore through the sides of the *Georgiana* from the *Wissahicken* as other Union gunboats closed for the attack. The iron-hulled, two-hundred-foot-long brig-rigged steamship *Georgiana* was hit by an exploding shell from the *Wissahicken.* Using a ruse of surrender, Capt. A. B. Davidson waited until Union naval boarding parties approached his ship, then opened his throttles and sped away in the darkness. Fearing capture and hopelessly overpowered by the waiting Union blockading ships, the captain ran the *Georgiana* aground, scuttling his ship in fourteen feet of water and escaping to shore with the crew. As the *Georgiana* was sinking, the Union forces boarded it. Unable to prevent the scuttling, the sailors set the ship on fire.

The area where the *Georgiana* was scuttled is replete with other shipwrecks. Dr. Spence found records of three other ships, the *Norseman,* the *Mary Bowers,* and the *Constance Decimer,* all blockade runners that struck the submerged hulk of the *Georgiana* and sank. The *Mary Bowers* was found sitting right on top of the *Georgiana* and the *Constance Decimer* farther offshore where its captain ran it. Thinking he had only touched bottom, the *Constance's* captain was unaware that his collision with the *Georgiana* had torn a gaping hole in the side of his ship.

Years of work and arduous research paid off for Lee Spence who has recovered original 2.9-inch Blakely rifled cannons stowed in the *Georgiand's* cargo holds, as well as Dutch earthenware china, clay beer bottles, glass shirt buttons and pins, cannonballs, arms and assorted medicine bottles—some still corked with their contents inside. A treasure trove of history from the romantic era of blockade runners of the Civil War.

Research compiled by Dr. Spence revealed that Spanish ships wrecked off South Carolina's coast as early as 1520, when the nao captained by Don Lucas Vasquez de Ayllon was lost, followed five years later by the loss of another of Vasquez Ayllon's caravels. These wrecks supposedly carried treasure from the New World. They have not been salvaged, although claims have surfaced that Spanish shipwrecks have been secretly discovered but their whereabouts carefully concealed.

While the myriad of shipwrecks off the Carolinas are legend, one ship, the *Anamaboo,* a slaver, recalls a darker side of American history. Heading for Rhode Island with a cargo of African slaves chained and shackled belowdecks, the *Anamaboo* was caught in a violent Atlantic storm off St. Helena, South Carolina, in 1757. The *Anamaboo* struck a bar, was thrown on its side, and sank. All but a few crew members perished with the ship, the human cargo chained together and shackled to the ship belowdecks.

The *Anamaboo,* like the thousands of other phantoms of the fathoms has been lost to time. These wrecks represent history captured in an instant of tragedy, present-day mysteries being unraveled by marine archaeologists like Dr. Lee Spence and other Carolina divers.

THE HENRIETTA MARIE

Another South Carolina marine archaeologist, David Moore, worked closely with the late Henry M. Taylor III and Mel Fisher to conserve finds made off the Marquesa Keys of the slaver *Henrietta Marie.*

Located by Fisher during his more than eleven year search for the treasure galleons *Atocha* and *Santa Margarita,* the slave ship was ignored by Fisher and his divers in their quest for the more famous treasure galleons. Veteran diver Henry Taylor contracted with Fisher to work the *Henrietta Marie* shipwreck site located in the New Ground north of The Quicksands, where Mel Fisher discovered the *Atocha.*

Taylor, the late Duke Long, and Jim Amoroso recovered the ship's bronze bell, bearing the vessel's name and the date, 1699. With this provenance, the divers were able to search historical records, revealing that the ship was registered in London as a 120-ton square-sterned vessel mounting eight guns, assumed to be the same ship although the record lists the vessel as the *Henrietta Maria*. Divers recovered many shackles and ivory tusks. It was clear from the macabre cargo of irons, that the ship was engaged in the slave trade.

Research done by Neptune Explorations, Taylor's salvage company, revealed that there had been a monopoly on the English slave trade through the Royal African Company, which claimed exclusive domain to supply slaves to the British colonies. Others broke into the monopoly in 1698, and these separate traders, as they were called, paid a ten percent tax on their outward-bound cargoes to defray the Royal African Company's provision of soldiers and forts in West Africa. While this gruesome trade flourished, slaves were chained to the planking belowdecks, as close together as possible to assure the maximum profit for each voyage.

Records indicate that a ship logged as the *Henrietta Maria* was cleared from the port of Jamaica. It is probable that the *Henrietta Marie* was en route to Jamaica or Virginia with its human cargo when the ship wrecked. Cruelly chained as they were, it is unlikely that any of the slaver's human cargo ever survived wrecking.

While Taylor and his divers unraveled the mystery of the slave ship, the artifacts were carefully inventoried and preserved in the conservation laboratories of Treasure Salvors in Key West. Pewter bottles and pewter bowls recovered from the wreck site bear hallmarks or touchmarks that Henry Taylor was able to trace to the original craftsman. "On the bottle it was John Ames of London. He was authorized to strike a touch in November 11th of 1700, so that is the latest date of any artifact we've had on the *Henrietta Marie,* so we know she had to sink after 1700," Taylor said.

Timbers and wooden structures recovered from the shipwreck have been identified by David Moore as the uppermost section of the ship's wooden bilge pump. The wooden pump measures about nine inches square with a five-inch-diameter hole and three-inch discharge port, strapped around at the top. The pump is a rare find that has been preserved by the salvors. One pewter tankard was encrusted with small trade beads. Other trade beads were discovered by the divers around the wreck site, proof of the ship's nefarious slave trafficking.

Describing his find, Henry Taylor said, "The first indication we had of the name of the ship was when we recovered the bell, and upon clearing away the encrustation around the waist of the bell, and to our surprise, we found the actual name, the *Henrietta Marie* and the date 1699. When Mel and his group worked it in 1972, they had no indication what ship it was; however, they did surmise it was a merchant slave ship." "The ivory tusks and the trade beads and other artifacts showed it had been in the slave trade in Africa,'" Jim Amoroso added, describing how the wreckage was scattered over a large area on the site.

Duke Long related the discovery of the bronze bell: "What we were doing was running a metal detector search, and as we were going across the bottom we got a metal detector reading and slowly started fanning. I thought it might be some more iron shackles or iron spikes as, all of a sudden, I saw the lip of the bell. It was kind of exciting. Realizing what it was then bringing it up off the bottom, I first tried to get it up with a buoyancy compensator. It was way too heavy and I had to get it up with a line and bring it up to the boat. I handed the iron clapper up first to Jimmy and said wait until you see the rest of it. Everybody was pretty excited to see the actual bell of the ship," Long said, running his finger along the embossed lettering on the bronze bell.

"The pewter basins were very beautiful items. They were very large and deep and they were actually traded on the slave coast, too—used there as well as being sold to the colonies in the New World. We found some very interesting forks and spoons, and there are some beautiful pewter spoons that Jim Sinclair cleaned up recently that had the bust of William the Second on there and also had the touchmark of Stephen Bridges. This is all very fascinating to me," Henry Taylor said. He showed some of the artifacts he and his divers have recovered from the site.

"To me it is what I call an artifact wreck; we won't know until we finish working it. There'll probably be no treasure as such, but to me I love to get in there and find the artifacts and also add to the history of the slaving business back then. It's a fascinating thing. I am undertaking the financing of the salvage. It's what I call a minisalvage expedition. I think I'll be very happy to break

even on it, but I will do it again on the same basis," Taylor said, sharing his
excitement in the new discoveries from another shipwreck lost to time.

THAILAND'S SHIPWRECKS:
ANCIENT POTTERY RECOVERED FROM THE SEA

It was one of the most exciting finds of archaeological significance in modern
history. Fishermen from the village of Pattaya were casting their nets off the
coast in southern Thailand. The nets snagged. One of the fishermen dove down
to recover his net. When the fisherman surfaced, he held up pottery vessels that
had been submerged for almost six hundred years.

From that moment in September 1974, the story of the recovery of thousands of pieces of early Chinese and Thai ceramic ware, porcelain, pottery, coins,
and early artifacts from the Gulf of Siam unfolds like a story of international
intrigue. Smugglers, amateur divers, treasure hunters, fishermen, Chinese antique
dealers from Hong Kong, and finally the Royal Thai Navy descended on the
underwater sites and began helter-skelter recovery efforts that left archaeologists reeling in disbelief and dismay.

The pottery and ceramic objects found on these shipwrecks in the Gulf of
Siam have been dated to the thirteenth and fourteenth centuries AD. What is most
interesting, from a historical point of view, is that most of the pottery originated
in Thailand, not China.

Thailand is rich in history. Artifacts including bronze tools and implements
have been recovered from archaeological land digs in the north, where the sites
have been dated back five thousand years.

Legend has it that the king of Sukhothai, in what is now Thailand, visited
the emperor of China sometime around the latter part of the thirteenth century.
The Sukhothai king, it is said, was so impressed by the quality and development
of glazed pottery making in China, that he returned to Thailand with five hundred craftsmen to establish pottery and ceramic works in the Thai kingdom.

Chinese documents analyzed from the Mongol reign record several diplo-
matic visits by Sukhothai officials in this period. None of the early writings,
however, have been able to prove or disprove the visit of the king of Sukhothai
to the court of the emperor of China. Some of these early Chinese writings have

been lost and others are incomplete, compiled only in the late eighteenth century, leaving gaps in the documentary accounts of this entire period.

The legend of the Chinese artisans being imported into Thailand to establish the ceramic industry remains one of the most fascinating art mysteries. The subject is frequently debated by historians and art detectives. The fact that kilns were built in the Sukhothai kingdom is established beyond question by archaeological evidence.

Around 1230 AD, Sukhothai became the first independent kingdom in the Khmer empire. The kingdom was established in an area that lies about 280 miles north of today's city of Bangkok. Visitors to the archaeological ruins of the ancient cities of this early Sukhothai empire will find the remains of 129 kilns at Sri Sachanalai and remnants of 49 kilns outside the walls of the old city of Sukhothai.

Pottery produced in the Sukhothai kilns bear the name Sukhothai pottery, but ceramics from the district of Sri Sachanalai are called Sanghaloke or Sawankhalok ware. During this period of history, Angkor, located in what is now Cambodia, was at the height of its development and culture. Angkor is located near Sri Sachanalai. As a result of archaeological data found at Angkor, historians conclude that the Sri Sachanalai or Sanghaloke kilns were not constructed before 1350 AD.

Since the Sanghaloke pottery has been found to be more technically advanced in manufacture than the Sukhothai varieties, it is thought that the Sulthothai was made earlier, before better clay was discovered twenty-four miles farther north at Sri Sachanalai.

Relatively little is known about the trading that went on during this period. There is a close relationship between the Thai Sanghaloke celadon ware and Chinese Lung Ch'uan ware. The finds of these pottery-containing shipwrecks in the Gulf of Siam therefore took on important significance. The haphazard recovery of these valuable finds, the dispersal of many of the important porcelain artifacts by treasure hunters, and the destruction of the shipwreck sites by overzealous divers made the job of reconstructing the evidence obtained from the wreckage difficult.

Divers on the wreck sites recovered bags of Chinese coins. So many coins were recovered as to make the divers think they were being used as ballast in the ships. None of the divers assigned much importance to the coins, often casting them aside, preferring instead the porcelains. The ceramics found underwater were erroneously thought by many to be Ming dynasty ware, probably because of their ignorance of Thai history.

The mad scramble for these treasures was not without tragedy. There were tales of divers suffering agonizing bends. According to reports, three Thai divers and one Greek national supposedly died as a result of diving accidents over the wrecks. It was reported at the time that when one of the wrecks was discovered at a depth of 165 feet, divers would descend, fill bags to the brim with pottery and porcelain, then ascend to the surface by means of inflating their safety vests, without regard for the requirements of decompression.

When word of these finds leaked out through antique shops in Bangkok—whose proprietors had been buying up the pirated wares from divers and fishermen—Chinese antique dealers from Hong Kong commissioned seagoing junks with divers to work the sites. These looters returned with their finds directly to Hong Kong without even landing the artifacts on Thai soil.

Finally, but only after a great deal of damage was done and many of the valuable artifacts were lost to pillagers, the Thai Fine Arts Department took charge of the shipwreck sites. The government ordered a Royal Thai Navy ship to guard the wrecks until they could be explored by government frogmen.

Unfortunately the lack of experienced underwater archaeologists and conservators resulted in destruction or damage to many of the priceless porcelains once government recovery efforts were undertaken. One amateur archaeologist reported that persons at the site were using a marking pen to number and identify the porcelains recovered. The ink penetrated through the porcelain and became impossible to eradicate. When Fine Arts Department personnel discovered to their horror that the ink markings on hundreds of porcelain bowls would not come off, they frantically telephoned from Bangkok, urging a change in the identification procedure. Because of failed communication, divers at the site simply thought Bangkok wanted marking on the inside of the bowls to stop. The divers then adopted a procedure of using the indelible marking pen on the outside bottoms. The ink still penetrated the porcelain and was seen through. This tragic episode was reported as having affected many of the most beautiful finds.

One of the shipwrecks contained both Sukhothai and Sanghaloke pottery. Thai Fine Arts Department experts, as a result of this find, speculated that the kilns at both Sukhothai and Sri Sachanalai were producing pottery vessels at the same time. The Sanghaloke pottery found was celadon ware while the Sukhothai pottery on this same wreck site was decorated with black designs.

Thai police officials seized quantities of pottery from shipwreck pirates, but inaccurate or nonexistent information accompanied their recovery, and experts were unable to draw any inferences from the artifacts. The police seizures included pottery boxes with lids, small brown bottles with delicate earlike handles at the neck and glazed pottery bowls.

For the most part divers made no effort to hide their activities and openly recounted stories of finding piles of broken shipwreck pottery in Thai fishing villages along the coast. These broken shards had been abandoned by fishermen who had recovered the pottery from submerged wrecks. The broken pottery apparently had no resale value to the antique dealers or Hong Kong art merchants and thus was discarded by the fishermen as worthless.

As a result of the initial flurry of interest in the pottery found among the wreckage of Chinese junks sunk off Pattaya and Sattahip, several other shipwrecks were found off the coast. A number of these sites were already known to local fishermen. Once rumors of treasure and wild tales of gold and silver began to circulate throughout Thailand, fishermen converged on the wrecks and began salvaging pottery.

Members of the Thai Fine Arts Department found brown and copper glazed Chinese pottery among the wreckage of one of the ships off Sattahip. Divers reported finding fine blue and white porcelain on the same wreck site before government frogmen arrived. Thai experts felt that this was a trading ship, outward bound from Ayudhya. Since the vessel was heavily laden with Sukhothai pottery, the experts felt that the captain had taken the surplus Chinese ware aboard in Thailand for transshipment or sale elsewhere.

This theory is quite feasible since by the middle of the fourteenth century the Thai city of Ayudhya, built on the edge of the Chao Phya River north of Bangkok, became a center for Asian trade. Fine Arts Department officials further theorized that Thai pottery wares would undoubtedly not be shipped to

China, where sales could not compete in the market place with Chinese wares. These experts felt that the ship containing these artifacts sank on its way to the Malay, Philippine, or Indonesian peninsulas.

The shipwreck was discovered some twenty-two nautical miles south and west of the island of Koh Khram near Sattahip, a location that lends credence to this theory. Thai officials, after driving off the artifact hunters and treasure seekers, recovered some four thousand pieces of pottery from the Koh Khram shipwreck. They assumed their recoveries accounted for about sixty percent of the total cargo.

Navy divers measured the site and determined that the ship had been about sixty feet in overall length and about seventeen feet wide. Large pottery jars and jugs were found stratigraphically near the surface layer just under the sand. The more delicate bowls and dishes were found deeper, indicating that the more fragile wares were stowed in the ship's hold while the larger ceramic storage jars were carried as deck cargo.

Royal Thai Navy divers brought up wood from the ship. The cut beams posed another mysterious circumstance that experts have yet to unravel: the ship's beams appeared to have been hewn with saws that had fine teeth. Experts in Chinese archaeology have urged that the implements used in this period for Chinese shipbuilding caused a coarser cut in the wood. This presented the possibility that the ship was a European trader. Most experts have discounted this theory because the earliest recorded evidence of European ships in this part of Asia occurred when the Portuguese visited the area and established a trading post on the west coast of Malaysia in 1511.

This is later than the dates established for the Thai pottery found on the wreck. Portuguese archives do not reveal trade in Sukhothai or Sanghaloke pottery from Thailand. More probably, experts conclude, this particular vessel may have been an Arab ship that called on Ayudhya on its way to Indonesia or the Philippines.

Discovery of the ancient shipwrecks has enabled historians to confirm the existence of at least three early trade routes from the Sukhothai kingdom. Ships would sail down the Chao Phya River, plying their trade along the coast of Sattahip, Pattani, and Pattalung. There was also the eastern trade route toward

Cambodia and the southern trade route along Thailand's Sattahip coast to Chumporn and Pattani. Each shipwreck discovered was laden with fine Sukhothai and Sanghaloke ceramic wares, the principal export of the region. Ten shipwrecks have been found along the trade route near Sattahip. Eight additional wrecks have been confirmed by the Thai Fine Arts Department in areas plied by the eastern traders, and, additionally, Thai authorities are investigating reports that many more shipwrecks exist in waters off the Gulf of Siam.

Tales of fisherman and divers secretly working other wrecks have given rise to the estimate that about forty wrecks in total have been thus far discovered in Thai waters.

Wood recovered from some of the other wrecks leads marine historians to conclude that they were constructed with teak wood and that most of the vessels were built along the lines traditional to Chinese junks of that period.

Examples of this Thai pottery recovered from the wrecks included black, glazed celadon bowls, small, round storage jars with beautifully turned lids, and ceramic jars. Where edges of pottery were broken, one could recognize the flecks of white impurities, characteristic of the clay used in these early Thai ceramics.

These Thai pottery wrecks are probably among the most interesting finds of modern times. The wrecks log a period of history about which relatively little is known. Unfortunately much of the archaeological significance has been destroyed by haphazard looting of the wrecks by unauthorized persons. Even with the pillage and destruction, these finds have yielded knowledge of the cultural heritage of Thailand. The Thai Fine Arts Department has prepared special exhibitions of this shipwreck pottery that is on display in the Thai National Museum in Bangkok.

Sabordage: Death of
the French Fleet at Toulon

It was the last boat to sink. Fishermen gathered around the crew of the tug *Dardennes* and gave Captain Franceschi and his men civilian clothes. In their fishermen's garb, they left their boat at the dock, slipping away unnoticed, having first opened the sea cocks. The *Dardennes* sank upright where it was moored, right under the noses of the German army.

That one day, 27 November 1942, saw the most dramatic event in French maritime history unfold in the naval anchorage at Toulon, on France's Mediterranean coast. The incident with the *Dardennes* mirrored the heroism and the despair of France since the country was overrun by the Nazis on 16 June 1940. The Germans had occupied the whole country except for regions of central and south France.

Marshal Henri-Philippe Pétain collaborated, forming a government at Vichy. The French fleet remained under the control of Vichy as did the naval yards and arsenal at Toulon. The French-German Armistice Agreement provided, under Article 8, that the French fleet would be demobilized, assembled in ports, and disarmed. The ships that were necessary to guard France's empire—mine sweepers and coast patrollers—were excepted. The Germans agreed under Article 8 never to use the demobilized French fleet in the continuing war effort.

On 24 June 1940, Adm. Jean-François Darlan, minister of the navy and commander in chief of French naval forces, issued a special order under his secret signature, Xavier 377. The order provided that "Under no circumstances will the French fleet be left intact for the enemy." Darlan's order instructed commanders to make preparations for a sabordage, or scuttling, in the event that enemies or foreigners attempted to take the ships by force. For Captain Franceschi and his men on duty aboard the tug *Dardennes* on the morning of 27 November 1942, the finesse of war diplomacy meant nothing. Mariners' tradition and courage meant everything. Yet Captain Franceschi, too, was apparently torn between his duty and his honor.

It was 5:05 AM. At the docks, French submarines were still fast to their moorings when an alert sounded through the boats. German soldiers were on the quays. Nazi machine gun fusillades sprayed the wharf. Planes from the Luftwaffe were dropping flares to light up the anchorage. Capt. Jean L'Herminier, commander of the submarine *Casabianca,* later wrote, "The enemy is there firing at us. That's the only thing certain, and the enemy, good god, is German."

One French submarine officer drew his pistol and fired back at the Germans on the docks as the crews worked feverishly to loose the compressed air lines and cables to cast off. The electric engines needed no boilers—they started immediately and five French submarines headed out of the anchorage under fire. The port was closed with antisubmarine nets, with a second barrage pulled across the entrance to the port to prevent surface ships from entering. The first obstacle the escaping submarines had to pass through was the antisubmarine nets that closed the pass between the Mourillon jetty and Saint-Mandrier. The antisubmarine net was opened and closed by the tugboat *Dardennes.*

"Tugboat, open," the commander of the submarine *Casabianca* shouted across the space of water as the French tugboat crew and captain hesitated, at first confused about what to do. It was reported that Captain Franceschi called back that he needed "superior orders." In the hesitation and confusion of the moment, with fire raining down from the air and shore, an officer standing on the *Casabianca*'s prow pulled out his pistol, menacing the startled tug crew. A violent explosion shook them from a bomb dropped by one of the attacking Luftwaffe planes. The tugboat captain understood in that moment that "the enemy is German," and opened the antisubmarine net.

The *Casabianca* passed through, diving to evade the second barrier, the anti–surface ship nets. The *Casabianca* was followed by the French submarines

Marsouin, Iris, Glorieux, and *La Venus.* From the end of a nearby jetty, French gunners fired back at attacking German planes. The bombers retaliated, destroying the lighthouse on the jetty and silencing the loyal French gunners. Four men were killed and eight wounded in the explosion, the first victims of the day.

The water was phosphorescent as the tug *Dardennes* maneuvered in the dark of early morning; after the submarines passed through the ambient water glowed with phosphorescent particles. German planes mistook the tug for an escaping submarine. Bombs exploded around it as Captain Franceschi maneuvered his tug against the jetty, sending men scrambling ashore to evacuate the wounded from the lighthouse.

One wounded man was brought back on board. The crew reported to their captain that another wounded man was trapped under concrete blocks and they could not free him. German planes were now dropping magnetic mines, which started to explode as they came in contact with the steel antisubmarine nets. Captain Franceschi left some of his crewmen on the jetty to help the trapped man, taking one of the wounded to Saint-Mandrier for medical help. At Saint-Mandrier, the injured sailor was taken off, but the Germans would not let Franceschi return to the jetty.

Local fishermen gathered around the tugboat captain for the news, aware of the explosions from the magnetic mines. The fishermen had followed the events with great interest, especially as Franceschi recounted how large numbers of dead fish were floating to the surface where the mines had exploded. Without hesitation, the local Toulonese fishermen rushed into their boats and headed out to gather up the dead fish. One of the fishermen stopped at the jetty, picking up Franceschi's two crewmen and the wounded sailor and returning them to Saint-Mandrier, where the fisherman gave them civilian clothes, before heading out again to join his colleagues "fishing."

In a parting gesture, Captain Franceschi scuttled his tug at the dock and walked away. It was reported, years later, that Madame L'Herminier, wife of the late submarine commander, apologized to the tugboat captain for the initial unpleasantness that passed between her husband's submarine and the tugboat, finally settling accounts between two courageous Frenchmen.

The unique bravery brought on by the exceptional circumstances during the escape of the five submarines was repeated many times during the early morning of 27 November 1942. Confusion, contradiction, and a crisis of conscience marked events leading up to the self-destruction of the French naval fleet at Toulon, touching every sailor and citizen alike.

Debated as part of the historic debacle surrounding the collaboration of the Vichy government, proceedings later held before France's High Court of Justice accumulated the evidence and reasons for the personal decisions of the principal officers who played a role in the drama that unfolded.

As a predicate to the scuttling of the French "Forces de Haute Mer," or High Seas Fleet, in 1942, the attitude of the French sailor and officer may be understood with reference to the defeat of French vessels at Mers el-Kébir. British naval forces under Adm. James Somerville attacked French ships at anchor in Mers on 3 July 1940. The French, historically naval antagonists of the English, suffered great losses at Mers el-Kébir, Algeria's port on the Gulf of Oran, during the execution of Operation Catapult by the English. On the same day the British seized French ships that had sought refuge in English ports. Operation Catapult was a British assault to neutralize French forces in the Mediterranean and prevent their use by the Germans.

Winston Churchill ordered the definitive seizure or permanent destruction of all French ships at Mers el-Kébir. While the French and English were trying to negotiate after the British admiral tendered an ultimatum an Italian unit appeared and firing broke out. The result was 1,297 French sailors killed or missing in combat and 351 wounded. Three capital ships in the French fleet were knocked out of commission.

After the assault, even those in the Vichy government who had been favorably disposed to the British were hardened and dismayed at the senseless attack. From the disaster at Mers el-Kébir, Vichy regrouped and reconstituted French naval forces at Toulon. Some of the ships damaged at Oran were refloated and repaired.

With the events at Mers fresh in history, Hitler made provision to invade the south of France as early as 10 December 1940. The secret plan was dubbed Operation Attila by the Germans. By December 1941 the Americans had entered the war, launching Operation Torch, to occupy French North Africa.

Almost a year later, on 11 November 1942, Hitler put Operation Attila into action, moving with the Italians into Vichy-governed areas under the guise of defending France, stating that they would be better able to protect Corsica from assault. That same day Adm. Jean de Laborde issued an Order of the Day, demanding loyalty to Marshal Pétain. The communiqué described German actions after the events in North Africa, stating that the French fleet under no circumstances was to fall into the hands of foreigners intact.

Admiral Laborde commanded the entire French Forces de Haute Mer from his flagship, the *Strasbourg*. On 12 November he assembled his admirals and commanders in the salon of his flagship. Laborde demanded the word of honor of every officer assembled that they would obey his orders without reservation. The one officer who refused was relieved of command. The rest were instructed to return to their ships and demand the same loyalty of their subordinate officers.

By 19 November Hitler prepared the working order for the execution of his plans to occupy the south of France. The new plan, Operation Lila, called for the taking of the French fleet intact. At this time there were some 150 navy ships berthed in the port of Toulon, ranging from the battleships to harbor vessels. What transpired over the next few days as German tanks approached and surrounded Toulon, cutting telephone lines, is worthy of a place in the annals of great wartime events. Gendarmes rode their bicycles into town to give the alarm, while colleagues tried to lead the Nazi Panzer divisions in the wrong direction.

The naval duty officer, an ensign, remained at his post, passing messages over the marine telephone system, which was not cut by the Germans. The ensign was able to destroy classified documents and even rescue sacks of mail coming by train from Vichy to the naval authorities in Toulon the next day. The Germans captured one of the Toulon naval outposts, Fort Lamalgue, but at 4:30 AM on 27 November 1942, an alarm was telephoned in that the Germans had taken over French positions and were advancing on the port. Fifteen minutes later, Admiral Laborde was awakened. He ordered his fleet cleared for action.

In their cribs, five submarines broke their moorings and left the docks. Aboard the other vessels, plans that had been made to scuttle and destroy the ships were put into effect. Explosive charges had been prepared and all had been placed at the ready to destroy critical machinery in the event of foreign intervention.

At the Hotel du Parc, headquarters of France's Vichy government, President Pierre Laval huddled with Adm. Maurice Le Luc, head of France's maritime forces. The men were confronted with Hitler's letter and the news that the Germans were occupying Toulon and that Fort Lamalgue was occupied. Le Luc telephoned Toulon, questioning the duty officer, Ensign Pieters. Ensign Pieters held the phone away from his mouth so that the listeners in Vichy could hear the explosions outside. "The ships are blowing up," the duty officer told the admiral. Le Luc dictated to Ensign Pieters an order for Admiral Laborde on behalf of himself and President Laval. The order, hastily scribbled down by the youthful ensign, stated, "Avoid all incidents. This order modifies all orders previously received."

At this moment, German soldiers pushed into Ensign Pieters's office, taking over the building. Pieters was able to slip away from the Germans temporarily. He telephoned Vichy back and was connected to Admiral Le Luc. Pieters interrogated the admiral to be sure that he was in fact speaking with the French commander of maritime forces.

The order was confirmed. It was subsequently modified to "Avoid bloodshed and unnecessary destruction of property." But the order came too late, and probably would not have been obeyed in any event. At 5:30 AM, when Admiral Laborde was informed that German tanks had broken into the arsenal, he immediately sent out the signal, "This is Admiral of the F.H.M., scuttle the fleet . . . scuttle the fleet." The signal was flashed from the mast of the flagship as well as by radio. "Execute immediately the scuttling of your ship. Admiral Laborde, C.E.C. les F.H.M."

German forces advanced toward the French ships. As a tank approached the admiral's flagship, the *Strasbourg,* gunners fired on it, hitting several German soldiers, forcing it to retreat. The tank advanced again, this time firing its 88-mm cannon. The shell found its mark, striking the turret of one of the *Strasbourg's* guns. The officer in charge, fatally wounded, his legs blown off by the explosion, continued to give orders to his men, five of whom were also wounded.

Around the fleet, every commander responded to the orders to scuttle their ships. Aboard the *Bayonnaise,* a torpedo patrol boat guarding the jetty, Capt.

Nicolas Barrelon ordered the colors raised and began firing at the German planes. Aboard the *Provence,* the Germans boarded the ship. The soldiers were distracted by French officers while scuttling operations were completed. While a German officer was arguing with the commander, the *Provence* canted over and began to sink under them. As the list increased, the German lieutenant lost his footing, still arguing with French Admiral Jarry, and fell into the water as the French sailors laughed.

Around the anchorage, sailors took up "La Marseillaise." On Admiral Laborde's flagship the *Strasbourg,* a German officer demanded, "Admiral, my order says you must render this ship intact." "The ship is sunk," the French officer replied, saluting.

In the submarine cribs at Missiessy, five submarines were scuttled at their moorings. A submarine mechanic, leaving the base, detoured a German Panzer column which stopped to ask him directions to the submarines. At the Vaubin docks, French crews only managed to scuttle two submarines; four others fell into German hands. In the submarine anchorage at Mourillon, French officers and men put up resistance to the German advance, managing to scuttle three submarines under fire and partially flooding a fourth before the Germans boarded and prevented its sinking.

Of the five submarines that broke away from their moorings and escaped, one boat, *La Venus,* was scuttled by its commander once outside the anchorage. The submarine *Casabianca* lay off the port of Toulon hoping for action and waiting for Italian shipping. Others made for Spain to refuel then escaped to North Africa to serve in the war on the side of the Allies. The *Casabianca* later was the first submarine to land on Corsica, supplying the secret army of resistance with badly needed men and supplies, distinguishing its captain, Jean l'Herminier, and crew for exceptional patriotism and courage.

In Toulon, the anchorage and city were engulfed in smoke billowing up from the dying fleet. Admiral Laborde refused to leave his flagship in spite of German demands. Marshal Pétain sent him a message. "I learn that your ship is sinking. I give you the order to leave it." The 26,500-ton battleship *Strasbourg* settled in the water as Nazi propagandists ordered what was to be printed about the scuttling in French newspapers.

In the aftermath of the scuttling, which left six French sailors dead and twenty-six wounded, 101 ships were sunk or destroyed, amounting to more than 232,000 tons. Apart from the derelicts that served only as floating pontoons, and 17 patrol vessels excepted from the scuttling order to serve as coast guardians, only 22 French ships survived the mass suicide. When the tally was in, the French had scuttled 3 battleships amounting to 75,189 tons, 7 cruisers totaling 62,800 tons, 1 aviation transport ship, 29 patrol and torpedo boats, 12 submarines, 4 naval cranes and floating docks, 11 patrol ships and fuel carriers, as well as numerous smaller vessels.

Destruction was everywhere. Along the coast, shore batteries had been destroyed. The reaction of Comdt. Philippe Tailliez, at the time a young naval officer, was typical. As he flung open the shutters from his apartment in Toulon to look out at the anchorage, his eyes flooded with tears.

On 8 June 1945, Marshal Pétain penned a note to the minutes of his oral testimony before the French High Court, stating that he had not ordered the French fleet to escape to North Africa on 11 November 1942 because he had feared German reprisals and escape would not have been possible in any event.

The conflict in orders and the interpretation of Le Luc's vague order to avoid bloodshed and unnecessary destruction of property were the subject of court inquiry after the war. Whether obedience of an order is demanded regardless of the justice of failing to obey continues to preoccupy debate of the acts surrounding the scuttling of the French Fleet at Toulon and the conduct of the Vichy government.

Did Le Luc's order come too late to retract the command to scuttle and too late to prevent major destruction of the fleet? Would it have been obeyed in any event by Admiral Laborde and other French officers? These questions are still asked by those who consider the facts surrounding one of the world's maritime debacles unique in history. Perhaps the romantic statement of French writer Charles Péguy, who died in 1914, expresses the view that the world after the Second World War seems to have taken of the incidents at Toulon.

Péguy wrote, "I would disobey if justice and liberty required it." A decision the writer was not alive to make at Toulon in 1942, but whose sense of honor may have been possessed by brave Frenchmen who chose destruction of their fleet over what they viewed as dishonor.

Eventually the scuttled ships were salvaged and cut up for scrap. Tons of salvaged steel was shipped off to Italy to fuel the Axis war machine. French land and naval forces were disarmed and decommissioned by German order. Only ghosts of the fleet that died at Toulon remain, haunting reminders of the horror and destruction of war.

CHAPTER TWELVE

The Scilly Isles:
Sunken Ships and Sea History

Scilly is a region of sunken ships. Craggy granite cliffs face the sea on stark, beautiful islands, where hearty islanders have for generations put out in their launches to claim salvage. Located some twenty-eight miles off Land's End at the tip of England's Cornish coast, the Scillies are a place where wrecking is a tradition, and, for as long as anyone can remember, the Gibson family has chronicled the maritime tragedies of ships that have washed up on Scilly's rocks. Indeed Gibson family photographs are today stark reminders of both Scilly's past and its present.

Just as great sailing ships wrecked on Scilly's coast from the first days of ocean exploration, ships continue to put up on their shoals, violently succumbing to the relentless sea. There is great treasure in these waters—perhaps the greatest treasure trove of sunken ships to be found anyplace in the world. And with this booty of gold and silver thousands of lives were lost. The fortunes of war and national pretension vanished beneath the waves. With great sailing ships vying against steam to do commerce, hopes have been dashed never to surface again after wrecking on Scilly's shoals. But even iron hulls and great motored ships have come up frail and fragile in the storm-tossed winter seas.

In this part of the ocean gales lash the water into such fury that men like Richard Lethbridge, who have spent their lives at sea, declare that the sea off Scilly has no equal, not even in the tempest of Cape Horn. For this is the sailors' inferno, the place where the ocean converges with submerged rocks that first disembowel then swallow up and crush great ships and small.

One of these ships, part of a fleet sailing back to England from having besieged the French port at Toulon, carried the admiral and commander in chief of Britain's Mediterranean Fleet. The commander, Sir Cloudesley Shovell, paid off in winter. It was the habit of warring nations of that time, prior to the Seven Years' War, not to risk men or ships at war in foul weather. The English were engaged in the War of Spanish Succession. They had fared well in 1707, and the spoils of warring were loaded aboard the ships of the line heading home.

Sailing from Gibraltar on 10 October 1707, Shovell, with a fleet of twenty-one ships, made into the ocean and headed for England. The weather was stormy, ill affording navigators the opportunity to take observations. Edmund Herbert, sent to the Scilly Isles two years after the incident, recorded events aboard Shovell's flagship, the HMS *Association,* on 21 October 1707. "Abt. one or two aft. noon on the 23rd [an incorrect fact recorded by Mr. Herbert, it was the twenty-second] Octr Sir C. call'd a council & examd ye masters wt lat. they were in; all agreed to be in that of Ushant on ye coast of France, except Sr, W. Jumper's Mr of ye *Lenox,* who believ'd 'em to be nearer Scilly."

Refusing to heed the *Lenox* navigator's advice, Shovell, thinking that his fleet was a hundred miles from the Scilly Isles, proceeded on his perilous course. In three hours the fleet was among the rocks. In the midst of the tempest, the admiral dispatched the *Lenox, La Valeur,* and the fire ship *Phoenix* for Falmouth. The *Phoenix* struck and was damaged, going ashore on Scilly. The two other ships slipped through the shoals, arriving at Falmouth on 25 October 1707.

Herbert's commentary of what happened continues: "The weather being stormy, they could not see the light on St. Agnes; not yet knowing where they were they fir'd, soon after wch they struck on ye Ledge, and bilg'd; the *Rumney* also struck immediately and stav'd on the Guildstone. The *Eagle* was lost on ye Gunnar or thereabouts, by wt of ye wreck floated to St Just and other places at ye Lands End & up ye North Channel."

Lost on the rocks of the Gilstone Ledge and Bishop Rocks were the flagship HMS *Association* of ninety-six guns, the seventy-gun *Eagle,* and the fifty-gun *Romney.* The *Firebrand* was badly damaged on the rocks; the *Phoenix* was holed; and the *St. George* struck rocks but was lifted clear again. Some two thousand men perished with their ships, including the commander, Rear Adm. Sir Cloudesley Shovell, whose body washed up on shore on Porthellick Bay on St. Mary's Island the next day with his pet greyhound.

Edmund Herbert was assigned to the Scilly Isles to attempt to recover property from the shipwrecks. He was not successful in doing so, although his written reports show that islanders and members of the squadron in port at the time recovered such goods as floated ashore. Herbert reported that a ring was taken off Shovell's finger and never recovered, the mark of it still on the hand when the body was put aboard the HMS *Salisbury*, before the corpse was conveyed to an embalmer in Plymouth and then returned to London.

A report in a Scottish newspaper, dated 9 July 1710, described a salvage operation in the following terms, "We hear from Scilly that the gentlemen concerned in the wreck where Sir Cloudesley Shovell was cast away have taken (from the bottom) several iron guns and seven brass guns, with a cable, and have found the *Association* in four fathoms at low water, the hull of the ship being whole, wherein there is vast treasure——the Queen's Plate, several chests of money, besides ten chests of Sir Cloudesley's own, with great riches of the Grandees of Spain."

The report went on to detail the salvage, stating, "The divers go down in a copper engine, and continue two hours underwater, thirty fathoms deep, where they have also met the Fireship (cast away at the same time as the *Association*, I don't know her name). Had not the winds been westerly, which occasioned the seas to be very high and boisterous, all the Treasure before this, had been fished out," the newspaper account concluded.

But all the treasure was not fished out. The report of high and boisterous seas tells more than its author's understatement, writing in 1710. It has required almost three centuries to plumb the depths where the *Association* struck on the Gilstone Ledge on Scilly's western rocks and for technology of the modern age to extricate the ship's remains from under huge boulders cast upon the wreckage of the 165-foot-long by 45-foot-wide ship.

The vessel was lost in an area of ripping tides, frigid water, and perpetual bad weather that at best permits twenty-eight working days a year on the site. Divers are excavating the wreckage, in spite of danger and hardship. The salvors in possession, modern day Scillonians with "wrecking in their blood," have set about locating and bringing up Shovell's treasure.

Terry Hiron and James Heslin began searching for the treasure of the *Association* in 1968, when they visited the Scilly Isles on a diving holiday. Both men, Hiron a chartered surveyor and Heslin the owner of a small garage in London, decided then and there to chuck their jobs and set about searching for the fabled wrecks of the *Association, Eagle,* and *Romney.*

It was a rather bold adventure, with little hope of success—after all, the location of the shipwreck off the Gilstone Ledge on Scilly's western rocks was widely known. Many salvors had tried before to recover the wealth of artifacts and treasure. The work proved quite difficult, compounded by a sea state that had pounded the remains of the *Association* in a rock basin and tossed huge boulders on top of the wreckage of the old wooden ship.

Some cannons were recovered, including a magnificent bronze gun with ornate engraving. The British government gave Heslin and Hiron rights to the shipwreck as salvors in possession, and they worked the wreck as much as they could each summer, given the sea conditions. The two divers were joined by Terry Roe and Mac Mace, the latter trained in the use of controlled explosives and a designer who devised a customized dive support vessel.

Mace developed special mining techniques that enabled the divers to drill into huge rocks lying on top of the wreckage, set a bolt with an epoxy type resin, and lift the rocks safely out of the way using air bags inflated underwater. Rocks too big or unwieldy to be lifted off the wreckage in this manner had to be split and blasted with submarine plastic explosives. The men worked carefully to avoid damage to artifacts located under the boulders. It was like burrowing in a mine, although the mining took place sixty feet below on the *Association* wreck site in a tide that coursed through the area at six to eight knots at times. There were places on the reef below where the muzzles of iron cannons protruded from solid boulders that must have weighed a hundred tons. It was not uncommon for the men to crack through rocks that weighed fifteen tons, lifting the sections away with great difficulty. The divers, once through burrowing under the rocks, would work the site with airlifts and then would fan by hand once the larger pieces of debris were removed.

As the work went on only a handful of coins rewarded the salvage efforts. The results would not pay the expenses of the archaeological support vessel, let alone the divers' time. Mace decided to blast through some rocks that had been blocking access in one of the caves created by a rockfall perhaps two centuries ago.

Hiron and Heslin dove down to check the site and set the charge as the salvage operation was documented on film. Mace connected an electric primer as Heslin protected his ears from reverberation. It detonated. The divers waited until the debris cleared below before going back on the site.

Mace and the author entered the cave without expectation, hoping to film the airlift in use. In a moment, as the first piece of crud was lifted out from under the broken rocks, it was clear that this was a new discovery and that Shovell's ship was yielding up more of its cargo than any of the divers had imagined possible.

The thrill of discovery spread aboard the small support vessel as the first bags of concretion were hauled aboard. Then anticipation as Dave Holland and Mac Mace dumped the heavy sacks out on the metal deck. It was science, it was discovery, it was treasure, it was adventure, it was the excitement great explorers feel when a new discovery is made.

Heslin reached into the material brought up on deck, ignoring the hundreds of coins, some in clumps, some loose, including English crowns and shillings, Spanish pieces of eight from Mexico and Peru, and minted pieces of eight from Spain. Heslin extracted a set of brass navigational dividers covered with black from the silver coins. He washed the dividers in saltwater and handed them to Mace. Whatever value experts might place on the dividers, there was no greater value or esteem for them than in the explorers' hands as they passed them around and each in turn admired them.

Hiron next discovered a long silver probe with a hook on the end, which he recognized as a silver boot lacing device. In one of the clumps Mace recovered a round sounding weight, a lead probably hove overside as the admiral waited, trying in vain to determine their true position, realizing too late that they had miscalculated their course and were in harm's way.

As the work went on to recover and document the finds, the divers brought up thousands of coins. More boulders were moved off the underwater site and clumps of concretion were revealed. One lump contained cannonballs, coins, and, perfectly preserved, a brass sector or gunter's scale. The sector was used for measuring angles on navigational charts and working out mathematical problems to calculate a ship's position.

To understand the fascination with the navigational instruments one must understand the inexact state of that art in 1707. As a direct result of the sinking of the *Association,* the British Admiralty ordered verification of all compasses on their ships. Of all of the compasses on the surviving vessels of Shovell's fleet, none of the wooden boxed compasses were found to be accurate within acceptable limits, and only one or two of the brass boxed compasses were found to give acceptable readings out of some seventy-five tested compasses. In 1707 there was little accuracy in shooting the sun's position to gauge latitude, and because the chronometer was not yet invented, longitude was unknown. The early navigators depended on sailing close to shore where possible and sounding with lead weights to determine depth. Hollow wax–filled cavities in the base of the sounding weights told the consistency of the bottom, thus the probable location.

Danny Owen, a diver the late Terry Roe took on the wreck of the *Eagle* near Bishop Rocks, swam down the anchor line to a depth of about 120 feet. Without swimming more than a yard from where the anchor lay on the sea floor, Owen lifted a broken shard of glass from an onion bottle on the bottom, ran the side of his hand over the sand beneath it, and found a pure gold ring studded with emeralds. The stones were small but dark, apparently taken as the spoils of war from the Spanish who brought it from New World emerald mines in Colombia.

There is a tendency to presume that the secrets of the sea have been discovered. Some even go so far as to infer that exploration of the ocean will yield few great treasures. Yet in Scilly, where ships have wrecked since humans have put to sea, there shall always be discovery. The islands, while remote, have been made accessible by frequent British Airways helicopter service from Penzance on the Cornish coast. Passing low over the rocks and islands as the helicopter sweeps above the dark green water, the impression of the islands takes on a new dimension.

From the air the elements of nature that have torn the bottoms out of countless ships depicted in Frank Gibson's family pictorial chronicles become animated and three dimensional. They are also beautiful and stunning memorials to the sea's challenge. They are, as the early charts proclaimed of Scilly's western rocks, "fearful to behold," yet beautiful, mysterious, and mystical. The kelp beds and rocky reefs play host to hundreds of shipwrecks, and some continue to give up their secret treasures from the deep. On Scilly, explorers with modern technology add to our knowledge of history—history beneath the sea.

Bibliography

Amundson, Katherine. *The Story of the Spanish Galleon Nuestra Senora de Atocha*. Key West, Fla.: Salvors, Inc., 1987.

Anderson, Nina, and William Anderson. *Southern Treasures*. Chester, Conn.: Globe Pequot Press, 1987.

Bankson, Ross. *Hidden Treasures of the Sea*. Washington D.C.: National Geographic Society, 1988.

Bascom, Willard. *Deep Water, Ancient Ships: The Treasure Vault of the Mediterranean*. New York: Doubleday & Co., 1976.

———. *The Great Wave: Adventures in Oceanography*. New York: Harper & Row, 1988.

Bass, George F. *Archaeology Beneath the Sea*. New York: Walker & Co., 1975.

———. *Archaeology Under Water*. London: Thames & Hudson, 1966.

———. *A History of Seafaring Based on Underwater Archaeology*. London: Thames & Hudson, 1972.

———. *Ships and Shipwrecks of North America*. London: Thames & Hudson, 1988.

———. *Shipwrecks in the Bodrum Museum of Underwater Archaeology*. Bodrum, Turkey: Museum of Underwater Archaeology, 1996.

Bischoff, William L. *The Coinage of El Peru*. New York: The American Numismatic Society, 1989.

Blassingame, Wyatt. *Diving for Treasure*. Philadelphia: Macrae-Smith Co., 1971.

Blot, Jean-Yves. *Underwater Archaeology: Exploring The World Beneath the Sea*. Paris: Editions Gallimard, 1995.

Bound, Mensun. *The Archaeology of Ships of War*. Shropshire, U.K.: Anthony Nelson, Ltd., 1995.

———. *Lost Ships*. New York: Simon & Schuster, 1998.

Bowman, Gerald. *The Man Who Bought a Navy*. London: Harrap & Co., 1964.

Breeden, R.L., and D. J. Crump. *Undersea Treasures.* Washington, D.C.: National Geographic Society, 1974.

Brown, Joseph E. *The Golden Sea: Man's Underwater Adventures.* New York: The Playboy Press, 1974.

Budde-Jones, Kathryn. "Coins of the Lost Galleons." (Self-published, 1993).

Buranelli, Vincent. *Gold: An Illustrated History.* Maplewood, N.J.: Hammond, Inc., 1979.

Burgess, Robert F. *Gold, Galleons, and Archaeology.* Indianapolis, Ind.: Bobbs-Merrill Co., 1976.

————. *Man: 12,000 Years Under the Sea.* New York: Dodd Mead & Co., 1980.

————. *Sinkings, Salvages, and Shipwrecks.* New York: American Heritage Press, 1970.

Burton, Hal. *The Real Book About Treasure Hunting.* Garden City, N.Y.: Garden City Books, 1953.

Chorlton, Windsor. *Buried and Sunken Treasure.* London: Marshall Cavendish, 1974.

Codinach, Guadalupe Jimenez. *The Hispanic World, 1492–1898.* Washington D.C.: Library of Congress, 1994.

Coffman, F. L. *Atlas of Treasure Maps.* New York: Thomas Nelson & Sons, 1957.

Cooke, James Herbert. *The Shipwreck of Sir Cloudesley Shovell on the Scilly Islands in 1707.* London: Isles of Scilly Museum, n.d.

Cousins, Geoffrey. *The Story of Scapa Flow.* London: Muller & Co., 1965.

Craig, Alan K. *Gold Coins of the 1715 Spanish Plate Fleet.* Tallahassee: Florida Bureau of Archaeological Research, 1988.

Davis, Robert N. *Deep Sea Diving and Submarine Operations.* London: St. Catherine's Press, 1955.

Deagan, Kathleen. *Artifacts of the Spanish Colonies of Florida and Caribbean, 1500–1800.* Washington, D.C.: Smithsonian Institution Press, 1987.

Dean, Martin, et al. *Archaeology Underwater: The NAS Guide to Principles and Practice.* London: Nautical Archaeological Society, 1992.

Delgado, James P. *Encyclopedia of Underwater and Maritime Archaeology.* New Haven, Conn.: Yale University Press, 1998.

————. *Lost Warships: An Archaeological Tour of War at Sea.* Vancouver, B.C.: Douglas & McIntyre, Ltd., 2001.

DuBois, Bessie Wilson. "Shipwrecks in the Vicinity of Jupiter Island." (Self-published, Jupiter, Fla., 1975).

Dumas, Frederic. *Thirty Centuries Under the Sea.* New York: Crown Publishers, 1976.

Fine, John Christopher. *Sunken Ships and Treasures.* New York: Atheneum-Macmillan, 1986.

————. *Sunken Treasure.* New York: Richard C. Owen Publishers, 2000.

Foreman, Laura. *Napoleon's Lost Fleet: Bonaparte, Nelson and the Battle of the Nile.* New York: Roundtable Press, 1999.

Frost, Honor. *Under the Mediterranean.* London: Routledge and Kegan Paul, 1963.

Garrett, Charles. *Treasure Recovery from Sand and Sea.* Dallas, Tex.: Ram Books, 1988.

George, S. C. *Jutland to Junkyard: The Raising of the Scuttled German High Seas Fleet From Scapa Flow.* Cambridge, U.K.: Patrick Stephens Ltd., 1973.

Gibbon, Mason. *The Triumph of the Royal Navy. Official Record of Surrender of German Fleet.* 1919.

Gold & Silver Treasure. Plymouth, U.K.: W.H. Lane & Son, 1979.

Harris, Simon. *Sir Cloudesley Shovell: Stuart Admiral.* Kent, UK: Spellmount, Ltd., 2001.

Horner, Dave. *The Treasure Galleons.* New York: Dodd Meade & Co., 1971.

Larn, Richard. *Cornish Shipwrecks—The Isles of Scilly.* Newton Abbot, U.K.: David & Charles Publishers, 1971.

Larn, Richard, and Peter McBride. "Sir Cloudesley Shovell's Disaster in the Isles of Scilly October 1707." (Self-published, United Kingdom, 1985).

Lincoln, Margarette. *Shipwrecks: Learning through Underwater Archaeology.* Greenwich, U.K.: National Maritime Museum, 1993.

Lyon, Eugene. *The Search for the Atocha.* New York: Harper & Row, 1979.

————. *Search for the Mother Lode of the Atocha.* Port Salerno, Fla.: Florida Classics Library, 1989.

Mace, Mac. *H.M.S. Association—Sank 1707.* Isles of Scilly, U.K.: Scillonian Diving Service, n.d.

Marken, Mitchell W. *Pottery from Spanish Shipwrecks 1500–1800.* Gainesville: University Press of Florida, 1994.

Marx, Robert F. *The History of Underwater Exploration.* New York: Dover Publications, 1990.

————. *Into the Deep: The History of Man's Underwater Exploration.* New York: Van Nostrand Reinhold Co., 1978.

————. *In the Wake of the Galleons.* Flagstaff, Ariz.: Best Publications, 2001.

Marx, Robert F., and Jennifer Marx. *Shipwrecks of the Western Hemisphere.* Cleveland, Ohio: World Publishing Co., 1971.

McKee, Alexander. *History Under the Sea.* London: Hutchinson & Co., 1968.

McKenzie, T. "Marine Salvage in Peace and War." *The Institution of Engineers and Shipbuilders of Scotland* 93, Paper 1122.

Peterson, Mendel. *The Funnels of Gold.* Boston: Little Brown & Co., 1975.

————. *History Under the Sea.* Washington, D.C.: Smithsonian Institution, 1965.

Potter, John S. *The Treasure Diver's Guide.* Garden City, N.Y.: Doubleday & Co., 1960.

Pradeau, Alberto-Francisco. *Numismatic History of Mexico.* New York: Sanford J. Durst, 1978.

Reisberg, Harry E. *The Sea of Treasure.* New York: Frederick Fell, Inc., 1966.

Sedwick, Frank. "The Practical Book of Cobs." (Self-published, Maitland, Fla., 1987).

Silverberg, Robert. *Sunken History: The Story of Underwater Archaeology.* Philadelphia: Chilton Books, 1963.

Singer, Steven D. *Shipwrecks of Florida.* Sarasota, Fla.: Pineapple Press, 1992.

Taylor, I. D. M. "The Salving of the Ex-German High Seas Fleet at Scapa Flow." Scotland: The Institute of Mechanical Engineers Scottish Branch—Graduate Section, November 1961.

Throckmorton, Peter. *The Lost Ships.* Boston: Little, Brown & Co., 1964.

———. *Shipwrecks and Archaeology.* Boston: Little, Brown & Co., 1970.

Von Reuter, Vice Adm. L. *Das Grab der Deutscher Flotte.* Leipzig: R. F. Roehler.

Wagner, Kip, and L. B. Taylor. *Pieces of Eight.* New York: E.P. Dutton & Co., 1966.

Weller, Robert. *The Dreamweaver.* Charleston, S.C: Fletcher Publishing, 1966.

———. *Galleon Alley: The 1733 Spanish Treasure Fleet.* Lake Worth, Fla.: Crossed Anchors Salvage, Inc. 2001.

———. *Galleon Hunt.* Lake Worth, Fla.: Crossed Anchors Salvage, Inc., 1992.

———. *Salvaging Spanish Sunken Treasure.* Lake Worth, Fla.: Crossed Anchors Salvage, Inc., 1999.

———. *Sunken Treasure on Florida Reefs.* Lake Worth, Fla.: Crossed Anchors Salvage, Inc. 1987.

Index

About the Author

A lawyer and expert in maritime affairs, John Christopher Fine has handled many issues involving the law of salvage. He has contributed to numerous dive and ocean-related magazines and is the author of twenty books, focusing on ocean issues, environmental pollution, and underwater archaeology. He served and continues to serve on several boards, including acting as liaison officer with the United Nations Environment Programme for Ocean Matters. Mr. Fine's underwater photography has won the first prize in the International Underwater Photographic Competition on the island of Malta. He currently resides in Scarsdale, New York.

The Naval Institute Press is the book-publishing arm of the U.S. Naval Institute, a private, nonprofit, membership society for sea service professionals and others who share an interest in naval and maritime affairs. Established in 1873 at the U.S. Naval Academy in Annapolis, Maryland, where its offices remain today, the Naval Institute has members worldwide.

Members of the Naval Institute support the education programs of the society and receive the influential monthly magazine *Proceedings* and discounts on fine nautical prints and on ship and aircraft photos. They also have access to the transcripts of the Institute's Oral History Program and get discounted admission to any of the Institute-sponsored seminars offered around the country. Discounts are also available to the colorful bimonthly magazine *Naval History*.

The Naval Institute's book-publishing program, begun in 1898 with basic guides to naval practices, has broadened its scope to include books of more general interest. Now the Naval Institute Press publishes about one hundred titles each year, ranging from how-to books on boating and navigation to battle histories, biographies, ship and aircraft guides, and novels. Institute members receive significant discounts on the Press's more than eight hundred books in print.

Full-time students are eligible for special half-price membership rates. Life memberships are also available.

For a free catalog describing Naval Institute Press books currently available, and for further information about joining the U.S. Naval Institute, please write to:

Membership Department

U.S. Naval Institute

291 Wood Road

Annapolis, MD 21402-5034

Telephone: (800) 233-8764

Fax: (410) 269-7940

Web address: www.navalinstitute.org